The Herald's History Of Los Angeles City

CHARLES DWIGHT WILLARD

JUERGEN BECK

The Herald's History of Los Angeles City, C. D. Willard
Jazzybee Verlag Jürgen Beck
86450 Altenmünster, Loschberg 9
Deutschland

Printed by Createspace, North Charleston, SC, USA

ISBN: 9783849691349

www.jazzybee-verlag.de
www.facebook.com/jazzybeeverlag
admin@jazzybee-verlag.de

CONTENTS:

PREFACE

The career of a city contains as much good material, out of which an entertaining history may be constructed, as does the life of an individual, or the development of a nation; but, for some reason, it has come to pass in America that the preparation of city, or "local", history has usually fallen into the hands of schemers who exploit the "prominent" citizen for his biography, and throw in something of a narrative, merely as an apology for the book's existence. The volume thus produced is a huge unwieldy affair, that circulates only among the hundred or two victims, and is not read even by them, except as to the pages where each one finds the story of his life set forth in a flamboyant and patronizing style. It not infrequently happens that in the history portion of these monstrosities there will be found evidence of careful, conscientious work on the part of the (usually anonymous) writer, but it is buried under such a mass of rubbish, and the volume itself enjoys such a limited circulation, that the judicious reader grieves to see such good labor wasted.

The experience of Los Angeles in the matter of local history has been no different from that of other American municipalities. Of these biographical albums there has been no lack; they have come in cycles of every seven years. Two of these have been — as far as the history portion is concerned — considerably above the average standard. That of Thompson & West, written by J, Albert Wilson, and appearing in 1880, gave subsequent students cause of gratitude for the amount of valuable material gathered together and preserved. One published by the Chapman Company in 1900 contains a history written by that conscientious and devoted searcher in the local field, J. M. Guinn, Secretary of the Los Angeles Historical Society. Mr. Guinn's portion of the volume is an admirable piece of work, but the 780 pages of biography that accompany it contribute to the document a weight of ten pounds — and very little else.

The present book is an attempt to supply in convenient and portable shape the material facts in the history of Los Angeles city. It contains nothing in the form of paid or biographical matter (strange that such a statement should be needed!), and it is offered for sale at the bookshops on its merits as a book. The writer lays no claim to any great amount of original research, his work being chiefly that of collecting, arranging and presenting in logical order the established facts. As the volume employs only 80,000 words to cover a period of nearly a century and a half, there is not much opportunity for detail work. It is, however, carefully indexed.

The work was undertaken by the writer partly on the suggestion of Mr. R. H. Chapman of the Los Angeles Herald, and it was published during the months from July to December (1901) in the Sunday magazine of that

1

excellent journal. It is for that reason called the Herald's History of Los Angeles.

The writer desires to express his thanks to the following: Miss Anna B. Picher of Pasadena, who read the manuscript, and assisted in collecting the pictures, and whose advice and suggestions were of great value; Homer P. Darle of the Stanford Faculty, who also read the manuscript; Mrs. J. D. Hooker, whose beautiful collection of Mission photographs (never before published) were placed at the author's service; Miss Jones, librarian, and Miss Beckley, her assistant; Harry E. Brook, W. S. Hogaboom, Miss Bertha H. Smith, J. M. Guinn, D. O. Anderson, G. G. Johnson, C. C. Pierce, and Putnam & Valentine.

CHAPTER 1. SONS OF THE SOIL

The original name of Los Angeles was Yang-na, and its population consisted of about 300 human creatures barely above the animal plane. They were called Indians, a general term bestowed by the discoverers of this continent upon all aborigines, although those in Los Angeles bore no more resemblance to the brave and intellectual Iroquois and Tuscaroras than the Turk does to his fellow-European in London. They were undersized and squat in stature, of a dingy brown color, with small eyes, flat noses, high cheekbones and large mouths. The general cast of their features was Asiatic rather than Indian, and although the trivial character of their institutions, and the meagerness of their language makes it quite impossible to classify them ethnologically, it is evident that they are more nearly related to the Alaskan and Aleutian tribes that crossed from Asia when the northern rim of the continent was yet unbroken by the sea, than to the distinctively American Indian of the eastern coast and the interior valleys.

The center of Yang-na was somewhere about the corner of Commercial and Alameda streets and it straggled south as far as First street, and north to some point near Aliso. California Indian villages had a habit of creeping about, due to a peculiar, but, on the whole, commendable practice of their residents. The huts were small, insubstantial affairs, constructed of light poles, bound together and interlaced with twigs and tules. The dwellings of the more fastidious were sometimes roughly plastered with mud. Now when one of these habitations was completely overrun with parasitical insects of all sorts the householder would order his wife to fill the place with dry leaves and branches, and, having himself secured a torch from the vanquech, or temple, where the embers smoldered continually, but where women were not admitted, he would then set fire to the house and cremate its many-legged inhabitants. A new dwelling was presently erected in the vicinity of the old one; sometimes it was built on the same spot, as soon as the ashes were cooled.

There were from 25 to 30 of these Indian villages scattered about Los Angeles county, the largest being at San Pedro or Wilmington, which was said to contain 500 people. Probably 4000 of the aborigines were to be found in the district bounded by the mountains, the sea, and the San Gabriel river, this being one of the most thickly settled portions of the state. Each village was a tribe in itself, possessing its own chief, its specific manners and customs, and, in many cases, its own individual language. There were not many of the missionaries that took pains to study the Indian tongue, but one who did so declared that there were seventeen absolutely distinct languages in Alta California, besides several hundred different dialects, some of the latter being, in effect, separate languages. A

3

few hundred words comprised the whole of their vocabulary, and their talk seemed to the Spaniards to be made up of gruntings and slobberings.

The people of Yang-na were probably on friendly terms with the people of the neighboring villages — at Pasadena, San Gabriel, Cahuenga and Clearwater. They were too timid and too indolent to fight unless the occasion was urgent. When some foreign tribe or combination of tribes undertook to enter and seize their lands, they would fight like rats in a trap, for to leave their homes meant death. They had bows and arrows that were well made, and their marksmanship seemed to the Spaniards extraordinary, but it was probably no better than that of most savages. There were sometimes bitter feuds between adjoining tribes that lasted for many generations, but actual conflict seems to have been rare, a peculiar ceremonial of cursing and extravagant threats being substituted, as less dangerous and perhaps quite as gratifying. Captured enemies after a real battle were put to death with dreadful tortures.

Chieftainship was hereditary, and carried with it the power to practice polygamy, which, considering the extremely fragile nature of the marriage vow, must have been of little advantage, even from the savage point of view, except that it gave the chief more household drudges, and allowed him to maintain a higher degree of dignity. The older men of the village were the chief's counselors, and met with him in the temple to discuss questions of state, which latter consisted, for the most part, in setting the date for the next general rabbit hunt, and arranging for the initiation of some newly grown-up youth into the tribe. Decision on many of these matters was likely to be left to the sorcerers, who formed a distinct aristocratic class, quite as powerful as the chief himself, and passed down their crude and disgusting rites from one generation to another. These were the spiritual guides and physical guardians of the tribe, and it is difficult to say which was the worse, their religion or their therapeutics. The primeval curse of the savage lies not so much in his poverty as in his superstition — in the unfortunate perversions of his vacant mind.

The head of their scheme of religious belief was a demi-god named Chinigchinich, from whom the order of priests or sorcerers was descended. Most of the legends connected with this being have been transmitted to us through the memoranda left by Padre Geronimo Boscana, who lived at San Juan Capistrano during the first quarter of the nineteenth century, but the later historic criticism has decided that either the good father drew somewhat on his imagination, or else he was imposed upon by the Indians from whom he secured his alleged facts. The close resemblance of the cosmogony which he outlines to that of the ancient Greeks does not occur in any other savage religion, and the delicate strain of transcendentalism that runs through the legends, as the padre presents them, is entirely out of keeping with the known limitations on the Indians' intellect. The practical

4

worship of this divinity consisted of dances and slow rhythmical jumpings about the sacred place or vanquech. The sick were treated with lugubrious incantations, to which were added some simple remedies. Rheumatism was treated with blisters made by nettles. Inflammation was met by bloodletting and the fever patient received a huge bolus of wild tobacco. The sweathouse was applied for lumbago, and also as a general tonic, and to get rid of vermin.

The male inhabitants of Yang-na went entirely naked, when the weather was warm, and even on the coldest days of the year the only garment likely to be worn was a cloak of badly-tanned rabbit skins. The women were partially covered, and were not without some sense of modesty. Paint was liberally used on the bodies of both sexes. As the houses were not built to withstand the wind and rain, these people must have suffered to some extent from inclement weather, although not as severely as the savages in less favored climates. Mortality among them bore a close approximation to the birth rate, and the population of Yang-na varied little in number from year to year, or, for that matter, from century to century. The check on increase lay, however, not so much in death from disease as in prospective famine, which always operates as a natural deterrent on births among savage peoples. It must be remembered that this region is by no means luxuriant in its natural state. It does not teem with animal and vegetable life as the tropics do. Its rainfall is uncertain, and its soil not extraordinarily rich. The California Indian sowed nothing and cultivated nothing. If, through the graciousness of nature, he was nevertheless permitted to reap, he had not even the judgment carefully to bestow what he gathered, but after gorging himself to repletion, he allowed the remainder to go to waste. He found various edible seeds, among them wild barley. He soaked and baked the roots of the flag. Acorns he dried and ground to powder, and filtered out the bitter by allowing water to trickle through. This served him as a kind of flour, but when the Spaniards tried it, in some of their starving times, it made them very ill. The Indians killed deer, coyotes, squirrels and snakes for food, and they caught fish. The flesh was eaten raw, or nearly so. Grasshoppers and even grub worms were devoured in dry years.

The Indian man looked upon himself as a hunter and warrior; any other occupation than these — unless he was a sorcerer and practiced medicine — he regarded as beneath his dignity. At rare intervals he would go with the tribe on a short expedition in search of seeds and acorns, but that was rather in the nature of a civic function, and was preliminary to a special feast. The daily round of food was supposed to be provided by the women, who went on long marches over the fields and through the woods, laboriously hunting where others had already gleaned before them. She ground the acorns in a stone mortar, and rolled the seeds on a metate. She built the fire, cooked the cakes, and then went to summon her husband, who was drowsing in the warm sunshine, or playing "takersia" in the level plain near the village.

The games and amusements were restricted to the men, although women participated in some of the semi-religious dances. The favorite pastime, which is named above, was played in a space about 30 feet square. One man rolled a ring about three inches in diameter across the course, and another, his opponent in the sport, undertook to throw a wand five feet long through it, as it rolled. If he succeeded in doing so, without stopping the ring, he was given one point. Three points constituted the game. Another favorite pursuit was to knock a small, hard, wooden ball several hundred yards with a stick that had a knob at the end, which would seem to provide the modern game of golf with an ancient though none too creditable origin. It is said the players grew so excited at times over this pursuit that they would even stake their wives on the achievement of a good score, which, considering the special utility of the creatures, would indicate a remarkable degree of enthusiasm for the game.

The people of Yang-na had no form of writing nor hieroglyphics. Their artifacts are of limited variety and simple construction, and are all of the stone age. One of the finest collections of these ever gathered may be seen in the west gallery of the Chamber of Commerce in Los Angeles. It is the work of Dr. F. M. Palmer, and was obtained, for the most part, in the Channel islands, where the natives were more energetic and ingenious than on the mainland. A careful examination of these six large cases of artifacts, which were gathered and arranged with the trained judgment of the ethnologist, while it recalls the extreme simplicity of the life led by our predecessors, at the same time impresses us with astonishment at their patience and skill in working so difficult a substance as stone.

Dirty, ignorant and degraded as the California Indian was, there are still some things to be said in his favor. His first behavior toward his white visitor was that of the kindly host, offering him such food and shelter as he had at his command. This seems to have been done not through fear, but in good humor and admiration. Christianized Indians testified afterwards that when they first saw the Spaniards they believed them to be gods. A rude shock to this idea came when they beheld the strangers wantonly killing the birds, for these poor savages argued that no power which could create life would wish thus to destroy it. Only when driven to extremity by repeated outrage did the Indian attack the soldiery, and the padres traveled about among them without fear.

It is interesting to consider to what extent the condition of these people — degraded even below the average of their kind — was due to climatic environment. The California Indian did not build a warm wigwam, because few days in the year were inclement; and he did not cultivate the soil, nor store away grain, because there was no season, like the eastern winter, when nature entirely deserted him. His immediate successor, the Spaniard, followed the same easy and dreamful life, notwithstanding the many centuries of civilization that had been placed to his credit; and it yet remains to be seen what effect the eternal spring softness of this climate will have on the life and character of the Anglo-Saxon, when it comes to the test of successive generations.

CHAPTER 2. THE EDGE OF THE SPANISH EMPIRE.

When the fact for which Columbus had contended — that the earth was a globe — became finally established in men's minds, and navigators from all the leading European nations were out on the ocean, discovering and claiming strange lands, his holiness the pope, the senior power of Christendom and the representative of Peace on Earth, endeavored to settle all disputes over the titles to new territory by dividing the world with a great meridian circle drawn one hundred leagues west of the Azores. All the globe west of the line was to belong to Spain, and all the globe east of it was to go to Portugal. This arrangement, which had at least the advantage of extreme simplicity, was somewhat disturbed by the English, Dutch and French, who took possession of the Eastern portion of the North American continent, and of a few islands here and there; but the pious and adventurous Spaniards certainly did their best toward carrying out the pope's program. During the sixteenth century they overran nearly all of South America, and the islands of the Mexican gulf; and on the northern continent they set up a stable government in Mexico, and by exploration and to some extent by actual occupation they secured control of about two-thirds of the present area of the United States. Whatever may have been the mistakes and the misfortunes of that country since those days, Spain is entitled to rank in history as the discoverer and the conqueror of the new western world.

The history of California begins in the history of Mexico, for, of all the explorers that visited the state prior to its colonization, only one, Sir Francis Drake, came from European waters; the others came up from Mexico. And the settlement of the country, which was finally undertaken with the authority of Spain, was accomplished through Mexico, of which country California, upper and lower together, constituted a province.

Hernando Cortes, the conqueror of Mexico, landed at Vera Cruz in 1519, and within a few years had established a government that was felt from the isthmus to the Rio Grande. In 1524, he describes California in a report to the king of Spain, as an island of great wealth, abounding in pearls and precious gems. It is inhabited, he says, by women only. The origin of this strange idea undoubtedly lay in the romance, "Las Sergas de Esplandian," which was published in Spain about 1510, and which seems to have enjoyed a run of popular favor, much as a successful novel might in these days. It is purely a work of fiction, and the writer describes his imaginary island which is called California, as located somewhere to the right of India. This island, the story says, is entirely peopled with black women, having a queen named Califia. They use no metal but gold. Copies of this work undoubtedly found their way across the Atlantic, and formed, at last, the basis of one of those persistent rumors of wealth that floated about the ears of the Spaniards, and led them on into the wilderness. In the case of California, the story of gold happened to be true, but it was not for the Spaniards to profit by it.

Up to the year 1862, the origin of the name California was the basis of a great deal of learned discussion. Many explanations were offered and imaginary etymologies were supplied for the word. It remained for Edward Everett Hale, the author of "The Man Without a Country," to set all doubts at rest, and trace the name to its veritable source in the romance, "Las Sergas."

In 1534, Cortes sent an expedition in search of the gold of this wonderful island. The vessels were skirting the mainland, along the gulf of Lower California, when a mutiny broke out. A part of the company seized one of the ships, and, crossing to the peninsula, landed at a point about ninety miles north of Cape San Lucas, where afterwards a Spanish settlement was located and named La Paz. The leader in this affair was Fortuno Ximenes, who is entitled to be recorded as the discoverer of Lower California. A year later Cortes came up the gulf himself, and, landing at La Paz, formally took possession of the country. Four years later, in 1539, he sent Ulloa with orders to sail around the island, as it was supposed to be, and to discover, if possible, the passage, back to Atlantic waters. Just as the English, French and Dutch navigators, working along our eastern coast, were constantly on the lookout for the fabled "Northwest Passage," which would give them a shorter way across to India, so the Spaniards on the Pacific coast made their way into every bay and river mouth, hoping always to discover the "Straits of Anian," which were recorded on all the charts of the time as crossing this continent somewhere to the north of the limit of exploration.

Ulloa did not find the desired passage, but he came to the head of the gulf, and explored the pearl fisheries, which, for over two hundred years afterwards, enriched the Spanish court favorites to whom they were granted as monopolies. He came back to Cape San Lucas, and worked north on the western coast to the middle of the peninsula.

In the year that Cortes returned to Spain, 1540, the viceroy, Mendoza, sent two vessels under Alarcon to the head of the gulf, and they managed to sail some distance up the Colorado river. It is not improbable that Alarcon came near enough to California to catch a glimpse of the country, and he is regarded by some writers as the discoverer of the state.

A great expedition had been planned by Mendoza and Alvarado to go up the Colorado in search of the treasure which was supposed to exist somewhere in the interior, but the return of some of the people who had explored this region dissipated the viceroy's hopes in that direction. He had the fleet that had been prepared for this scheme still on his hands, and more to keep it busy than for any definite purpose, he sent Juan Rodriguez Cabrillo, a navigator whose bravery had been tested in many shipwrecks and battles on the Spanish Main, with instructions to sail up the California coast as far north as practicable, keeping always a sharp lookout for the "Straits of Anian." He had two boats, the San Salvador and the Victoria, short, top-heavy affairs, on which no modern sailor would risk his life. With these he set sail from Navidad, on the western coast of Mexico, June 27, 1542, just fifty years after the discovery of America.

Cabrillo is the Christopher Columbus of California. When he passed Cedros island, which is about the middle of the peninsula, he entered upon a stretch of waters as full of strange and terrible possibilities as those that lay before the intrepid Genoese when he went forth into the broad Atlantic with his three little boats. For all that Cabrillo knew the sea on which he sailed might presently terminate in a huge sink or maelstrom, and the shores where he was expected to land and make explorations might be peopled with hideous monsters. The utter commonplaceness of the events of his voyage makes it seem a small achievement now, but we may be permitted, nevertheless, to pause and admire his courage, as he ventures out into the unknown.

In the month of September he entered the bay of San Diego, and the soil of California bore for the first time the impress of a European foot. The record does not inform us who led the way ashore, but it requires no great strain on the imagination to suppose that it was Cabrillo himself.

The Indians at San Diego were friendly, except that their suspicions seem to have been excited by the attempt to land a hunting party at night, when they fired on the boat and wounded two sailors. At no place in his many landings along the coast does Cabrillo seem to have had much trouble with the natives. After a short stay at San Diego, he sailed north to San Pedro bay, which he named the Bay of Smokes, from the great clouds of smoke that hovered over the mainland; the Indians of Wilmington were evidently engaged in one of their great rabbit hunts, in which they burned off the dry grass, to drive in the game. Here he landed to obtain water, and he probably climbed the hills back of where San Pedro now stands, that he might obtain a view of the country inland. If he did so, he was able on a clear day to see the site of Los Angeles. This was over 350 years ago, and more than two centuries were destined to pass before the white men should come down into this valley.

Winter was now at hand, and with it came storms and head winds. He visited the islands of the channel, and on one of them met with a fall that broke his arm. The trip further north was made under hard conditions; and after working up the coast as far as San Francisco, though he did not enter the bay, he returned to the island of San Miguel, opposite Santa Barbara, where the explorer finally died from the unsuccessful surgery practiced on

10

his broken arm. He was buried m the shifting sand of the harbor afterwards called Cuyler's, in San Miguel, and if any sign was left to mark his grave it has long since disappeared.

With his latest breath Cabrillo urged his chief lieutenant, the pilot Ferrelo, to continue the exploration to the north. His wish was respected, and the San Salvador and Victoria under their new commander went up the coast a second time, but as they passed Cape Mendocino they were driven back by storms. Ferrelo then returned to Mexico and made his report to the viceroy. This was in 1543.

In 1579 Francis Drake sailed along the coast of California in the famous Golden Hind, then two years out from Plymouth, England.

He had been overhauling the Spanish galleons in the West Indies and on the Mexican coast, and had taken so much treasure — so his chaplain says — that he used the silver to ballast his ship. His fleet of five having been reduced to one, he had no desire to meet with any of the Spanish men-of-war that might be prowling about in Atlantic waters, so he was making his way westward around the globe.

He anchored in the bay north of San Francisco, now called by his name, evidently failing to recognize in the Golden Gate the entrance to a great harbor. As his ship drew only 13 feet, the upper bay would answer to his description of "a fit and convenient harborough." Here he remained 36 days, finding the Indians friendly and the climate pleasant. He named the country New Albion, and claimed it for his queen. Several of the "gentlemen adventurers" of England visited Lower California, following in the wake of the Golden Hind, but they accomplished nothing beyond a few successful robberies, and the claims set up by Drake were allowed to lapse.

It is not impossible that the visit of Drake and the other Englishmen to this coast may have stimulated Philip H of Spain to plan to tighten his hold on the Californias. In 1596, the viceroy, acting under direct instructions from the monarch, sent Sebastian Viscaino with three ships to go on with the work that Cabrillo had so bravely begun, more than fifty years before. He sailed from Acapulco to La Paz, where he became involved in difficulties with the Indians that caused him to abandon the expedition. The nature and cause of these difficulties is indicated by the fact that when he started again, this time with two vessels in the year 1602, he ordered the death penalty for any soldier that should cause a disturbance among the Indians.

His journey was in a considerable degree a replica of that of Cabrillo. Like the former explorer, he met with stormy weather, and was finally turned back when he had worked his way a little north of Cape Mendocino. He explored the port of Monterey, but placed it on his chart too far north by two degrees. He changed the names of the islands of the channel, from those bestowed by Cabrillo to the ones they now bear, even robbing his

11

predecessor of the poor honor that lay in the title Rodriguez (Cabrillo's middle name) on his island grave.

Viscaino transmitted to the king an account of his visit to California, in which he declared that the country was rich and fertile and admirably adapted to colonization, and he urged that he be allowed to undertake an expedition for its permanent settlement. The king hesitated to grant the required powers, but finally did so, in 1606. Before the plan could be carried out, however, Viscaino died, and it was abandoned.

Now follows a period of one hundred and sixty years, during which no more white men came to California. In that time the thirteen colonies were planted on the Atlantic coast, waxed strong and were preparing to revolt from the mother country. England passed through the revolutions that cost Charles his head and James his throne. Germany endured the horrid struggle of the thirty-years' war, and witnessed the rise to power of Frederick the Great. France was sinking lower and lower under the rapacious and imbecile line of Bourbon, and Spain, once the ruler of the seas, was priest-governed and impoverished. There was no more wealth to be wrung from the new world — therefore it was neglected and almost forgotten.

CHAPTER 3. VIA CRUCIS.

Philip II of Spain, whose rule extended through 40 years of the period of most active exploration and acquisition in the western hemisphere, received from the pope the significant title of "His Most Catholic Majesty"; and all his successors on the throne down to the present have cherished this phrase as part of their official name. It must be admitted that the title has not been misplaced, for no country on the globe has been more rigidly faithful to the church of Rome than Spain. It was the originator of the inquisition; in Spain the church was the largest owner of property, and the priesthood outnumbered all other professions and intelligent occupations combined. It was natural, therefore, that the colonial system of this country should be permeated with the religious idea, and that a large part of the work of organizing the new territory should be turned over to the hierarchy.

This work possessed lively attraction for the young and ardent members of the priesthood, because the new country was peopled with heathen, whose souls seemed to be crying out for salvation. The order of the Jesuits, founded by Ignatius Loyola in 1540, threw itself with boundless enthusiasm into the new missionary fields, and no corner of the earth was too remote, and no tribe of savages too fierce for the Jesuit to enter, bearing the standard of the cross. The conquering soldier came first, it is true, but his act of "taking possession" was little more than a formality. The real work of colonization, of controlling and organizing the Indians and of producing at least a semblance of civilized order, fell to the priest.

The Californias, upper and lower, were at the extreme northwestern edge of the great Spanish empire, and the tide of colonization, which flowed slowly across the new world, reached them last of all. In the first period of conquest great quantities of wealth were drawn from the western continents, and poured into the lap of Spain, and with this increase of fortune came an undermining of the moral, and finally of the material, forces of the country. The energetic and progressive artisan class, from which colonists for a new country would naturally come, had died out in Spain.

One viceroy after another was sent out from the mother country to govern the province of Mexico, and at times a "visitador general" was delegated to make a tour of the territory, and transmit a special report to the king. A long line of mediocre monarchs were occupying the throne. Efforts at colonization by the government were fitful. The Spanish soldiers intermarried with the native women of Mexico, and the half-breeds, or mestizos, increased in number. Gradually paganism died out, and the spiritual rule of the church was accepted.

13

A few colonies had been established by the government in Lower California, but they were too far from the base of supply to continue successfully. Only those established by the church, where the natives were controlled by religious awe, as well as physical force, managed to survive. It was discovered that the Jesuits were most successful in establishing permanent locations among the Indians, and in the last years of the seventeenth century the whole of the territory of Lower California was turned over to them to manage as they saw fit. It was not a very promising piece of country — dry and sterile, and peopled with a race of savages quite as degraded as those further north on the Pacific coast. By this time the Spanish government had become impoverished, and could afford no funds for the undertaking. In the decree of February 5, 1697, whereby the plan of the Jesuits for colonization was adopted, it was agreed that the royal treasury was not to be called upon to meet any of the expense. This led to the establishment of the famous "Pious Fund," which, within the memory of the present generation, formed the basis of some remarkable international litigation.

The leaders in the movement were two priests named Kino and Salvatierra. They went about Spain enthusiastically describing this beautiful land, where thousands of heathen waited to be led into the church. Contributions to the fund began to flow in, the first one being $10,000 from the congregation of a church where Salvatierra had preached, and the second, $20,000, from an individual Spaniard. A wealthy nobleman and his wife made wills, leaving their entire fortune to the fund, and others followed their example. The money was well invested, and only the income was used — after the expense of establishment was defrayed. It was not long before some of the missions began to be self-supporting.

Salvatierra and Kino confined their work to Lower California, where they founded a complete system of missions, numbering finally sixteen in all. One of their fellow-laborers, the Padre Ugarte, seems to have possessed a veritable genius for what might be called the worldly portion of the work, teaching the Indians all the trades — even to that of ship-building — and accomplishing marvelous results with pitifully poor material. By the middle of the eighteenth century the scheme of organization had run its course to practical completion; that is, the Indians of the peninsula were largely under the control of the missions; a full complement of buildings, both for religious and temporal purposes had been erected at each location, and the church was pre-eminent over the whole system of government. There were a few rebellions, but on the whole the Indians were tractable, and were a few steps nearer civilization.

These matters have a direct bearing on the history of Alta California in two ways: First, in the fact that the "Pious Fund" raised by the Jesuits was used to defray the expenses of the work in Alta California, and, second, in the fact that the Franciscans, when they came to found missions in this state, had immediately before them, as a model, the institutions already existing in the lower peninsula.

About this time the feeling against the Jesuits, which had been slowly spreading throughout Christendom, culminated in their expulsion from several Catholic countries, as they had already been driven out of Protestant states. In 1759 Carlos III, the ablest of all the kings of Spain, came to the throne. During his reign of twenty-nine years that country made the first genuine progress it had accomplished since the days of Ferdinand and Isabella. He gathered about him wise advisers, and among these were several that believed the government to be too much under the influence of the priests. The Jesuit played the same part in the religious system that the party boss does in our politics, and the wave of reform reached him first of all. In 1767 an order was promulgated expelling the Jesuits from Spain and all her colonies. All temporalities held in their name were ordered to be seized for the crown. However justifiable this decree may have been with reference to the Jesuits of the mother country, it was certainly a harsh and cruel act as applied to the padres who had labored faithfully for over half a century on the arid soil of Lower California, and who, as they left the missions, where they had grown old in the service, were followed by crowds of weeping Indians.

The American religious outposts were to be placed in the hands of the two orders that were, next to the Jesuits, most active in missionary work — the Franciscans and Dominicans. It was at first proposed that the Lower California missions should be divided equally between the two orders, but later — at the suggestion of Father Junipero Serra — it was decided that, to avoid all possibility of friction, the Dominicans should be placed in charge of the Lower California institutions, while the Franciscans should be allowed the honor of beginning the work in the new territory.

The order of St. Francis was one of the oldest and most popular of the many priestly fraternities. It was founded in 1209 by an Italian monk, a preacher of extraordinary fervency and persuasiveness, who was subsequently canonized as St. Francis of Assisi. Its adherents were sworn to poverty and extreme simplicity of life. The dress was originally a coarse gray serge robe, tied with a hempen rope. Later on some portions of the order changed from gray to brown. The foundation principles were humility, voluntary mendicancy and abhorrence of controversy. The members desired to be known as peacemakers, and their influence was generally for harmony and for the existing order in temporal affairs. In this respect they differed materially from the Jesuits, who, as we have seen, had achieved an unenviable reputation in Europe for intrigue and mischief-making.

The Franciscan order grew with great rapidity from its founding, and by the end of the thirteenth century had over 200,000 members. At the time the order was placed in charge of Alta California it had over 8000 colleges and convents scattered about the world. Their headquarters on this continent lay at the college of San Fernando, in the City of Mexico. Here a great majority of the padres that were sent to California for service in the missions received their education, and to this institution were referred all difficulties and all matters of serious importance regarding the missions.

Junipero Serra has appropriately been called the "Eighteenth Century St. Francis." There is little doubt that had his career fallen five hundred years earlier his supreme devotion of purpose and his heroic efforts to advance the cause of the church which have been rewarded by canonization. He was born in the island of Majorca in 1713. His parents were laboring people, but he was given an education that fitted him for the priesthood; and because of his exceptional abilities a professorship of theology was bestowed upon him. From his early boyhood he had yearned to undertake the career of a missionary; and when, in 1749, word came from the College of San Fernando that recruits were wanted to work among the savages and half-breeds of Mexico he enthusiastically volunteered for the service. His friend Palou accompanied him, and the two were fellow-workers and intimates through all the California campaign.

When Serra's ship arrived at Vera Cruz there were no pack animals to convey the recruits to the City of Mexico, so he set out on foot, unwilling, in his fiery zeal, to wait for proper means of conveyance. During this trip overland he contracted an ulcer in his leg that tormented him through the remainder of his life, but which he endured with the fortitude of a martyr. During the first nine years after his advent to Mexico he served at the lonely mission of Sierra Gordo, where he gathered a large congregation, and where he built a splendid church structure. Without doubt, his experience with the Indians at this place, both in spiritual and in worldly affairs, was of great service to him in his subsequent labors in California.

The priests of the college of San Fernando noted the success that Brother Junipero had achieved at Sierra Gordo, and determined to try him in a new field. He was summoned to the City of Mexico and put over a congregation which was made up not of untutored Indians, but of the wealthiest and most refined people of the district. Crowds flocked to hear him, and his zealous preaching is said to have brought many to repentance.

In 1768, when the order to expel the Jesuits from the missions of Mexico was carried into effect, Junipero Serra was appointed president of the California district. This included Upper and Lower California, although as yet no establishment had been located north of the peninsula.

Whether it was the report on the expulsion of the Jesuits from this region, or the news that the Russians were working down the Pacific coast from the north that aroused the king, or whether it was merely the outgrowth of his natural energy and desire to promote the welfare of his country, is not known, but about this time Carlos III issued instructions to Marquez de Croix, the viceroy of Mexico, and to Jose de Galvez, the visitador general, or inspector, to undertake the colonization of Upper California, the government to act in conjunction with the priestly orders. Galvez, who was entrusted with powers second only to those of the king himself, went over to Loreto in Lower California, to direct the expeditions to the new country, and Father Junipero Serra repaired to the same spot. They were both men of tireless energy, and both possessed the same consistency of purpose; therefore they worked well together. They had at their disposal three vessels, the San Carlos, the San Antonio and the San Jose, all appropriately named for the pious work they were about to undertake. There were available, besides the ships, a couple of hundred soldiers, a score of artisans and a few priests. Supplies were to be obtained from the missions in Lower California. It was decided that there should be four expeditions — two by land and two by sea — each independent of the others, and that all should meet at the port described by Cabrillo and Viscaino, which we know now as San Diego. These preparations were made near the close of the year 1768.

CHAPTER 4. HOW GOVERNOR PORTOLA CAME TO LOS ANGELES.

The unpleasant task of expelling the Jesuits from the chain of missions they had established in Lower California was committed to Capt. Caspar de Portola, who landed at Cape San Lucas with a small detachment of soldiers in October of 1767, to begin the work. He was made governor of both the Californias, and in the expedition that was presently begun for the occupation of the northern territory, he represented both the military and the civil features of the government, subject, of course, to the orders of the visitador general, Jose de Galvez.

Portola was a good-hearted and popular man, not without considerable natural shrewdness, and he performed his duty toward the Jesuits with gentleness and sympathy. There was no resistance on their part, and no outbreaks among the Indians. The treasure, which it was supposed the padres had laid away, failed to come to light, and Portola reported to Galvez that it was quite impossible that the simple agricultural pursuits of the missions should have yielded any great wealth. Nevertheless, he assured Serra that these establishments were fairly well stocked with cattle and provisions, and that enough could easily be spared to supply the expedition to the north. Serra himself, in the year 1768, made a tour through the missions of the peninsula, of which he was now president, and inspected their stock of ecclesiastical paraphernalia, on which he proceeded to levy for the new institutions that he was planning to found.

Captain Rivera y Moncada, who subsequently filled an important function in the founding of the pueblo of Los Angeles, was appointed chief of the commissary department of the expedition, and was sent out to make a round of the missions, for the purpose of collecting cattle and stores, and was ordered to work toward the north, that he might be ready early in 1769 for the general movement into new territory. He had been the local commander for several years at Loreto, and was well posted on the geography and the climatic conditions of the country. He was therefore a most valuable man in the work, all the other leaders being strange to the region.

The headquarters of the undertaking were at La Paz and Loreto. Here through the last six months of 1768, Galvez, Serra and Portola toiled and planned, until by the first of the following year everything was ready. In January of 1769 — the year in which the history of California begins — the San Carlos put to sea, loaded with stores and carrying sixty-two people. Of these twenty-five were soldiers in command of Lieutenant Pedro Fages, who later held the office of governor of California, and the remainder were, for the most part, sailors and artisans.

In February the second expedition by sea started — the San Antonio, which, although it set sail a month later than the San Carlos, arrived at San Diego three weeks before its predecessor, Galvez's instructions to the commanders were that they should keep out to sea until they sighted the islands of the channel, and should then work down the coast to the bay of San Diego. It is difficult to realize that the San Antonio, which made the best time of the two, consumed sixty days in doing a distance that would now seem to call for less than a week of sailing. In the case of the San Carlos, however, the delay is easily explained in the one dreadful word — scurvy. This disease, which was at that time a common visitor on shipboard and in prisons and camps, was due to impure water, monotonous fare, uncleanliness and bad sanitation. It has very nearly passed out of existence among civilized people in these days, and it is not easy to appreciate what a terror it once had for all who followed the sea. The water casks on the San Carlos were leaky, and the springs of Cedros island, where the vessel stopped to replenish, yielded water that proved unwholesome. By the time San Diego was reached the disease had taken possession of the crew.

The first of the land expeditions was under the command of Rivera, who had collected a quantity of horses, cows, mules and general supplies from the Lower California missions. He set out for the north in March of 1769, and arrived at San Diego in the middle of May. By this time the people from the ships had constructed a camp and hospital on shore, and the crew of the San Antonio were taking care of the crew of the San Carlos, all of whom were now afflicted with the scurvy. About sixty deaths occurred, to the great demoralization of the whole company.

On the first of July the last of the land forces arrived. Governor Portola in command, accompanied by Father Junipero Serra. The delay had been occasioned partly by their stopping to found a new mission in Lower California and partly by Serra's inability to travel, owing to the condition of his ulcerated leg. He refused to allow the Indians to carry him in a litter, because he was unwilling to cause them such a labor, and he would not be left behind. At last a muleteer applied the same poultice that he would have used on an animal and the leg was made enough better for the padre to go on. This incident is set down at full length in the narrative in much the same way that a miracle would be recorded.

Galvez had issued instructions to the soldiers that the Indians should be treated with kindness, and he threatened severe punishment to all that failed to comply with this order. It was believed that little gifts of brown sugar and of cloth and beads would please the natives and induce them to accept Christianity — that is, submit to the form of baptism, as their brethren had done in Mexico and Lower California. The cloth and the beads were found

19

to be acceptable, particularly the former, but the sugar was declined, or if taken at all, was merely carried to the bushes and buried there. The same treatment was accorded all other articles of food that were offered to the Indians, the reason being that they connected the sickness so prevalent among the first Spaniards that arrived with their diet; and this fear of European food clung to the Indians for some time, and, with regard to the brown sugar, was never entirely removed.

It had been intended that the expeditions should be reorganized at San Diego, and that one of the ships and half the land forces should go north to Monterey, and there found a mission at the upper end of the territory, with San Diego as the limit on the lower end. Between these two points a series of institutions were to be established. But the havoc wrought by the scurvy interfered with this plan, and compelled the immediate return of one of the ships to Lower California for additional sailors — there being scarcely enough left to work one ship — and also for supplies. The San Antonio started back July 14, two weeks after the arrival of Portola. In the meantime Galvez, as though anticipating the wants of his colonists, had dispatched the third member of his little fleet at Loreto, the San Jose, well-filled with provisions and articles for the use of the settlers, and manned by a complete crew. What became of it? No one ever knew. No storm ever washed it ashore on the California coast, nor was it ever sighted on the high seas. Probably its crew became infected with the scurvy, like those of San Carlos, and after drifting about aimlessly for a time, it may have foundered in some storm and sunk in the open sea. Immediately after the departure of the San Antonio southward, Portola started north with an expedition of sixty-four persons, made up of soldiers, mule-drivers, a few Lower California Indians, and two priests. One of the latter, Father Crespi, kept a daily record of the journey, which has come down to us in the documents collected and treasured by Serra's friend, Palou. With the expedition were two future governors of the territory. Pages and Rivera. Junipero Serra did not accompany them, partly because his lame leg rendered such a trip difficult and dangerous, and partly because he wished to establish the mission at San Diego, and begin on the work of converting the Indians. The good father chafed, no doubt, under the delay and the interference to his plans which had been brought about by the prevalent sickness of the camp.

The purpose of the expedition led by Portola was to find the Bay of Monterey and establish an outpost there, to be held until Father Junipero should arrive and found a mission in due form. The round trip from San Diego to Monterey consumed over six months. It could now be made by rail in about three days. The party averaged from eight to fifteen miles a day, with frequent rests. Their route lay along the coast, except where the broadening of the valleys allowed them to make their way inland without the risk of losing their bearings.

On the nineteenth day after leaving San Diego, to wit, on the second of August, this party of white people crossed the Los Angeles river at about the point where the Buena Vista street bridge is now located, and passed around the hills of Elysian park, and out into the Cahuenga valley. It is not improbable that they came up toward the center of the modern city, and it was doubtless somewhere near the Plaza that they met with a party of Indians from the village of Yang-na. Father Crespi records the fact that the savages came out toward them with loud howling, but that they made no really hostile demonstration. On the contrary, they showed their good will by offering their visitors handfuls of seeds, which the latter refused, for the reason, the padre says, that "they had no place to bestow them," but perhaps also because they were a little suspicious of the Indians' motives. The savages were evidently displeased at the rebuff, for when the seeds were refused they threw them contemptuously on the ground.

Now the second day of August is, in the calendar of the Roman Catholic church, the special feast day of Our Lady of the Angels, that is to say, the Virgin Mary. As the party passed along through this unknown country, they made the most of the explorer's privilege to bestow names on the various features of the landscape, and also upon each spot in which they camped. The Spaniard being an individual who is rarely in a hurry, has a fondness for long and sonorous titles. The modern hidalgo, or Spanish gentleman, usually has half a dozen family names fastened together with a "Y" or an occasional "De" and in his original geographical titles he was no less prodigal. For example, when the party came upon the Santa Ana river, several days before they reached Los Angeles, they decided, for some reason, to name it after the Saviour of men. Now an American or an Englishman would have felt this to be somewhat sacrilegious, but if he had been compelled to do it, he would probably have called the stream merely the "Jesus river." The name bestowed by Father Crespi was "El Rio del Dulcisimo Nombre de Jesus," the River of the Sweetest Name of Jesus. While they were encamped on its banks, a series of light earthquakes took place, and it was decided to incorporate this fact in the name, and it was finally called "The River of the Sweetest Name of Jesus of the Earthquakes." Still it is not much of a river. In the eastern states it would be called a creek — or worse yet, a "crick." The Los Angeles river was named the Porciuncula, after a little stream in Italy that was dear to the heart of St. Francis; and the spot which the Indians called Yang-na was named from the second of August feast day, Nuestra Senora de Los Angeles. Twelve years later, when Governor Felipe de Neve founded a city there, he prefixed the word "Pueblo" to the title already on record, and it struggled along under that name, until the Americans took possession and chopped it down to the last two words; and now these seem to be in a fair way to be telescoped into L'sangl's.

21

Governor Portola and his party continued their way northward, with the sea on their left hand, until they came to the bay of Monterey, which they failed to recognize as the perfect harbor described by Viscaino. As they rambled about the adjoining country, in the search for Monterey, a small detachment under the lead of a lieutenant named Ortega, afterwards the founder of the Ortega family of Santa Barbara, came in sight of the bay of San Francisco, which one might suppose would have satisfied their desire for a harbor; but they had been sent out by Galvez to found a settlement at Monterey, and they proposed to obey orders. At length they abandoned the search, and returned to San Diego, passing for a second time through the Los Angeles region, this time by way of Pasadena and over the San Gabriel river. The party were footsore and almost without supplies, and Father Crespi records with gratitude the hospitable treatment accorded them by the Indians of the Hahamog-na tribe in that vicinity.

CHAPTER 5. THE BANNER OF THE VIRGIN.

The Mission of San Diego was formally dedicated on the 16th of July, 1769, by Junipero Serra and his attendant priests, just as Portola was leaving for Monterey. It is, therefore, the oldest of the establishments founded by the Franciscans in California. The location was in the vicinity of the camp, in what is now called the Old Town. The beginning was not auspicious. No Indians presented themselves to be converted; on the contrary, they regarded the ceremonial with suspicion and disdain. The discharge of musketry, which had frightened the savages in the beginning, was treated with indifference when they found that it brought them no harm; and they hung about the camp, incessantly begging for cloth, and stealing any article that was not carefully guarded. At last matters came to a crisis. Several of the Indians entered the camp where the sick lay, and undertook to tear the clothing from the beds. They were driven out by force, whereupon they returned in considerable numbers with bows and arrows and began open warfare. Obedient to the warnings of Galvez, the soldiers refrained from firing directly at the Indians, until a volley of arrows killed one European and wounded several others. Then they shot into the crowd, with a slaughter that terrified the savages into immediate submission.

From their account of the case, the Spaniards do not appear to have been at all to blame, but the result of the bloodshed was disastrous to the kindly intentions of the padres. It gave the soldiers an excuse to adopt harsh and often outrageous measures toward the Indians, and it put off, for an indefinite period, all possibility of winning them over to the standard of the church. A whole year passed before a single conversion was accomplished.

Early in 1770 Governor Portola returned to San Diego, with the disappointing information that he had been unable to find the bay of Monterey, and had effected no settlement in the north. We may suppose that Serra was grieved and annoyed, particularly when Portola came to describe the place that he admitted bore some resemblance to Monterey, and which the mariners who had remained at San Diego declared must be the spot that was sought. The distress of the ardent founder of missions became still more acute, when Portola presently announced that unless relief came from the peninsula by the middle of March, he proposed to take the entire company back to Loreto and abandon the expedition.

What happened then reads like a leaf from the early days of the Christian era — the days of saints and of frequent minor miracles. The exact time for departure was set, and Father Serra and his fellow priests prayed without ceasing that something might happen to prevent the governor from carrying out his threat. Argument, entreaty, and even tears had proved unavailing to shake his purpose. Finally, when the last hours of respite were passing, a sail was seen far out at sea, going north. Four days later the San Antonio came into the bay of San Diego. It had been laden with stores at Loreto by Galvez, and dispatched with orders to go north to Monterey, where the visitador general supposed a settlement had been located. Landing at the Channel islands for water, they learned from the Indians that Portola and his party had returned to the south.

Here was an interesting succession of chances that might, by the turn of a day, have completely changed the history of California. Had the San Antonio passed San Diego in the night, unseen, or had it delayed at Loreto a day or two longer, San Diego would have been abandoned, and Galvez perhaps have reported to the king that the occupation of Upper California was difficult and unprofitable. The Russians were already working down from Alaska, and a little later the English made fur settlements around Vancouver. It is not impossible that, had the Spaniards retreated from the country in 1770, some other nation would presently have taken possession, from whose hold California could not have been so easily wrested as it was from that of the Spaniards' legatee — the Mexicans.

The return of the San Antonio with ample provisions convinced Portola that Galvez was thoroughly in earnest about the settlement at Monterey. Two expeditions were immediately planned; one by sea, the San Antonio, with Serra on board, and one on shore with Portola in command, accompanied by Fages, the future governor, and Father Crespi, the faithful keeper of the diary of travels. Again the natives of Yang-na turned out to witness the passage of white men through their domain — and a very uneasy sort of a person they must have considered Portola, to be eternally wandering up and down the coast in this fashion. When the San Antonio arrived at Monterey, the land party had been on the ground two weeks, and a permanent camp was established on the shore. Here, on the 3rd of June, 1770, the second California mission was founded in the name of San Carlos Borromeo, although it was commonly spoken of as the Mission of Monterey,

The account which is given us in detail of the ceremonial is probably applicable, with a few small changes, to all the mission foundings of the period. A rude altar was constructed, and several of the bells brought from Lower California were hung in a framework of branches erected near by. Then all the Europeans assembled, the Indians surveying the performance a few hundred yards away. Chimes were rung upon the bells, and the congregation kneeled. Dressed in complete vestments. Father Serra asked a blessing and consecrated the place, while the hymn "Veni Creator Spiritus" was chanted. The cross was elevated and adored, holy water was sprinkled about, and mass was celebrated at an altar above which hung a banner painted to represent the Virgin Mary. In the absence of instrumental music there were salvos of musketry. Junipero Serra then preached a sermon, in which he exhorted those to whom the care of the mission was about to be committed that they should labor faithfully for the conversion of the heathen in their jurisdiction, and uphold the noble traditions of the Franciscan order. Prayers were offered to the Virgin and the ceremonial closed with the chanting of the "Te Deum Laudamus."

Messengers were dispatched to report to Galvez and also to the viceroy in Mexico the success of the enterprise in the founding of the two missions of Monterey and San Diego. The San Antonio presently set sail for San Bias, then the principal port on the west coast of Mexico, carrying Governor Portola, who now turned over to Pedro Fages the charge of affairs in California, as its military governor. This ends all connection of Portola with the enterprise of colonizing Upper California.

When the San Antonio returned, it brought ten more priests from the college of San Fernando in Mexico, and a load of fresh supplies. Orders were sent to Serra to proceed with the founding of more missions — or perhaps it would be more correct to say that consent was given to his wishes in that respect. The newcomers rested for a time at Monterey with Serra and Crespi, and were instructed in the work they were to undertake. It was decided to select a point midway between Monterey and San Diego, and locate a mission there. Again, between that point and San Diego, another should be placed. To this latter. Padres Somera and Cambon were assigned, and when the San Antonio went south, it carried them as far as San Diego.

The third mission to be founded was San Antonio de Padua, which was situated about sixty miles south of Monterey, and was another link in the chain of stopping places on the land route. The ceremony was performed by Serra himself, on the 14th of July, 1771.

San Gabriel was the fourth mission to come into existence. While Father Junipero was busy founding San Antonio, and advising with the new padres there, Somera and Cambon set out from San Diego on the 6th of August, 1771, with a mule train of supplies, fourteen soldiers, and four muleteers, or helpers.

It had been intended to locate the mission on the river described in a previous chapter as the "River of Jesus of the Earthquakes," which we now know as the Santa Ana, but the fathers were not pleased with the site for some reason, perhaps because they preferred higher ground. They went on until they came to the river that Portola had called the San Miguel, but which we now call the San Gabriel. Here they selected a site, about three miles south of the present location, in the midst of a fertile, well-wooded plain covered with shrubbery and flowers. Among the latter, the padres found what they called "wild Castilian roses."

The Indians appeared in great numbers and with what the padres took to be hostile demonstrations; but when the banner of the Virgin was raised before them, according to the account given by the priests, it received

25

immediate homage from the savages, who knelt and offered their necklaces to the beautiful painted image. The apparent submission, however, was probably a mixture of astonishment — for they had never beheld a picture before — with a fear of witchcraft.

The acting governor, Pedro Pages, did not accompany the expedition, owing to the fact that a number of desertions had taken place among the soldiers at San Diego, and general demoralization and disorder prevailed. He was engaged in a struggle to re-establish discipline. The soldiers that acted as a guard to the San Gabriel party were commanded by some petty officer, who seems to have exercised very little control over them. The formal founding of the mission occurred September 8, 1771, and just a month later a serious conflict took place between the Indians and the soldiers, owing to the latter's gross maltreatment of the native women. According to the statements afterwards made by the padres, it was the custom of the soldiers to ride into the neighboring Indian villages, lasso the females and drag them to the camp. The Indians finally attacked the mission, but their chief being slain in the fight, they begged for peace. Then the same condition ensued that existed at San Diego; the padres were unable to induce the Indians to come to the church, or to present themselves for baptism. As the only samples of the finished product of Christian civilization shown them were the cruel and licentious soldiers, it is not surprising that they hesitated to accept the doctrine.

Shortly after the breaking out of hostilities, Fages came up from San Diego with a body of soldiers and a pack train, on his way north to assist in the founding of some more missions. He remained at San Gabriel several months, during which time things were somewhat reduced to order.

The first building constructed was of wood, plastered with adobe and roofed with tules. It measured forty-five feet long by eighteen wide, and was surrounded by a palisade, the latter of such weak construction as to be practically worthless. This building came to be called the "Mision Vieja," or old mission, when the modern site was selected a few years later. The exact spot on which the first buildings were located is not known with certainty. There were some adobe ruins on the Garvey ranch which were for a long time pointed out as remnants of the first building, but as it was built of wood, and as Chapman, who came to San Gabriel in 1818, has declared these ruins to be from an old ranch house that he remembers there, it may as well be admitted that no vestige now remains of the "Mision Vieja," and its exact location will probably never be known. The record gives us no reason for the change of site, but it is probable that the padres, who had set up their establishment on the bank of the San Gabriel in the summer time when the water was low, were frightened at the sudden rise during the winter rains, and thought best to move back a few miles to construct the permanent buildings.

CHAPTER 6. THE PUEBLO PLAN

The very time that Great Britain was learning through her experience with thirteen rebellious provinces how colonists must be treated to be held in allegiance, Spain was maturing her plans for the settlement of the present state of California, and was falling into the same set of errors that Great Britain had made; the only point of contrast being that "His Most Catholic Majesty" went several degrees further to the wrong than did the English monarch. The saving grace of the Spanish system of colonization was that it was largely a matter of theory. It was never carried out as planned, else it could not have lasted even as long as it did.

The one purpose that actuated Spain in the establishing of colonies was to secure some direct and immediate advantage to herself. The welfare of the colonist was considered, to be sure, and considered with great care and particularity, but it was merely with reference to his producing value for the crown. The new territory was supposed to belong to the king, and to be subject to his direct control without interference from the cortes — the Spanish representative body. So far was this theory carried in the case of the early California colonists that they were given no title to the lands they obtained, but were treated as mere sojourners thereon, at the king's pleasure, having no right to give a mortgage or to transfer the occupancy without his consent. Right to live in the colonies was restricted to the aborigines and to Spanish subjects, the privilege of the foreigner being of a doubtful and precarious nature. With reference to California, it was especially decreed that any foreigner who entered the territory did so at the forfeit of his life. The institutions of the original owners of land in the Spanish colonies — whether Indians, Aztecs or Incas — were treated as though they did not exist. They were absolutely ignored. In this, Spain differed radically from Rome, whose example in most other respects she followed — for the Romans based their colonial strength on an adroit mingling of their own laws and customs with those of the conquered nations. Although the church was allowed to lead the way into the wilderness, and bring the savages to Christian civilization, it was never intended that any temporal advantage should accrue to that institution in return for its work. Fundamentally the policy was imperial, not ecclesiastical. The mission system, as it presently shaped itself — a scheme of paternal government among the Indians, with all the fruits of their industrial effort passing into the hands of the church — was something that the Spanish king never contemplated when he sent the Franciscans into California, and something that his successors were taking active steps to bring to an end at the time when the territory slipped out of their control. Although he was as faithful a Catholic as any of his subjects, Carlos III kept a watchful eye on the priesthood. He was ready to concede the highest spiritual authority to the church, but in temporal matters he would brook no infringement of his imperial power and dignity. The theory on which the California missions rested was that they were mere temporary religious outposts, whose function it was to bring the savages to the Christian faith. No definite time limit was set upon them, but it was generally assumed that ten years would be sufficient to carry out the contemplated work, and that then, the Indians all being baptized as good Christians, the missions would become parochial institutions, of the same rank and character as the churches in other portions of the realm.

The scheme failed to come out in this shape, because the Franciscans found it necessary in the practical work of Christianizing the natives to take on some elements of temporal authority, and having once assumed this, they never found the exact moment when it seemed to be possible — or at least desirable — to lay it down.

Now if the mission was to be a mere accessory of the government, it was evident that there must be some form of colonial development distinct from that; and this came in two forms, the pueblo and the presidio. The first of these was, in theory, purely civil — the town — and the other purely military — the fort. As the plan worked out, however, each partook in some measure of the properties of the other. The pueblo was under a semi-military rule, for the reason that one of the purposes of its existence was to supply provisions for the army; the presidio, on the other hand, was finally surrounded by a town made up of retired soldiers and their families, and of people who sought the safety and the trade that came through the presence of the military. Monterey, San Francisco, Santa Barbara and San Diego were the presidial towns; and the three regularly established pueblos were San Jose, Los Angeles and Branciforte, or, as it came to be called later, Santa Cruz. Towns also naturally came into existence in the vicinity of the missions, but these were regarded as accidents, not as part of the general plan.

The year after the establishment of the mission of San Gabriel, 1772, Father Junipero Serra founded San Luis Obispo, the fifth of the series, and the work having now advanced to a point where he felt it could be left alone for a time, the conqueror of the wilderness journeyed to the City of Mexico, to confer with the new viceroy, Bucareli. A conflict had already begun between the military authority, represented by Fages, and the Franciscans; and Serra wished to have the lines drawn more closely as to their respective powers. Bucareli seems to have arrived at the conclusion that the difficulty was due in some measure to the bad judgment of his military representative, for he straightway removed Fages and put in his place Rivera — the same officer that had taken charge of the commissary in the first expeditions. A suggestion of Serra's that a new land route to

California be opened by way of Sonora and the Colorado river was adopted, and an experienced Mexican officer named Anza was sent through that way. A mission post was presently established on the Colorado river which a few years later met with a tragical fate,

In 1774 Serra returned to California with increased authority and renewed hope and enthusiasm, and set about preparing for the establishment of more missions. He found that the Franciscans in Lower California were involved in a quarrel with the governor of that province, De Barri, who possessed a nominal jurisdiction over Alta California, and it is very probable that he asked Bucareli to make a change there as he had in the upper territory. At all events Bucareli removed De Barri, as he had Fages, and to him there succeeded one of the most remarkable and interesting characters of this whole period, a man second only to Serra himself in force, energy and foresight, Felipe de Neve, the founder of Los Angeles.

In 1775 the Indians of the San Diego district attacked the mission, and set it on fire. Father Jaume and two artisans were killed, and all the buildings were destroyed. There is no evidence that the Indians had been ill-treated by the soldiers, nor did the investigation, which was presently carried on by Rivera, reveal any special cause for complaint on their part, other than that the padres were baptizing their brethren. The outbreak seems to have sprung from the erratic impulse of a crowd. It struck terror into the hearts of the missionaries all over the state, and tightened the lines of discipline in the camps and around the Indian villages.

This affair led to a falling out between Rivera and the Franciscans, in consequence of which the former was removed from his position. He insisted upon entering the church edifice at San Diego and dragging thence an Indian who, he asserted, had participated in the rebellion, but whom the fathers regarded only as a fugitive seeking the sacred privilege of sanctuary. For this violation of the laws of the church Rivera was excommunicated. He chose to make light of this for a time, but at last it began to prey upon his mind, until there was a rumor among his soldiers that he was going mad. In 1776 the new governor, Felipe de Neve, was ordered to make his headquarters at Monterey, and to send Rivera south to Loreto. The next year the change was effected, with Monterey as the capital of the two Californias. It was now only eight years since the founding of the upper territory, but Galvez, who was a member of the king's colonial council, had come to believe that its development would soon surpass that of Lower California, and for that reason it was given the preference.

De Neve came up by land, inspecting the missions as he passed along, and studying the needs of the country. He arrived at Monterey in February of 1777, and the first boat that went south carried a report to his superior of what he had seen and what he desired to recommend. The missions of

San Francisco and San Juan Capistrano had been established in 1776, and that of Santa Clara in 1777 just before the governor's arrival. This made eight in all. The governor advised that three more missions be located on the Santa Barbara channel at the center of the chain, and that one of these be made also a presidio. The sites selected were those subsequently occupied by the missions of Purisima (near Point Concepcion), San Buena Ventura and Santa Barbara. The latter place was, in accordance with the advice of De Neve, made the military headquarters for all the central portion of the state.

The new governor was a thoroughly business-like individual, and the practice which prevailed — even after eight years of occupancy — of bringing all the supplies for the presidios by vessel from San Bias struck him as absurd, especially in view of the reported fertility of the California land. Before leaving Lower California, he had explained to the viceroy that the only way to remedy this state of affairs was to import settlers to till the fields, gathering them into cities for the sake of safety and to make life in the wild country more endurable. The process of settlement recommended by De Neve, and subsequently employed, was entirely different from that followed on the eastern coast, and throughout the middle west of America. In California the town or pueblo was made the unit of settlement; elsewhere in the union, the country received the pioneers, and the cities did not come into existence until the farming land was largely taken up. The California system showed the influence of Rome, coming down through the ancient province of Spain. The Roman empire was a city governing the territory that surrounded it, and throughout its provinces a similar system was employed; the city governed the country. Therefore it did not occur to De Neve to import settlers to go on farms. He must bring in people to found cities.

In his tour of the state, he noted two sites of striking beauty and fertility, each supplied with plenty of water and surrounded by open, level country. These were the site called Nuestra Senora de Los Angeles, on the Rio Porciuncula, and a location near the mission of Santa Clara, on the river Guadalupe, which has since become one of the most famous fruit districts of the world. At the latter site he founded the city of San Jose, named for Jose de Galvez, the original patron of California, as well as for the saint of that name. The settlers numbered sixty-six persons in all — fourteen families, the heads of which were, for the most part, retired soldiers from Monterey and San Francisco, special care being exercised to select those that knew something about agriculture. The date of the establishment of this first California pueblo is November, 1777, and it thus precedes by four years the pueblo of the south, Los Angeles. The plan pursued in the allotment of lands, and the treatment of settlers was very nearly identical with that employed later at Los Angeles, and the description given in the next chapter will do for both cities.

CHAPTER 7. GOVERNOR DE NEVE
COMES TO LOS ANGELES.

Heretofore the governor of California had reported to the viceroy direct, but about the time that De Neve was sent to the capital at Monterey a new arrangement went into effect, whereby the northwestern provinces of Mexico, including the two Californias, were joined in one district under a commandant general. The first to occupy this position was Teodoro de Croix, nephew of the De Croix who had been viceroy when Galvez was sending the expeditions into California. He was a man of energy and progressive ideas, and he seems to have reposed a large amount of confidence in Colonel Felipe de Neve — and wisely. The latter was fitted by natural inclination to be a jurist and a lawgiver. His state papers are, for the time and circumstances of their production, models of fairness, prudence and foresight. He found the governmental system of California in confusion, with the representatives of the church, the army and the civil authority continuously working at cross purposes. During the seven years of his administration — five of which were spent in Alta California — he codified the existing laws and rulings with regard to these provinces, and drew up a detailed plan for their military and civil government, touching in some degree, moreover, on the relation of the church to other elements of authority.

As was stated in the preceding chapter, the project for the founding of civil settlements was an important feature of De Neve's plan. The reason which he set forth in his first communication to De Croix on this subject, viz., that of producing supplies for the consumption of the army, was doubtless not the only element in his calculations. While preserving always a friendly and courteous attitude toward the Franciscans, he saw far enough along the line of policy they were pursuing to comprehend that it would never produce a legitimate industrial community, such as the colony needed for permanent prosperity. Being a man with some education, as well as a high degree of intelligence, he was probably not unfamiliar with the development that was taking place on the Atlantic coast, where the settlements founded by the English had increased in wealth and population to such a degree that they were now demanding for themselves the right of self-government; and he felt that if Spain was to hold its own in the final struggle for territory it must people the country with something better than a horde of timid and childish savages.

Immediately after the founding of San Jose, the governor set about preparing for the city in the south. He readily obtained the enthusiastic co-operation of De Croix, who transmitted to Galvez the recommendation of

De Neve, and by Galvez they were transmitted to Carlos III. When they came back from Spain they were in the form of a royal regulation, or order, and the new ruler of California was commended for his energy and good judgment. All this consumed time, and it was not until 1781 that the actual founding of Los Angeles took place. It was, therefore, the first legally ordained city of California, San Jose being rather in the nature of an informal, preliminary experiment.

The greatest difficulty with which De Neve had to contend — an almost insuperable one, as the subsequent history of the colony showed — lay in securing the right kind of material for citizenship. The whole policy of Spain for three hundred years had tended to drive out or destroy the progressive artisan class — the sturdy, independent yeomanry that had made England great on land and sea. There is reason to believe that De Neve was not pleased with the conduct of the ex-soldiers at San Jose; at all events when he came to establish Los Angeles he preferred to experiment in a new field, and he asked De Croix to send him some agricultural people from Mexico. Orders were dispatched to Captain Rivera at Loreto to come over to the mainland and secure twenty-four settlers with their families to form the new city in California. The requirements were that they should be healthy and strong, and men of good character and regular lives, that they might set a good example to the natives. There must be among the number a mason, a blacksmith and a carpenter. Female relatives should be encouraged to accompany them, with a view to marriage with the bachelor soldiers already in California. The term for which all were obligated was ten years.

The proposition that Rivera was empowered to make to the possible settlers, in accordance with the plan laid down in the regulations, was a fairly liberal one — vastly more liberal, in fact, than any that was ever offered to colonists on the Atlantic coast. Each settler was to be given enough land to engage his personal labor, though no extensive land grants were at this time contemplated. It was not his to mortgage or sell, but he owned it through life, and at death it descended to his children on the same terms. But this was not all. In addition to the land, each settler was to receive an allowance of $116.50 per annum, for the first two years, and $60.00 for each of the next three years, these sums to be paid in clothing and other necessary articles at cost prices. Each one was to receive, moreover, two horses, two mares, two cows and a calf, two sheep, two goats, a mule, a yoke of oxen, a plow point, a spade, a hoe, an axe, a sickle, a musket and a leathern shield. Breeding animals were to be provided for the community, and also a forge, an anvil, crowbars, spades, carpenters' tools, etc. The cost of all these articles was to be charged against the recipients, to be paid for at the end of five years in stock and supplies taken at the market price for the consumption of the army.

The regulations drawn up by De Neve provided that the pueblo which these settlers were to occupy should contain four square leagues, or thirty-six square miles; and the original boundaries of Los Angeles measured six miles each way. Near the center of this area there was to be a plaza, measuring 275 by 180 feet, around which building lots should be assigned the settlers, 111 by 55 feet in size. About half a mile from this plaza a series of fields were to be laid out, each containing about seven acres, and the settler was entitled to two of these for cultivation. He had, besides, a community right in the general area, both within and without the city, for pasturage.

Such were the privileges and the opportunities that Rivera was authorized to present to the people of Sonora and Sinaloa, along the west coast of Mexico, to induce them to come to California. The reputation of the Spanish government as paymaster not being first-class, he was advised by De Croix to explain specifically that funds had been set aside out of the royal treasury to meet these obligations; and as an earnest of good faith the first payment was made in advance. By this means, he was enabled to enter into a final contract with those who would agree to come, and to punish as deserters any that took the king's money and then failed to respond to the call.

Rivera was, without doubt, an excellent man for an undertaking of this kind. Having been in charge of the commissary for several expeditions, he knew the country and understood its people, and having served eight years in Upper California, he was probably well equipped with the usual stock of adjectives to describe its beauties and the excellence of its climate. There is, we believe, no case on record of any one living in California eight years without becoming enamored of its climate. Then there was a particular reason why Rivera should do his best to please De Croix at this piece of work. De Neve had accepted the governorship of California rather under protest, and his resignation was now on file with the commandant general. He had cause to hope that his influence at the Spanish court would procure him a more exalted position — a hope that was presently realized. Rivera was next in rank, and the position was now, under the new arrangement of provinces, of much greater importance than when formerly held by him.

We may therefore assume that the captain exerted himself to the utmost to secure the required number of settlers, and to make the best possible selection of material. He consumed nearly a year in the work. Nevertheless, the net result of his labors was not the twenty-four families demanded, but twelve, and of these there was one that probably never came to Los Angeles at all. While the writer naturally hesitates to say anything that can be construed as a reflection upon the "first families of Los Angeles," historical verity requires the fact to be set down that Rivera, at the end of his search, seems to have taken what he could get, rather than to have selected what he desired. A list of these people will be given presently, together with some particulars about them, and the reader may judge for himself.

It was in the beginning of the year 1780 that Rivera crossed over from Loreto to Sinaloa, and it was not until a year and two months later, March, 1781, that his settlers arrived at Loreto to undertake the trip to the new country. They were in charge of Lieutenant Jose Zuniga; for Rivera was to go north with the live stock and supplies, accompanied by some soldiers that he had enlisted, by the new route across the Colorado river. Zuniga and his party arrived at San Gabriel on the 18th of August, and they were quartered some distance from the mission — probably at the old buildings — for the reason that one of the colonists was just recovering from the smallpox, and a temporary quarantine seemed advisable.

Now comes the end of poor Rivera. Two years before this time, a small settlement had been established by the Spaniards on the Colorado river, and two churches were founded there, under the special patronage of the commandant general, De Croix. These latter were in the nature of an experiment, for they differed radically from the missions of the Californias, in the respect that padres were forbidden to direct the industrial efforts of the Indians, or to exercise any form of temporal authority over them. De Croix, like many other civil and military officers of the provinces, viewed with mistrust the increasing power of the priestly orders, and he proposed to try here a system that was more in accord with what he considered the legitimate function of the church. He was most unfortunate, however, in the locality that he selected for his experiment, the Colorado, or Yuma, Indians being fiercer and more treacherous than those nearer the coast.

Letters written to De Croix by the priests stationed in this district were full of forebodings of disaster, but the commandant translated these to mean that the restrictions on the temporal powers of the padres had ruffled their pride. When Rivera arrived at the settlement with his train of cattle, he laughed at the fears of the fathers. He judged these Indians by those he had known along the coast, and, as if to show his contempt for the warnings, he sent all his soldiers on ahead, except a small bodyguard, and even turned back the detachment that the governor had sent down from San Gabriel to meet him.

On the 17th of July the Indians attacked the settlement and the churches, slew all the men except five, and captured the women and children, whom they held for ransom. The number killed is estimated at forty-six, among whom was Rivera, who died fighting bravely. Three months later De Neve sent an expedition into the district headed by Pedro Fages, now returned to California as a lieutenant colonel. The captives were ransomed, as it was found impracticable to attack the Indians. The attempt to colonize the Colorado river district was, however, abandoned.

Much as he regretted the disaster, De Neve saw in it no reason for postponing the foundation of the pueblo of Los Angeles. On the 4th day of September, 1781, therefore, the expedition set out from San Gabriel, the governor leading the way in person, followed by a detachment of soldiers bearing aloft the banner of Spain. Then came the settlers, forty-four persons in all, eleven being men, eleven women, and twenty-two children of all ages. The plaza had already been laid out, and the boundaries fixed for the building lots that faced it. As they neared the selected spot a procession was formed, made up of the soldiers, with the governor at their head, the priests from San Gabriel, accompanied by their Indian acolytes, then the male settlers, and, lastly, the women and the children, the former bearing a large banner with the Virgin Mary painted upon it. We may suppose this banner to have been loaned by the mission authorities, and it may have been the same one that had so miraculously brought the natives to submission when Padres Somera and Cambon first met them on the banks of the San Gabriel, ten years before.

The procession marched slowly and impressively around the plaza, followed, no doubt, by the wondering gaze of the Indians from Yang-na, who had assembled for the event. When the circuit was completed the priests asked a blessing on the new city that was about to come into existence. Then Governor Felipe de Neve delivered a formal speech to the settlers, of which no report has come down to us, but which we may safely assume was full of excellent advice to the citizens, and of glowing prophecy for the pueblo's future. Prayers and a benediction from the padres concluded the ceremony, which was probably the most extensive and the most impressive that was ever held over the founding of an American city. The comparison is easily made, for the reason that probably not more than a half a dozen American cities ever enjoyed the distinction of being really founded. The great majority of them merely happened.

CHAPTER 8. THE ROSTER OF 1781.

HE demands of tradition and of imperial dignity having been satisfied by this ceremonial, the practical work of city building was begun. The plaza, which had been laid out by De Neve's orders a few days before, was an oblong space, with its corners turned toward the four cardinal points of the compass, the longer sides running northwest and southeast. The reason alleged for this apparent violation of the natural laws of direction was that, by this arrangement the winds would not sweep directly through the streets. This would involve a stupid assumption on the part of the governor or of some one else in authority, that the winds were accustomed carefully to consult the compass before they started out to blow. The present writer does not believe this to have been the real reason for the plan; and he may perhaps be pardoned a slight digression on this point, as it raises an important issue of architecture and health.

The streets of the original Los Angeles ran northeast and southwest, and southeast and northwest. The modern city has shifted from this a few degrees, but it is still considerably out of plumb. The city of Santa Barbara is exactly "on the bias," and others of the older cities of Spanish America were laid out on this same plan, although some sections of them, built in later years, have grown entirely away from it. People from the eastern states are accustomed to speak of this arrangement as "peculiar" and "awkward," and they point with pride to their own cities, which are as severely accurate and regular as a demonstration in Euclid. It is true that ninety-nine out of every hundred cities in the eastern states have their streets running to the cardinal points, the exceptions being those places — like Boston — that were never actually laid out, but that "just grew." To defend and to praise this plan, however, shows the easy triumph of conventionality over logic and good sense. The most charming guest that the householder can ever hope to bring into his home is the sunshine, for it drives away disease, and instills cheerfulness and good health. Now if the streets are laid out exactly "on the bias," this glorious visitor can find his way, in his daily course, to every room in the house. If the streets are drawn straight with the points of the compass he is forever shut out from one-fourth of the domicile. Especially is this true in the great cities, where the buildings are huddled together in indecent proximity. Had the city of Chicago, for example, been originally planned to lie as Santa Barbara does, who can say how many thousand lives might have been saved from the baleful ruin of diphtheria and pneumonia, and how much suffering from rheumatism and neuralgia might have been avoided?

It is not unreasonable to suppose that De Neve, with his extraordinary grasp of detail and his keen insight, comprehended this law of health and sanitation, and planned the location of Los Angeles in accordance therewith.

The original plaza must not be confounded with the existing park called by that name, although the latter grew, in a way, out of the former. The two tracts would touch, if marked out on the map, only at one corner, that is, at the northwest corner of the present plaza. The latter is an almost square piece of land, lying between Main and Los Angeles and Marchessault and Plaza streets. The ancient plaza began at the southeast corner of Marchessault and Upper Main (or San Fernando, as it has lately been named), near the Church of Our Lady of the Angels; its boundary continued along the east line of Upper Main almost to Bellevue, thence across to the east line of New High street, thence to the north line of Marchessault, and thence back to the starting point.

Most of that area, save what is used for streets, is at the present time covered with adobes, and it has been so covered as far as the memory of man runs back. How did the first plaza come to be thus occupied, and by what peculiar chance have we this modern plaza near to the other, and yet not of it?

There is no definite record of how this occurred, but it is not difficult to trace a probable course of events leading up to such a result. When the building lots around the plaza were assigned to the settlers, the land at the southeastern end, which is the tract covered by the modern park, was kept for public buildings and for a church. Land was so plentiful at that time that few people took the trouble to secure titles, and the boundaries established by such deeds as were executed were often of the vaguest character. The early adobe buildings were not very substantial, and when the first residences of the settlers around the plaza went to pieces the new structures were pushed forward a little into the open space. We know this was true, for complaint was made from time to time that the plaza lines were becoming obliterated, and that its land was being seized by the adjoining owners. The warnings issued by the ayuntamiento, o ' city council, were unheeded, and the gradual hitching forward process went on, each one endeavoring to outdo his neighbor, until none of the old plaza was left to tell the tale.

There still remained, however, the space in front of the southeastern side, which had been used for the guard house, the granaries, and the council room. While the house builders did not hesitate to steal the park, they scarcely ventured to push the city out of the land it had in active use. Early in the century the church was located about where it now is, and we may suppose that the space directly in front was kept open from a sense of decent religious observance. At all events, when people began to obtain titles from the ayuntamiento — a practice which did not begin until about

1830 — that body was careful not to give away the land to the southeast of the square, and out of that has grown the little plaza park of today.

There were eleven families to be provided with building lots about the original plaza, and at the rate of four locations to the side, three sides were occupied, leaving the fourth for public use, as we have said. We are not told of the exact process by which these sites were assigned, but as the fields for cultivation were drawn for by lot, it is reasonable to suppose that the same practice was employed in the division of the building sites. This being rather a delicate matter, it was probably attended to before Governor De Neve left the pueblo that day in September.

A map has come down to us showing the exact location of most of the settlers. Three are left in doubt, because they had moved out, by request, before the map was made.

Beginning at the western corner (New High and Marchessault), and making a circuit of three sides of the ancient plaza, let us see how the homes of the first families were located, and what sort of people they were that occupied them.

First, at the corner fronting New High street came the home of Pablo Rodriguez, an Indian, twenty-five years of age. His family consisted of an Indian wife and one child. Next adjoining was the home of Jose Vanegas, an Indian, twenty-eight years old, with an Indian wife and one child. He was the first to hold the office of alcalde, or mayor, in the pueblo, being elected to that honor in 1788, and re-elected in 1796.

Next to the house of Vanegas a narrow street cut across at right angles to the plaza front, and then came Jose Moreno, a mulatto, twenty-two years of age, his wife a mulattress. This couple had no children. The fourth location on that side was taken by Felix or Antonio Villavicencio, a Spaniard, aged thirty, with an Indian wife and one child. Around the north corner was an L-shaped lot, occupied originally by one of the expelled settlers. Next came two lots across from and facing the public side, which were taken by the two other banished families. The exact order of these three is not known, but they are described as follows: Jose de Lara, a Spaniard, fifty years of age, with an Indian wife and three children; Antonio Mesa, a negro, thirty-eight years of age, with a mulattress wife and five children. At the east corner was another L-shaped lot, taken by Basilio Rosas, an Indian, sixty-eight years old, married to a mulattress with six offspring.

Coming now to the front that corresponds to Upper Main street, we have first Alejandro Rosas, an Indian, nineteen years of age, whose wife is described as a "Coyote Indian" — which does not sound very promising — with no children. Next came a vacant lot, then a narrow street, and then the home of Antonio Navarro, a mestizo, i.e., Spanish-Indian half breed, whose wife was a mulattress with three children. Lastly, coming back to the side of the public land, we have the residence of Manuel Camero, a mulatto, aged thirty years, with a mulattress wife and no children. He was elected regidor, or councilman, in 1789.

Cataloguing this extraordinary collection of adults by nationality or color, we have: two Spaniards, one mestizo, two negroes, eight mulattoes and nine Indians. The children are even more mixed, as follows: Spanish-Indian, four; Spanish-negro, five; negro-Indian, eight; Spanish-negro-Indian, three; Indian two. Thus the only people of unmixed Caucasian race in the whole company were two Spanish men, on the purity of whose blood frequent aspersions were cast; and the only members of the coming generation with regular ancestry were the two Indian children.

There was one more member of this interesting party, a certain Antonio Miranda, who fell out by the wayside, at Loreto, and who probably never came to California. This is in one way regrettable, for we may believe, from the title bestowed upon him in the original catalogue, that he out-freaked all the rest. He is recorded in the list as a "Chino," which does not signify that he was a Chinaman, as many writers have erroneously stated, but that he was a mysterious tangle of all kinds of available ancestry — "compounded of many simples," as Jacques says of his melancholy — and that his hair was curly. He had no wife extant, so the data is not at hand on which to form even a rough estimate as to what his one child was like. However, it suffices for us to note the facts that Miranda was not a Chinaman, and that he was not of the Los Angeles party. A very fair ethnological composite was achieved, without the assistance of a "Chino." No information has reached us concerning the trades or lines of business of the various settlers, save that Navarro was a tailor. If Rivera obeyed orders in making his selection there was a blacksmith in the colony, and also a carpenter and a mason, but we do not know which members of the party filled these roles, nor, indeed, are we entirely sure they were filled. Little else is known of these early settlers beyond the few facts set down above. If there are any descendants of them now living in California, they are not known as such. The Los Angeles directory of 1901 fails to show anybody by the name of Vanegas, or Villavicencio, or Rosas, or Navarro, or Camero, and only one Mesa. The names Rodriguez and Moreno, which are common everywhere in Spanish America, occur respectively five and twenty-six times in the directory.

In the letters of the padres, these early settlers are generally referred to in terms of pity and contempt. It was originally intended by De Neve that they should enjoy a form of self-government by choosing their own mayor and councilmen (alcalde and regidores), but no election was held during the first seven years, the town being under the guidance of a petty military official, who came afterwards to be called a "comisionado." Evidently the founder of Los Angeles and his successors in the governorship felt that people of such a sort could not be trusted to look after their own affairs.

Work began with the building of houses around the plaza. The regulations required that within five years each settler must be provided with a substantial residence built of adobe; but the first houses were made of light stakes driven into the ground, with poles stretched across for the framework, the whole thatched with tules and plastered with mud, much after the fashion of the Indian "wicky-ups." These were a sufficient protection against the rains of the first season, and before the wet months came again a number of adobe dwellings had been finished.

The next undertaking was a communal one — the construction of a ditch to supply the pueblo with water for irrigation and for domestic use. A small dam was run out into the river at about the point where the Buena Vista street bridge now stands, and the water was carried over the line of the modern city zanja — the "zanja madre" — to the fields, which lay along lower Alameda street, occupying the ground where the lumber yards and Chinatown now are. Here a planting was made of wheat, maize and vegetables, and a palisade was constructed to keep off the cattle and the thieving Indians. This palisade was presently replaced by an adobe wall, which enclosed the houses and some of the fields.

During the first few years, those of the colonists who desired to attend church on Sunday were compelled to travel all the way to San Gabriel; but in 1784 a chapel was constructed near the corner of Buena Vista street and Bellevue avenue. Other public structures completed in the first years were the town house, the guard house, and the granary.

Before the city was six months old it was discovered that Rivera had made a sad mistake in some of the settlers he had selected; and Jose de Lara, the Spaniard, and the two negroes, Antonio Mesa and Luis Quintero, were formally expelled on the ground that they "were useless to the pueblo and to themselves." They went out, taking with them their families, and the number was thus reduced by sixteen. Some years later Navarro, the tailor, was expelled for the same reason. He took up his abode in San Francisco, but a descendant of his was living in Los Angeles in 1840.

In 1785 Jose Francisco Sinova, who had resided in California several years, applied for admission to the pueblo, and was taken in on the same terms as the original settlers. By this time two of the sons of Basilio Rosas had grown up to citizenship, and Juan Jose Dominguez, a Spaniard, had joined the little colony. The latter was given a special land grant by Governor Fages, De Neve's successor, including what was afterwards known as the San Pedro, or Dominguez rancho, which has descended through his brother, Sergeant Cristobal Dominguez, to the heirs of that family at the present time. He is, therefore, the first tangible link between the ancient city and the modern.

CHAPTER 9. THE MISSION SYSTEM.

The time of the founding of Los Angeles, in the year 1781, there were eight mission establishments in California. Within the next four years three more were added, making eleven in all that came into existence under the supervision of Father Junipero Serra. San Buenaventura was founded in 1782. Santa Barbara and Purisima (near Lompoc in Santa Barbara county) were not founded until after the death of Serra, which took place in 1784, but as most of the details of their establishment had been planned by him, it is right that they should be included in the list of the eleven missions of Junipero Serra. The period covered by this work was about sixteen years.

In the three decades that followed ten more missions were founded, making twenty-one in all. No one of these was farther than a day's journey from the coast. They covered a stretch of seven hundred miles, averaging about an easy day's journey from one another. Through the first half century of California's existence these institutions occupy the center of the historical stage, the other elements — civil, military, communal or individual — serving rather as accessories than as independent actors. To obtain, therefore, a correct perspective for the little pueblo of Los Angeles, whose founding we have just described, it will be necessary to examine into the unique social-religious system that was above and around it.

Although this system was in full operation from San Diego to San Francisco less than a lifetime ago, with its long chain of prosperous institutions involving directly and indirectly about fifty thousand human beings, no remnants of it now remain, save the half-crumbled ruins of the buildings. These being, for the most part, constructed not of stone or of brick, as are the churches of Europe, but of half-baked clay, their ultimate complete destruction is only a matter of a few years' time, unless individual or government enterprise intervenes to protect them. A local organization of Southern California, the "Landmarks Club," has checked the ruin of San Juan Capistrano and San Fernando, and is now devoting its energies to San Luis Rey. Such of the buildings as are in proper condition and are suitably located are used for parochial institutions by the Roman Catholic church. Santa Barbara and San Gabriel are examples of establishments that have been in almost continuous use for church purposes since their foundation.

Unfortunately many of the missions were located in districts that are now too sparsely settled to support them as churches, and these have gone into utter ruin. San Antonio de Padua, for example, which, not more than ten years ago was a handsome, substantial structure, having been preserved for church use up to that time, is now nothing but a stretch of ragged clay wall, which the rain and suit and wind will, in a few years more, completely obliterate.

Of the human elements that entered into the system, the remnants are even fewer. The original Spanish Franciscans are gone — a few German Franciscans have taken their places. The Roman church is here — as it is everywhere — but it holds now only a share of the population, where in the mission days it held all except the few roving Indians on the foothills. But the thirty thousand savage converts, the neophytes that gathered around the missions and served the fathers both as congregation for their spiritual ministrations and as toilers in the industrial development of the country — they have disappeared entirely as a class and almost utterly at a race. In the prosperous days of San Gabriel it embraced within the system of its industrial operations nearly two thousand Indians, and now not more than half a dozen Indian families can be found in that vicinity. Not only has the mission system itself departed, but the elements that entered into it seem to have been destroyed, root and branch.

Institutions that are planned for permanency and pass away usually rank as failures, but the Franciscan missions of California were not as utterly valueless as the wreck of them would indicate. Their projectors had a certain purpose in view, viz., the Christianizing and civilizing of the Indians — a worthy purpose, it must be conceded; and if they managed to accomplish it, or if they came as near to success as others engaged in the same work elsewhere, then the mission system is not to be hastily condemned as a failure, notwithstanding the fact that it exists no longer, and its materials have fallen into decay.

The question of the value of the missions and the wisdom and justice of their treatment of the Indians, has given rise to a great amount of controversy, with a variety of resultant opinions. The phrase "to civilize the savages" is easily written and glibly uttered, but when its full meaning is considered it will be found to contain one of the greatest of human problems. It is of about the same order as the squaring of the circle, or the achievement of perpetual motion. The frontier proverb that "the only good Indian is a dead Indian" puts into rough and brutal form the experience of the English-speaking peoples that about the only way to civilize savages is to put an end to their existence. This may be done by the swift and simple process of slaughter, or by the slower and more complex plan of driving them from their lands into inevitable starvation. If neither of these plans is available, there still remain the white man's deadly vices. Now to make a fair judgment of the system employed by the padres with the California Indians — a judgment which with most of us will labor under the unsympathy of an alien blood and a different religious belief — it might be well to use as a basis of comparison our own treatment of the Indians during a similar period of our development. Where are the Indian tribes that formerly held the land east of the Mississippi? Are they civilized or are they obliterated? Or, if the matter be brought nearer home, will the comparison be more favorable if we inquire into our methods with the Mission Indians, after California became part of the union? It is a heart-breaking story that has been told only too well by Mrs. Helen Hunt Jackson in "Ramona" and "A Century of Dishonor." Plainly these comparisons are out of the question.. But while the Anglo-Saxon will plead guilty to his own failure to civilize the savages, and will even admit that he and they cannot live in the same neighborhood without the latter coming to destruction, yet he does not hesitate to pass judgment on the efforts of others. The American historians that have handled the mission question have generally condemned the system employed by the padres with the Indians, although certainly no one of them would claim that the Anglo-Saxon has ever done the work any better.

The process by which the mission system came into existence was a logical one. A couple of priests, accompanied by a small squad of soldiers go into a strange country, peopled only by savages, but having great agricultural and industrial possibilities. Of these possibilities the priests are thoroughly cognizant, by reason of the resemblance between the climate of the new country and that of their own. The demands of religion must be considered first, and for that purpose a church building is to be constructed. Who will do the work? The soldiers will not; the priests alone cannot, and there are none others save the savages. The padres offer the natives little gifts of cloth and beads, and when their good will is established ask for their assistance in the work of erecting the church. This is frequently offered without the asking. Next comes the planting of crops for the support of the padres and of such of the natives as have worked faithfully at the building, for the Indian in his native state is always close to starvation. The cattle which the padres have brought with them must be cared for, so a few of the Indians are taught to ride horses and to serve as vaqueros. In the meantime the work of baptism and instruction in the rites of the church goes on, a little slowly at first, but more rapidly as the Indians learn that no harm comes of it. A series of buildings are constructed, not only for church work and the use of the priests, but also to harbor the Christian Indians, the neophytes, as they are called, who, having lost caste among their own people for doing the manual labor of the white man, must be cared for by the padres and kept from backsliding into savagery. In this way the industrial system is gradually built up, each undertaking laid upon its predecessor with inevitable logic and seeming necessity.

It is to be doubted whether any form of civilization could have been worked out among these savages that did not rest upon some sort of an industrial base. Had the padres confined themselves, as De Croix and other civil governors advised, to the purely spiritual side of the work, and had the savages been allowed to continue in their indolence and degradation, the religious instruction must have fallen on ears that would not hear. The

Indians would inevitably have become involved in conflict with the soldiers, from whom the padres with difficulty protected them, even under the mission regime; the savages would have grown fiercer and more crafty, and in the end would have proved a barrier to the advance of civilization, instead of assisting its progress. The doctrine that the Evil One is always at hand to find work enough for the idle, applies as well to the savages as to the civilized man. The fathers understood this; there was plenty of work to be done, and they could see no reason why the Indian should not do his share.

In the minds of these simple, earnest soldiers of the church a law was a law, and was to be obeyed. Both religion and worldly wisdom required that the Indian should be controlled and made to work; and the padres did not allow any idle question of sentiment to interfere with this policy. If discipline was necessary they were prepared to administer it. They found the savages to be very like children, and the only form of discipline then in vogue for the child was the rod. If the Indian would not work he was starved and flogged. If he ran away he was pursued and brought back. His condition was not exactly that of a slave, as is sometimes charged. He was not sold from hand to hand, nor separated from his family, nor denied a considerable degree of liberty, if he did not abuse it by bad behavior; neither was he treated with wanton cruelty, nor put to death, except for some capital crime. His condition was rather that of an apprentice bound to service for an indefinite period of years, and subject to the forms of discipline that were practiced upon apprentices all over the world at that time. He had stated hours of labor, usually not exceeding seven in the day, to which must be added three hours for religious exercises. His food and clothing were coarse and none too plentiful, but such as they were they improved upon the nakedness and semi-starvation of savagery. The conditions of life for the mission Indian varied, of course, greatly with the personal characteristics of the padres in charge of the establishment. Some of the superiors were hard and even cruel, and others kind and gentle. Some were successful in maintaining order without much punishment, and others believed in the lash for all offenses. At worst, the Indian's lot was somewhat better than slavery; at best it was happy though not very agreeable.

It happens that on the question of the padres' treatment of the Indians we have plenty of other testimony than that of the priests themselves. The civil and military authorities were ready at all times to criticize the methods of the padres, and the reports filed with the viceroy and the commandant general by the governors show that affairs at the missions were subjected to a close scrutiny. It was hardly to be expected that any system of discipline could be maintained over tens of thousands of ignorant savages without affording occasional instances of harsh treatment or injustice.

The mission system may be properly charged with the mistake of over-discipline, which brought two bad results; the one of occasional cruelty to the Indians and the other — more serious in the long run — of failing to make the natives independent and self-supporting. It remains to be proved, however, whether any form of policy would have accomplished the latter object. The charge that there was great mortality among the Indians under this system is true, but a large death rate is to be expected whenever savages are required to change from out-of-door freedom and nakedness to the civilized form of life.

On the other hand, it must be recorded to the credit of the mission system that order was established and maintained among a horde of degraded savages scattered along six hundred miles of frontier; that the men were taught agriculture, irrigation, cattle-raising, leather-working, carpentry, milling, building, blacksmithing, the care of horses, and many other useful pursuits; and the women were taught to cook and sew and weave, and were protected through girlhood and decently married to men of their own race or to the Spaniards; that an industrial community was created in each mission center, to redeem the land from an otherwise complete worthlessness and sloth; that the padres, almost without exception, led moral lives, setting an example of decency and sobriety not only to the Indians, but also to the white settlers; and, lastly, that the whole mission undertaking was founded in the beginning on a conscientious devotion to the teachings of Christ, and was carried on by the fathers with sincere motives, and according to their best judgment.

CHAPTER 10.
EIGHTEENTH-CENTURY LOS ANGELES.

The provisions under which each settler received his allotment of a building site and a piece of farming land was that within three years he should have a good adobe house constructed and the land cleared and that within five years he should have some chickens, a fair crop of corn or wheat growing and a good farm equipment. Not until the five years had passed was he to receive anything like a title to his land, and even then he would not be allowed to sell or mortgage, the king being the real owner and the colonist rather in the nature of a lessee.

There is reason to believe that these conditions were not entirely complied with by all the colonists; nevertheless, De Neve's successor, Fages, in 1786, thought best to issue the so-called titles, and he sent Jose Arguello, afterwards governor of the province, to perform this service. Arguello appointed two witnesses from the guard of soldiers at Los Angeles, one of them being Corporal Vicente Felix, who was an important factor in the city's affairs at this time. Summoning all the settlers to his presence, Arguello presented each one of the nine with: First, a deed to his house lot; second, a deed to his farm land; and third, a branding iron, by which he was to distinguish his stock from the others'. These nine settlers were the original eleven, minus De Lara, Mesa and Quintero, expelled for general uselessness, and plus Sinova, the emigrant picked up in California. Twenty-seven documents were thus distributed, for a description of each branding iron went with the implement, all signed by Arguello and his witnesses, and adorned with the "X, his mark," of the settler, for not one of the nine could write. In the case of the house lots, each location was described with reference to the plaza, showing that a rough survey had been made, and a map was filed with Arguello's report to the governor of the transaction. The location of the fields is left somewhat vague, the assumption being that each one knew about where his own land was, anyhow.

During the next four years considerable increase took place in the population, the newcomers being chiefly soldiers who had served out their time. Some of these were married to Indian wives, but others were attracted to Los Angeles, no doubt, by the fact that a number of girls were growing u:p in the families there, who would in time be ready for marriage. By 1790, the number of households had increased from nine to twenty-eight, with a total population of 139. All of the original settlers who had received titles from Arguello remained, except one, Rosas, who had departed for San Jose. On the other hand, Los Angeles had received one emigrant from San Jose, a certain Sebastian Alvitre, who, for nearly twenty years, enjoyed the reputation of being the worst man in the province of California. Most of the reports from the comisionado at Los Angeles to the governor, during this period, contain somewhere the interesting item of news that Alvitre is in jail again.

Among the names of the twenty new settlers there are several that are now common in Los Angeles; such, for example, as Figueroa, Garcia, Dominguez, Pico, Reyes, Ruiz, Lugo, Sepulveda and Verdugo.

No selection of an alcalde seems to have been made prior to 1788. Corporal Vicente Felix acted as general manager of the colony and arbiter of all disputes up to that time. The settlers found fault with him continually, and on one or two occasions formal complaint was lodged with the governor, but no change was made; on the contrary, Felix was presently given the title of "comisionado," and advised by the governor to make it his business to see that the laws were obeyed and good order maintained, although the pueblo had by this time an alcalde and two regidores, or councilmen, who were supposed to be the local administrative, judicial and legislative authority.

Jose Vanegas, one of the original settlers, was the first alcalde, Jose Sinova the second, and Mariano Verdugo the third. The list from 1790 to 1800 runs as follows: Francisco Reyes, Jose Vanegas (re-elected), Manuel Arellano, Guillermo Soto, Francisco Serrano and Joaquin Higuera. Through all these administrations Felix continued to hold authority, as the real representative of the governor, and the court of last appeal. Theoretically, the pueblo was entitled to local self-government, but practically it was under military control — that is, as far as it was controlled at all.

The records of the pueblo during this epoch are decidedly meager. In 1790 the fact is noted in the reports that the colonists of Los Angeles grew a larger crop of grain than any of the missions except San Gabriel. The amount is given as 4500 bushels, which does not seem large when it is divided by the number of heads of families — say 150 bushels to the settler. Most of this was corn. In 1796 it was nearly twice as large. By 1800 the crop had increased so far beyond local needs that a proposition was made by the pueblo to supply 3400 bushels of wheat annually for the market at San Bias at a price of $1.66 per bushel. This is especially significant in view of the fact that De Neve had advocated the founding of the pueblo because wheat was being imported from San Bias to supply the soldiers in California. In 1797 there was a drought, and only 2700 bushels were grown. About this time the governor sent down word that land must be assigned to every head of a family in Los Angeles, and that each one must be required to do his share of the cultivation. Fences were ordered constructed, so that cattle would not get into the grain, and each settler was compelled to subscribe three bushels a year to make up a fund for the city's improvement.

Horses and cattle increased with considerable rapidity. In 1790 there were 3000, and in 1800, 12,500. Sheep numbered 1700. A provision in the original regulations of the pueblo as drawn up by De Neve forbade the ownership of more than fifty cattle by any one person. This was for the purpose of preventing monopoly. It seems to have suffered the usual fate of legislation of that order, and was never observed. It had developed by this time that a man might have an abundance of cattle and yet be poor. In the annals of San Gabriel mission, in the year 1795, it is recorded that a man who was known to be the owner of 1000 horses came over from the pueblo to beg for a piece of cloth to make a shirt, as there was none to be had in Los Angeles. In an official price list published by Governor Fages we find the value of an ox or cow put at $5; of a sheep, $1 to $2; of a chicken, 25 cents; of a mule, $14 to $20, and of a well broken horse at $9. An attempt was made during Fages' time to arbitrarily fix the price of wheat at $1 a bushel. The value of horned cattle could hardly have been so great at this time as it was a quarter of a century later, when the Yankee traders began to frequent the coast to buy up hides and tallow.

During the decade from 1790 to 1800 the population of Los Angeles increased from thirty to seventy families, from 140 people to 315. By this time it had become the custom to send the superannuated and invalided soldiers from the various presidios to Los Angeles to end their days in its mild climate. In the census of 1790 there is a division of citizens by age, and out of eighty adults nine were over 90 years old, which is an extraordinary percentage. This same census gives the division of nationality as follows: Spanish, 72; Indians, 7; mulattoes, 22; mestizos, 30. The increase in the number of Spanish (which probably includes those of Spanish descent born in America) shows the large part now played by the army in the colonization; for the soldiers detailed in California up to this time were largely brought over from Spain, whereas the colonists from Mexico were, as we have seen, of mixed descent.

Los Angeles at the end of the eighteenth century consisted of about thirty small adobe houses, twelve of which were chistered around an open square, and the remainder huddled in the vicinity, without much system as to location. The houses were near together, not because land was scarce or valuable, but for sociability and for mutual protection against thieving Indians. Most of the new houses were to the southwest of the plaza, where are now Buena Vista and Castelar streets. To the north and east lay the lower land, and the space reserved for the public buildings. These latter consisted of a town house, where all the public business was transacted; a public granary, a jail, and the barrack, where the small detachment of the army that was assigned to Los Angeles: Vicente Felix, the comisionado, and his three or four men, had their headquarters.

The houses were one-story affairs, frequently containing but one room. The roofs were constructed of poles, thatched with tules, and at first plastered with mud; later brea was discovered in the fields to the west of the town and used for roofing material, as it is to this day. As the rafters had but little slope, considerable rain must have found its way into the houses in wet weather. Glass was unknown, the small windows closing with a shutter, if at all. The few pieces of furniture were crudely constructed of poles and strips of rawhide.

No attempt was made to keep the yards about the houses in decent sanitary condition, much less to make them beautiful. There were no flowers nor shade trees, except here and there a sycamore, that may have escaped the searchers for firewood, or a few wild blossoms in the springtime. Cattle were slaughtered for food right in the house yards, and the remains of the carcasses thrown about. The sole scavengers were dogs and chickens and the birds provided by nature for that purpose. In the summer time the roads and paths about the houses were deep in dust, which every passing horseman stirred up for the wind to drive through open windows and doors.

There does not appear to have been any planting of fruit trees until near the end of the century, when Governor Borica sent word to the authorities that orchards and vineyards should be set out and protected from cattle by fences and walls. The irrigating ditch was frequently neglected, until there was danger at one time that everything would dry up and die; so the governor ordered extensive and permanent repairs to be made. A great deal of the hard labor of the farms and households was done by Indians, who had been half civilized and half educated at the mission of San Gabriel, and who found life at the pueblo easier and more entertaining. Some of these worked the farms on shares, which gave the settlers plenty of time to attend cock fights and play the guitar.

The padres who came over from San Gabriel to take charge of the religious welfare of the citizens complained bitterly of the idle and worthless lives led by most of their parishioners. There was no school in Los Angeles, nor any attempt at instruction of the young. In 1784 an ex-soldier named Vargas opened a school in San Jose, and a few years later he was summoned to San Diego by a raise in salary — $250 a year was the improved figure — but Los Angeles did not put in a bid. A mail was carried to and from Mexico once a month, covering a distance of 3000 miles over the Camino Real or King's Highway, but as almost none of the settlers could read or write postal facilities were little used. There was a good deal of disorder of a mild type — drunkenness, quarreling and occasional fights — but murder seems not to have been frequent. The soldiers acted as policemen, and a guard was maintained night and day.

Foreign vessels were not allowed to visit the coast, and there was very little trade or commerce of any kind. Such as there was remained largely in the hands of the padres at San Gabriel, and was carried on through the port of San Pedro, where some years later a warehouse was constructed for the use of the mission.

This description seems to be carrying us back into the Middle Ages, and yet it was only one hundred years ago, in the administrations of Washington and of John Adams, the time of Pitt and Burke, and of Napoleon and Goethe.

CHAPTER 11. IN THE SPANISH PROVINCE.

Felipe de Neve was too valuable a man to be allowed to remain long in charge of so remote and unimportant a province as California, and within a year from the founding of Los Angeles, in 1782, he was transferred to a higher position. He presently succeeded De Croix as commandant general of the "Internal Provinces," an office independent of and very nearly equal to that of the viceroy of Mexico. Unfortunately, he died a few months after reaching this coveted honor. As the founder of Los Angeles city, and the first independent governor of California, he would be entitled to a prominent place in the locality's history, whatever his attainments; but the fact that he was a man of exceptional brilliancy and force, whose judicial powers and administrative skill were recognized at an early age by his government, will cause us, more than a century later, to revere his memory and to regret the untimely death that ended his career.

In the same year, 1784, died the other great man of this epoch and region — Father Junipero Serra. He had reached the age of 67, having labored zealously in California since 1768, during which time he had established and thoroughly organized the mission system of the province. He had many of the qualities of the soldier, the statesman, and the industrial leader, as well as those of the evangelist. When the smaller men — Rivera, De Barri and Pages — obstructed his path he brushed them aside; but in De Neve he had to contend with an individuality as powerful as his own. In spite of the guarded language with which De Neve, in his state papers, handles all matters relating to the missions, and in spite of the calm dignity of his demeanor towards the padres, it is evident that he was entirely conscious of the churchman's disposition to encroach on the confines of the civil authority, and his eye was ever on Serra as their leader. An incident that took place in 1779 with reference to Serra's exercise of the power of confirmation illustrates so admirably the character of these two men, and shows so plainly the attitude they held towards each other, that it is well worth relating. The administering of the rite of confirmation, i.e., the acceptance of converts into the church, was limited, both by ecclesiastical and civil law to the bishops. Although ranking as president of the California system of missions, Father Junipero was not a bishop, but he obtained by special arrangement through the college of San Fernando, Mexico, and the viceroy, the authority to confirm; and he proceeded to exercise it upon great numbers of Indians. It may have been that De Neve questioned the wisdom of receiving these ignorant savages into church membership, or it may have been that he regarded this as a usurpation of power on the part of Serra, which it was his duty to inquire into; at all events, finding no record anywhere of the granting of such a privilege, he wrote a courteous letter to

Serra, asking him the source of his authority. Serene in the consciousness that he was well within the law, and actuated, perhaps, by a very human wish to humiliate the governor, Serra paid no attention to the summons and continued with the ceremony of confirmation. Thereupon De Neve issued an order suspending all future confirmations, and in a letter entirely free from animus or personal feeling, he reported to De Croix, the commandant general of the provinces, what he had done. De Croix learning, in the meantime, either from the viceroy or from the College of San Fernando, that Serra had in his possession the documents showing his right to confirm, wrote to the ecclesiastic, and instructed him to deliver them to De Neve, and put an end to the controversy. But Serra had taken occasion to send the documents down to the College of San Fernando. Why? Our admiration for this conqueror of the wilderness is so great that we hesitate to accuse him of a trivial or ignoble act, yet his conduct through this whole affair is exactly that of a man seeking by every small device to put a conspicuous humiliation upon a rival in power. If that was his purpose he certainly failed, because De Neve was too great as a man, and too dignified as a ruler to notice the effort. In due course of time the papers were returned and submitted to the governor; whereupon he withdrew his order, acting both then and thereafter with even, unruffled courtesy toward Serra and the other priests.

De Neve's successor was Pedro Pages, a frank, good-hearted soldier, of no great intellectual attainments, but conscientious in the discharge of his duty. He served from 1782 to 1790. It will be remembered that Fages accompanied the first expedition sent out by Galvez to colonize California, and that he succeeded Portola as military ruler of the upper province. His removal from that position was caused through the influence of Serra, and it was scarcely necessary for De Neve to warn him, as he did in a formal state document, that the civil authority must be protected from the encroachment of the priests. He was, however, by no means so well qualified to hold his own in controversy with the padres as was De Neve, a fact which is well illustrated in the circumstances that attended the founding of Santa Barbara and Purisima missions.

These establishments had been planned by Serra, and would have been founded before the close of De Neve's term but for the disagreement between the governor and the padres regarding them. De Neve's estimate of the mission system shows in his desire to establish pueblos and permanent fortified camps, and in his determined efforts at civil colonization.

He seems to have regarded this industrial development among the Indians, with its hierarchical foundation, with suspicion and distrust, and although he manifested no hostility toward the establishments that already existed he was loth to assist in the upbuilding of new ones. He offered no objection to San Buenaventura, which was part of the original plan devised before his administration, but his influence was felt through the commandant general and the viceroy in the arrangements for the other two missions of the channel — Santa Barbara and Purisima. The regulations drawn up for the founding and management of these two institutions provided that the natives were not to be brought in from their villages by force, nor were they to be kept at the mission, except for a limited term and a few at a time. This was, in effect, an interdiction on the whole industrial scheme — which the Franciscans would not tolerate, their contention being, as we have seen in a previous chapter, that unless they could control the daily life of the Indians it was impossible to civilize them. De Neve agreed to provide plenty of soldiers to shield the fathers from harm, and he expressed some well-bred doubts as to the efficacy of a conversion that could be achieved only through material means. In the end, there was a deadlock, which is possibly what De Neve anticipated and desired. The padres refused to serve at the new establishments, and the governor maintained his position, in spite of their refusal.

But when Fages was governor, and after the death of De Neve, the question was reopened, and by some means the padres carried the day. In 1786 the two new missions were founded, and their plan of operation was exactly like that of the other establishments. The issue was never raised again, and all of the ten remaining missions followed the original plan.

The successor of Fages, on the latter's resignation in 1790, was Jose Antonio Romeu, who served as governor only two years, during most of which he was an invalid. During his administration two more missions were established, making thirteen in all. The new establishments were Santa Cruz and Soledad, the latter situated about thirty-five miles south of Monterey. On his death, and after a short interregnum, came Diego de Borica, who held the office until the beginning of the nineteenth century. He was a prudent, politic man, famous for his wit and comradeship, but industrious and capable. His attitude toward the padres and the mission system, while not partaking of the far-sighted doubts of De Neve, was no less independent and firm. He was also an advocate of the pueblo plan of colonization, and the Villa of Branciforte was founded near Santa Cruz mission during his administration.

On the death of Serra, Fermin Francisco Lasuen succeeded to the presidency of the missions. Point Fermin at San Pedro was named in his honor, a fact that should set at rest the question of its spelling, which has been variously written by map-makers and government engineers as Fermin, Firmin and Firmen. After the death of Serra, mission development was allowed to flag somewhat during the administration of Fages and Romeu, but shortly after Borica came into office it was taken up with new vigor. In 1797 three missions were founded, San Jose, San Juan Bautista and

San Miguel. The following year two more were added, San Fernando, near Los Angeles, and San Luis Rey in the San Diego district. This made a total of eighteen. All of these institutions were in a fairly prosperous condition, averaging about six hundred and fifty Indians and three thousand cattle to each establishment. At the end of Borica's term the missions were producing an aggregate of 75,000 bushels of grain, of which about three-fifths was wheat. There was much complaint at this time of the ill treatment of the Indians by the padres, which, in some cases, was clearly substantiated, and the necessary reform followed.

In his effort to found the new pueblo of Branciforte — named in honor of the viceroy then administering the government of Mexico — Borica was confronted by the same difficulty that beset De Neve, and his enterprise met with even a poorer degree of success than his predecessor's. It was one thing to draft extensive regulations for the governing of a pueblo, but quite another to find the people to occupy it. We do not know that Borica ever paid a visit to Los Angeles, but he certainly inspected San Jose, which was only a short distance from the capital at Monterey; and he was probably not much impressed with the outlook there, for he announced his purpose to build adobe houses for the settlers at Branciforte before they were asked to emigrate thither, lest they should follow the example of the colonists at the other pueblos and live in miserable tule-thatched huts. The mother country being involved in a war at this time he was obliged to devote all his energies to the coast defense, and the projected architectural greatness of Branciforte failed to come to pass. A few settlers were secured from Mexico, of about the same type as those of San Jose and Los Angeles, but the new pueblo presently became a refuge for transported convicts and other birds of the same feather, and in the end achieved the worst reputation of all the settlements of early California.

One of the chief difficulties in the colonization of California was the absence of women. Men came as soldiers and adventurers, but no women came, save those that were already married to the settlers of the pueblos. Governor Borica repeatedly urged the viceroy to send a shipload of healthy, respectable young women to become the wives of the male settlers. The request was never complied with, whence we may infer either that women were scarce in Mexico or that they were unwilling to experiment with this extra hazardous form of the matrimonial lottery.

The Spanish land grant system in California had its beginning about the time of the founding of Los Angeles, and the first tracts taken up were in the vicinity of that city. Shortly after Fages became governor, application was made to him for a grant of land to be used for stock-raising, and he applied to the commandant general for instructions. He was told that he might give land to individuals in areas not to exceed three leagues square, so located as not to interfere with the rights of any existing mission or pueblo.

The grantee was obliged to improve the place and put stock upon it, and to set up landmarks showing its extent. Under this arrangement, in 1784, the San Rafael ranch was granted to Jose Maria Verdugo, a tract which was described as across the river and four leagues distant from Los Angeles. In the same year Manuel Nieto received all the land between the Santa Ana and the San Gabriel rivers, from the sea to the hill land. The adjoining tract on the east side of the Santa Ana was given to Antonio Yorba in 1810. In 1784 Fages granted to Juan Jose Dominguez the tract along the ocean at San Pedro and up the estuary half way to Los Angeles. Lastly, at about the same time, the Enema ranch, a tract northwest of the city, was granted to Francisco Reyes, but this was later, in 1797, taken away from him and given to the new mission of San Fernando, founded at that time. The fact that the Encina grant was revoked without any apparent protest on the part of its owner, notwithstanding that he had made improvements upon it, evidences the uncertainty of the tenure as well as the small value attached to land at that time.

CHAPTER 12. EXIT SPAIN.

The first decade of the nineteenth century, which was for Europe a time of storm and stress, was for California a period of complete calm and quiet, and for Los Angeles — as far as the record shows — almost utter oblivion. During the second decade of the century, when peace and order were restored in Europe, the troubles of California began, culminating in 1821 in the revolution that made this a Mexican, instead of a Spanish province.

The Napoleonic wars, which tore the map of Europe to tatters, were scarcely noticed in this far-off corner of the world, and yet some of the effects that followed those wars bore heavily upon California. Although Napoleon was for a considerable period in complete control of Spain, with his brother Joseph on the throne, the performances of the Corsican were regarded only with horror and aversion by the Spaniards in California, and prayers were regularly offered for the restoration of Fernando to his rightful possessions. But when the monster was safely caged, and the frightened monarchs were creeping back to their seats, the king of Spain returned to find the ancient colonial empire undermined by neglect and tottering to its fall. By 1810 the rebellion of Mexico was well under way, and by 1815 the spirit of revolt had spread up and down the South American coast. At the end of the second decade of the century it was practically all over, and Spain's American possessions were reduced to Cuba and a few smaller islands.

On the resignation of Borica in 1800, Jose Joaquin de Arrillaga succeeded him as governor of California, and his rule extended through to 1814. He was a man of fair abilities and good intentions, but he lacked in energy and perseverance. It is charged against him by some writers on this period that he was dominated by the padres, but this does not seem to be borne out either by his deeds or his utterances, although he exerted himself somewhat more than his predecessors to keep on good terms with the mission authorities. There was ample justification for this policy in the conditions that had now come to prevail, for the wealth, energy and industry of the whole province seemed to center in these institutions. The pueblos had been in existence a quarter of a century, and their development seemed to have come to a dead halt. In the ten years from 1800 to 1810 the population of Los Angeles increased only from 315 to 365. Its flocks and herds diminished during that period, and its crops showed no particular improvement. Conditions at San Jose were even less promising, and as for Branciforte, it would appear from the accounts that come down to us from all sources that the more it gained in population the more disreputable and worthless it became. The pueblo plan of colonization apparently was not a success.

The missions, on the other hand, continued to increase in people and in the fruits of their toil. There were now about 20,000 Indians at work in these establishments under the guidance of padres who were as thrifty and intelligent in temporal matters as they were devout and conscientious in spiritual. Each mission was a veritable hive of industry, and the combined products of the whole system, small at first but presently increasing, represented whatever of wealth and prosperity there was to the credit of the province. The time was now almost at hand when this was to be demonstrated by an unquestionable form of proof: viz., the missions were to support the government of the province. Possibly Arrillaga foresaw this contingency, and was preparing for it. At all events he interfered but little with the affairs of the padres, and in all his acts seemed to favor the mission plan of government for the natives.

The events of the decade, 1800 to 1810, that are of record relating to Los Angeles, are so brief and meager as easily to be told. In 1805 the first American ship, so far as known, came to San Pedro. It was the Lelia Byrd, Captain Shaler, which in previous years had hovered about the coast, and after a trip to the Hawaiian islands now returned to California and ran into the harbor of Avalon, in Catalina. In his account of the voyage Shaler says that he found the island inhabited by about one hundred and fifty Indians, who were very friendly. After repairing his vessel he came across to San Pedro, where he obtained supplies in the shape of hogs and sheep, paid for in Yankee manufactured products. This was probably the first taste the people of Los Angeles had of the contraband trade, for all trade with foreign ships was contrary to law. But from this time forth Yankee traders came often to San Pedro, at first in search of otter skins — an animal that has since been practically exterminated in this region — and later for hides and tallow.

Another mission was founded in 1804, this being the nineteenth. It was located at Santa Ines, in Santa Barbara county. About this time there was some discussion over the establishment of a mission on Catalina island, but a severe attack of the measles among the Indians of the channel left Catalina almost without population, and the project was abandoned.

In 1806 a new form of agricultural industry was taken up, in the growing of hemp, an article for which there was a good demand from Spain. It was found that the labor required for its culture could be readily obtained from the Indians, and many of the colonists at the pueblos and presidios abandoned wheat and took up hemp. The product rapidly increased from only 1850 pounds in 1806 to 12,500 in 1807, 89,000 in 1808 and 120,000 in 1810. By this time the crop was paying the growers over $20,000 a year, which was an enormous sum for the time and the region. Suddenly the demand ceased and nearly 100,000 pounds of the last crop was thrown back on the hands of the growers. The revolution had broken out in Mexico;

Spanish trade was interrupted, and the colonists lacked the energy and intelligence to open new opportunities for its transportation. In the midst of the furore over hemp-growing, which prevailed more actively at Los Angeles than anywhere else in the province, an interesting question of the legal status of the neophyte as a laborer developed — a sort of a California Dred-Scott case. The settlers had obtained one hundred neophytes from the mission of San Juan Capistrano to labor in their hemp fields, but they were, for some reason, recalled by the mission authorities. The Los Angeles people thereupon besought their alcalde to issue a writ commanding that the neophytes be turned over to them, and the affair thus came up to the governor and the president of the missions. It was held that the colonists had no right to the labor of the neophytes, if it was against their will to work at Los Angeles, which it must have been assumed was the cause of their return to San Juan. It was furthermore held that the neophytes were entitled to religious instruction and care, which they could not receive at the pueblo.

During this decade there was some trouble between the San Fernando padres and the people of Los Angeles on the question of the use of the water of the Los Angeles river. The padres were accused of diverting some of the water by means of a dam above the Cahuenga. It was held by the governor that all the water in the river belonged to the colonists, and that if the dam constructed by the padres interfered with the pueblo's supply it must be removed.

In 1805 there was a pest of locusts that destroyed a large part of the crop; and in 1807, and again in 1809, there was a dry season. Although weather reports were sent in from various parts of the province to the governor, and were made matters of record, it is impossible to say what the actual rainfall was, because rain gauges were then unknown in this region.

Through most of this period Sergeant Javier Alvarado acted as comisionado and maintained order as best he could. His reports show that gambling, drunkenness, and all forms of bad behavior were largely on the increase. Each year an alcalde and two regidores were elected, the three forming a sort of a town council that enjoyed considerable dignity, but not much power.

We come now to the period from 1810 to 1820, which was the era of the rebellion in Mexico, culminating at last in the overthrow of the Spanish power and the establishment of the Mexican empire with Iturbide at its head, this to be followed almost immediately by the Mexican republic. Through this long contest California sided with Spain against the rebels, giving the mother country, however, no assistance, save an insubstantial moral support. The yoke of Spain had never rested very heavily upon the Spanish province. The suppression of commerce and of business enterprise brought about by Spain's antiquated and illiberal methods, while it strikes the modern reader as quite intolerable, was a matter of small consequence to these idle and thriftless people. The higher officials and the padres were, almost without exception, Spaniards by birth, and conservatives by training and inclination. A few seditious documents found their way into the province, but they were promptly seized and destroyed; and until the official announcement finally reached Monterey that the revolution was complete, no one of consequence in California believed that the rebels could succeed.

There was, however, one very tangible piece of evidence presented, by which these far-off loyalists might have known that something serious was happening. The pay and supplies for the army, for the padres and for the governor and his civil staff came to a sudden end with the year 1811, and in spite of a vast amount of hoping and longing and praying, they never came again. The annual pay roll of the army and civil list in California footed up to nearly $80,000, to which must be added supplies sent each year, or purchased from the missions with drafts on the Spanish authorities at Mexico, at a cost of $20,000 more. The total sum, therefore, was over $100,000. The revenues of the country amounted to barely $12,000, which was used in its entirety for other forms of local expense. The province was still on the wrong side of the ledger, as far as Spain was concerned.

This was the beginning of an era of hard times for California, and they grew harder and more desperate as the years passed with no relief. Even the Spanish trading vessels failed to come to the coast, fearing the Mexican and South American privateers, and the only chance for Californians to sell their products, or to buy what they needed, was through contraband trade with foreigners. This was the commencement of open commerce with American ships.

Something had to be done to supply the army with food, and the local government with cash, so the governor turned to the missions. They had plenty of wheat and live stock, and not a little coin put away in their strong boxes. He would pay for everything with drafts on Spain through the Mexican office, to be presented whenever this war with the rebels was over. The padres objected and complained a good deal at first, but in the end they came to regard it as a proper sacrifice to their patriotism and their veneration for "His most Catholic majesty." At the close of the epoch, the good padres held over $400,000 worth of drafts — utterly valueless save as mementoes of a duty bravely performed.

In 1814 Arrillaga died and was succeeded by Pablo Vicente de Sola, a Spaniard and an officer of the royal army. Although Spain could not afford to pay her soldiers nor provide supplies, she was still able to fill the offices of the province. Of all the Spanish governors of California, Sola was the one least qualified for the work, and the position came to him at a time when it was surrounded by difficulties. He was ill-natured, peevish and fussy, and was possessed of an exalted idea of his own importance.

In 1818 a hostile movement was undertaken against California, coming not from the rebels of Mexico, but from a privateer of Buenos Ayres, where also there was a rebellion in progress against Spain. The expedition, which consisted of two vessels, was led by a Frenchman named Bouchard, who was generally spoken of by the Californians as a pirate. He attacked Monterey, which he captured and destroyed. Three of his men were there taken prisoners, one of whom was Joseph Chapman, the first American resident of the Los Angeles region. Bouchard then came south, landing near Santa Barbara, where he sacked the Ortega ranch house, and at San Juan Capistrano, where he visited the mission and captured some wine and brandy. This ended the episode, which was California's only active experience with the rebellion.

In the month of March, 1822, a vessel arrived from Mexico, bringing official notice to the governor that the Spanish power was at an end in Mexico, and that Iturbide was on the throne as emperor. Sola immediately summoned a gathering of the principal officers of California, including the president of the missions. It was decided to take the oath of allegiance to the new government, and await further developments. Spain had been practically dead, as far as California was concerned, for ten years, and the change of government involved no disturbance in material affairs, and probably but little shock to the sentiments of the people of the province.

CHAPTER 13. THE PUEBLO BEGINS TO GROW.

Notwithstanding the hard times inflicted upon California by the Mexican rebellion, the pueblo very nearly doubled its population in the decade from 1810 to 1820, and in the next decade very nearly doubled again. In 1810 there were about 350 people in and around Los Angeles, and by 1830 this number had grown to over 1200. The holders of land grants in the vicinity of the pueblo regarded themselves as citizens, and, indeed, they were under the jurisdiction of the town council, or ayuntamiento, with reference to their local affairs. In this respect Spain and Mexico followed the ancient Roman custom, whereby the town governed the surrounding country.

This growth came largely from the natural increase of families. Life in the pueblo, although primitive, and without many elements of luxury, or even of comfort, from a modern point of view, had the one great advantage that starvation was well nigh impossible, even to the most improvident. There was an abundant supply of land for cultivation, and Indian laborers were cheap and plentiful. Cattle roamed over the plains in such vast numbers that the price of meat was almost nothing. On the ranches it was not required of a man that he should actually work to obtain subsistence; all that was necessary was that he should "hang around." Under such easy conditions of life there would be a natural tendency toward a rapid increase of population, and large families, or at least a large birth rate, was the rule in California during this period. This was, however, partially offset by the extremely unsanitary methods of living that prevailed, the absence of medical knowledge, and the frequent incursions of smallpox and other malignant disorders.

Los Angeles still continued to serve as the "Soldiers' Home" of this military district, although, as the army was now recruited largely from the province, there was no gain of Spanish population from this source. The only immigration received from Mexico was of a most unsatisfactory character. A shipload of foundlings and orphaned children from the asylums in the City of Mexico was accepted in Los Angeles without any serious objection, but when the viceroy, and afterwards the Mexican republic authorities undertook to make this region a dumping ground for criminals, and introduced "transportation to the Californias" as a form of punishment for the worst offenses, the various governors protested with great vigor; and while they were not able to prevent the occasional shipment of a few undesirable characters, the practice was never carried out on a wholesale scale. Those who did come, however, devoted their pernicious energies to the work of demoralizing the whole community, and the success they achieved must have given them a high degree of satisfaction.

Land for actual cultivation, either in or near the pueblo, was to be had almost for the asking, and yet a list of land owners and of landless persons in Los Angeles district made out by the local authorities in 1816 shows that a considerable element of the population was entirely willing to get along without assuming the burden of ownership. Out of a total of ninety-one heads of families seven were owners of large ranches or grants in the vicinity of the city; twenty were bona fide land owners in the pueblo, and twenty-four worked the commons. The latter had claims which, in due course of time, matured into ownership. This left forty to be entered as landless. Of these, twenty-five are said to work for others on their land, and the remaining fifteen simply existed. They are oppressed by no acres of their own, neither will they toil for anyone else. Happy fifteen! It is a hard commentary on the character of the city's population at that time that four-ninths, or nearly one half, lacked the energy to attempt farming on their own account, even under such favorable conditions, and that one-sixth had to be classed as no account at all.

Among land owners at this time we find only one of the original settlers of Los Angeles, Manuel Camero, the mulatto. There is a son of Navarro, the tailor, and a descendant of Basilio Rosas. The names of the other original colonists fail to appear anywhere in the list. This is only thirty-five years after the founding of the pueblo.

The instructions issued by Borica, near the close of the century, that the colonists should set out vines and fruit trees, seem to have been obeyed, at least as far as vines were concerned, for by 1817 there were over 100 acres of vineyard in and about the pueblo, and the manufacture of wine and brandy had begun on a considerable scale. Indeed, a few years later, the mission authorities complained to the governor that the citizens were being demoralized by this pursuit, as their local patriotism and their desire to patronize home industry caused them to consume a large part of the product, and drunkenness was in a fair way to be set up as a civic virtue.

In the year 1817 appears the first record of a school in Los Angeles city. It is possible that instruction may have been attempted for a short period prior to this time, but evidently not with much success, or some one would have made note of the fact. Governor Sola believed in education, and promoted the establishment of schools in all parts of the province. Not content with organizing a boys' school at Monterey, he even established a school for girls, which was a radical departure that must have caused a vast amount of wonder and foreboding.

The school at Los Angeles lasted only about a year, to be followed by a vacation of ten years. It was in charge of a retired soldier named Maximo Pina, who received $140 a year for his services. We have no detailed description of the school or of its master, but it is reasonable to suppose that it was of the same general character as the schools in the other towns at this time. Those at Monterey were fully described by some of the scholars after they had grown to manhood. The picture they present is a horrible one, but there is no reason to suppose it overdrawn. The teacher was almost invariably an old soldier, brutal, drunken, bigoted, and, except that he could read and write, ignorant. The school room was dark and dirty, and the pupils all studied aloud. The master's ferule was in constant use, even for blots on the writing paper or mistakes in reading. Serious offenses, such as laughing aloud or playing truant, or failure to learn the doctrina (catechism), were punished by use of the scourge, a bundle of hempen cords, sometimes having small iron points fastened into the ends of the lashes. It was a horrible instrument, that drew blood, and, if used with severity, left a scar for life. The only volumes used for reading were the books of religious formulae, which the pupils used cordially to hate all through their later life, for the torments of scourging they recalled.

In most of the Roman Catholic countries of Europe, schools were first organized through the church, and throughout the middle ages the clergy were almost the only learned class. It is a matter for natural comment and surprise that in the half century of mission activity in California nothing was done by the Franciscans for the cause of education. Why were no schools for the colonists opened at any of the missions, or, if that were not feasible, why did not the padres, who were, for the most part, fairly well educated, exhibit some interest in the schools opened by the settlers in the pueblos? Their attitude on this important question seems not only reprehensible, but it is even difficult to explain. We may suppose that the padres considered their undivided energies were due to the Indians, for whose conversion the order had set up these establishments in the wilderness; but such reasoning does not, of course, justify their attempt to ignore the thousands of people of their own race and nationality that had come into the province.

The year 1812 was signalized by a series of earthquakes all over California. The roof of the principal church building at San Juan Capistrano fell in, crushing forty neophytes. This structure, although large and imposing, was probably not built to stand much of a strain. The buildings at Purisima were destroyed, and at San Gabriel some small damage was done. Los Angeles escaped uninjured, there being no two-story buildings as yet.

In 1815 there was an excessive rainfall and a flood. The Los Angeles river left its bed and moved over toward the pueblo, running along San Fernando street to Alameda, and thence past the town. In 1825 came a still greater flood, when the river returned to its original channel — its present course — leaving an underground flow that came up in marshy springs on the Avila place, near the present site of the Kerckhoff-Cuzner mills. The worst part of the freshet came in the nighttime, and the roar of the water so terrified the people that they left their homes and went up on the hills above Buena Vista street. Prior to 1825 there had been considerable woodland between the city and the ocean, which the flood destroyed by cutting a definite channel for the river and draining the marshland where the trees grew.

In 1812 work was begun on a substantial and permanent church structure for the city of Los Angeles, which was located somewhere east of the Plaza. The formal laying of the corner stone took place in 1814, but when the river left its channel in 181 5 the governor advised that the location be changed to higher ground, and the site of the present Plaza church was chosen, it being city ground, adjoining the original Plaza, and in close proximity to the other public structures. Here in 1818 the church building was begun, 500 cattle being subscribed by the citizens to defray the expense. At $5 apiece, this would amount to $2500 in cash, which, considering the low price of labor, ought to have carried the work well toward completion. We note in the records, however, that the governor took over the cattle to be used as supplies by the army, and agreed in return to include the construction of the church in his next year's budget of expense. As the territorial government was entirely bankrupt, and was dependent on the missions for support that was half charity and half blackmail, this plan of Sola's presents in itself just ground for suspicion; and the latter is increased by the fact that operations an the church came to a sudden standstill the next year, nor were they renewed until the padres, in response to an appeal from the president of the missions, subscribed seven barrels of brandy, worth $575, to the building fund. In 1821 the work halted again, and a second appeal was made to the padres, and more brandy was subscribed. A number of cash subscriptions were made by the well-to-do colonists in all parts of the state, after Governor Sola had set the example. The conversion of the brandy into cash, drink by drink, was accomplished with the enthusiastic co-operation of the citizens of the pueblos. December 8, 1822, the building was dedicated with appropriate ceremony. The present Plaza church structure was built in 1861 out of the original structure.

The change from a royal province to a territory in the Mexican republic meant very little to the people of Los Angeles. There were a few slight changes in their political institutions — theoretical, rather than actual. California was now entitled to a representative in the Mexican national assemblage, to be elected by a local legislative body. Sola, who was anxious to be rid of the governorship, was chosen to represent the state in Mexico, and Luis Arguello was elected to fill the gubernatorial office. Los Angeles was represented in this — which we may call the first legislature of California — by Jose Palomares. In the second session, Jose Antonio Carillo, also of Los Angeles, was made a member. Palomares was probably elected by the people, and Carillo appointed by the body itself.

The Los Angeles ayuntamiento was enlarged by the addition of a syndico — treasurer and counselor — and a secretary. These, in addition to the alcalde and the two regidores, made a deliberative-administrative body of five. It was to be known hereafter as "Muy Ilustre" (very illustrious), and was to be surrounded with dignity and ceremonial. A gentle hint was presently thrown out to the comisionado that under the new order of things he lagged superfluous on the municipal stage, but it seems to have failed to take with Guillermo Cota, who was in charge of the local military. A clash of authority soon took place, the question of who was who went up to the governor, and he proceeded to rap the "very illustrious" over the knuckles. Order must be maintained in the pueblo, and the governor's representative should not be interfered with. A compromise was at last effected, by choosing Cota as the alcalde. Thus the civil authority finally absorbed the military.

Whether it was due to the spirit of revolution in the air, or to the increasing importance of local offices, about this time Los Angeles began to have trouble in municipal politics, with frequent election disturbances. In 1826 the election was ruled illegal, and ordered to be held over again; and in 1830 the returns were thrown out, on the ground that all the candidates were "vagabonds, drunkards and worse." Slow and stupid as the government of Spain had been, it was at least stable and dignified. That of Mexico, on the contrary, changed so constantly that it made itself ridiculous. In the era of revolution and local disturbance that was now beginning, California merely followed the example of the home government.

CHAPTER 14. THE EPOCH OF REVOLUTIONS.

California was a Mexican territory about a quarter of a century. The new oath of allegiance was administered on the nth of April, 1822, and on the 7th of July, 1847, the American flag went up over the old fortress at Monterey. During that period, eight regularly appointed governors administered the affairs of the territory (not to mention half a dozen irregular and self-appointed ones), and their terms varied from six months to six years. If we except the first of the list, Arguello, who was really inherited from the Spanish regime, every one of these governors had to contend with local rebellions during his term, and three were driven out of the country by revolution. One of the eight was a usurper, who seized the government without the shadow of a claim, rebelled from Mexico, set up an independent state of California, and was not only pardoned by the Mexican authorities, but, in the end, was regularly appointed to the position and allowed to serve out a considerable term.

To understand the disturbed condition of California during this epoch, it is necessary to bear in mind the demoralization that prevailed in the governing country, through its incessant revolutions and political plotting. Although California took no direct part in Mexican politics, but made haste to swear allegiance to whatever power came out on top, there was a natural undermining of the respect for authority, and a disposition to follow the bad example set at headquarters.

Party lines were drawn to some extent in California. The party division that prevailed in Mexico was modeled after that of the United States; which was logical enough, considering that the Mexican constitution was based on the American. The names, however, were not exactly the same. The opposing parties in Mexico were the Federalists and Centralists, the former representing the liberal idea, with a considerable element of local self-government, and the latter the conservative, with a strong central government, a large army, and a leaning to the Roman Catholic church. In California the great majority of the people were Federalists. Too far from the capital to participate in the home government, they were naturally in favor of local institutions, and of the party that would cherish them.

The pueblo of Los Angeles was the storm center for revolutions during this period. Most of the plots for the overthrow of one governor and the setting up of another had their birthplace in Los Angeles, and the chronic conspirators who, at irregular intervals, would work up a new scheme for making trouble, were, with a few exceptions, residents of Los Angeles. There were two reasons for this — one was that Los Angeles was the largest town in the territory, with a population whose idleness prompted it to mischief; and the other was that the southern metropolis was possessed of an idea that it ought to be made the capital of the state, and its failure to achieve the coveted honor kept it discontented and uneasy. In 1835, it succeeded in obtaining an order from the Mexican congress that the capital should be moved from Monterey to Los Angeles, and the latter place was given the formal rank of ciudad, or city, but the decree was not carried out until in 1845.

As we shall have occasion in the story of Los Angeles to refer to many of the governors of this epoch, and as the revolutions form an important part of the local narrative, this chapter will be devoted to brief enumeration of the eight Mexican governors, their terms, and the revolutions thereof.

On the 1st of February, 1825, Arguello was removed from office by the Mexican government, having administered the affairs of the territory with honesty and good judgment for nearly three years. He was followed by Jose Maria Echeandia, a man of small ability, but apparently possessed of good intentions. Echeandia undertook to move the capital to San Diego by the process of residing in that place himself. At the beginning of his term, he ordered the archives brought down from Monterey, and in spite of the opposition of Arguello, the command was obeyed. He contended that San Diego was the central point of the territory of the two Californias; but his real object in making the change was to live in a warmer climate at the southern end of the state. This snub to Monterey was resented by the people of that region, and in 1829, when a rebellion was started there by an embezzling office-holder named Herrera, and an ex-convict named Solis, it received some countenance. Governor Echeandia came up from the south with 150 men and met the conspirators near Santa Barbara. The battle was bloodless, as were most of the engagements of this period, and the rebels fled. The leaders were captured and exiled to Mexico, and Echeandia served the rest of his term in peace.

In 1831 Echeandia was removed, much to his disgust, to make room for a political adventurer from Mexico named Manuel Victoria, who, in his brief term of one year, succeeded in getting himself thoroughly hated for his arrogance and cruelty. He began by expelling Jose Antonio Carrillo and Don Abel Stearns, two respected citizens of Los Angeles, from the territory. He refused to assemble the legislature, or to submit any of his acts to the leading men for their opinion and advice. In November, 183 1, a manifesto was issued, containing the names of Pio Pico, Juan Bandini and Jose Antonio Carrillo, calling upon the people to rise and dispose of Victoria. About 200 men from San Diego and Los Angeles marched northward to meet the governor, who was coming down from Santa Barbara with all the men he could gather at that place — only thirty. The little armies met near San Fernando. A personal altercation took place between Captain Romualdo Pacheco of the Santa Barbara party and Jose Maria Avila, a prominent man of Los Angeles, and in the fight both were killed and Victoria wounded in the face. The governor was taken to San Gabriel, where he made a will, leaving the conduct of affairs to Echeandia, who was still living at San Diego. In the meantime, the legislative body of the territory had elected Pio Pico to be temporary governor until the Mexican authorities should be heard from. To get Victoria out of the state, for he was now quite ready to go, a fund was raised, to which Los Angeles contributed $125, on the understanding that it should be repaid by San Diego. It never was repaid, however, although frequent efforts were made by the Los Angeles ayuntamiento to collect the money.

Pio Pico does not count as a regular governor at this time; it was understood that he was to hold merely during the interregnum. Nevertheless, the brief period of his administration was long enough for two other governors to claim the seat — Echeandia on the south and Zamorano on the north, at Monterey. There was no actual fighting, although the armies at one time came within sight of each other.

In the spring of 1832, Jose Figueroa was appointed to succeed the luckless Victoria. He was the best of all the governors sent up from Mexico, and he managed to hold the office during three years with only one rebellion, and that a trifling affair. A few gambling vagabonds of the Los Angeles district assembled at the ranch house of Los Nietos, in the spring of 1835, and drew up the customary pronunciamento, but they failed to secure a decent following, were seized, thrown into jail, and finally sent out of the country.

In the fall of that year Figueroa died, and there followed him, after a short interregnum, the worst governor that California ever had, Mariano Chico, a Mexican politician who had to be "taken care of" by the administration then in power. He was a coarse, ignorant fellow, of violent temper, filled with hatred of foreigners, and contemptuous of local institutions and customs. He began his administration with a row with the people of Los Angeles. A citizen by the name of Feliz had been deserted by his wife, and when he undertook to bring her back, he was set upon and killed by the woman and the man with whom she had eloped. The murderers were captured and thrown into jail in Los Angeles, but a mob broke open the place, took them out, and, after a hasty trial, shot them to death. This is the first instance in California of the lynching of white malefactors. Indians were sometimes treated after this fashion for running off stock.

Now it happened that the man who had been killed was a fellow countryman of Chico, and the governor flew into a terrible rage against the people of Los Angeles. He ordered the arrest of the principal officers of the city, and threatened them with death. His courage seems to have failed him at the critical moment of the trial, however, and they were all pardoned with a reprimand.

When Chico had been in office about six months, and had succeeded in alienating all classes of society, he had an undignified altercation with the principal alcalde of Monterey, a very popular man, whom he insulted and then degraded from office. The next day the capital began to fill up with armed and mounted men. Day by day they increased in number, coming from greater and greater distances, until the place was invested with a band that seemed ready to take control at a moment's notice. Chico understood what it meant; he came from a country of revolutions, and when the legislature suggested that as more soldiers were needed for him to maintain order, perhaps he had better go back to Mexico and get some, he lost no time in taking the hint.

Gutierrez, being next in command, undertook to manage affairs until a new governor should be appointed; but the taint of the policy of Chico hung over his actions, and before two months had passed a new revolution was under way. It was led by a young man named Juan Bautista Alvarado, who, at this time, was an accountant in the custom house, and was the idol of the native element. Gutierrez had insulted and threatened the youth, using the manner of language that he had learned from Chico — and with the same result as befell the latter. Alvarado went out among the people and soon gathered a small army, with which he descended upon Monterey and drove Gutierrez into the presidio. The governor had removed all the powder from the armory, so he thought himself free from artillery attack, but Alvarado's men opened a number of musket cartridges, and, using the powder thus obtained, they managed to put a ball through the roof over the governor's head. He promptly capitulated, and went the way of Chico.

Alvarado was rather a unique character. He was born in Monterey, and at the time of his revolutionary experience was 27 years of age. His success in waging war against the incumbent seems to have been accepted by all the Californians as a legitimate title to the governorship, and in December, 1836, he formally entered upon the duties of the office. As he could not claim to represent Mexico, whose appointee he had driven from the territory, he announced himself governor of the "Free and sovereign state of California." But this effort at independence proved to be only a flash in the pan. The people looked askance at it, and there were immediate mutterings of rebellion in the direction of Los Angeles. The ayuntamiento of that city presently came out with a Statement to the effect that while they were ready to accept Alvarado as governor, his term should last only until Mexico could appoint, and, moreover, that a recent declaration of the governor in favor of independence and of toleration for other religions than that of the Roman Catholic church was entirely at variance with their views.

Alvarado hastily gathered a force of men and marched south to San Fernando. A conference was held with the Los Angeles forces, and Alvarado accepted the conditions laid down by the rebels. What he wanted at the time was to get himself firmly seated in the chair of the governorship, and then the future might take care of itself. In October of the same year, 1837, news came that Carlos Antonio Carrillo had been appointed governor. Alvarado refused to turn over the capital to him, and when Carrillo raised an army at Los Angeles and San Diego, and started for the north, the governor sent his chief of staff south with a considerable force to intercept them. The battle — so-called — took place at San Buenaventura; one man was killed and the southern army was routed. The engagements of these revolutionary times consisted chiefly in the discharge of artillery at safe range. Carrillo abandoned his claims, and the Mexican authorities seem to have decided that the easiest way to get rid of Alvarado was to accept him as governor. Possibly they figured that the Californians would soon tire of him, and throw him out; but if this was their idea, they were wrong, for he served his term of five years with credit to himself and advantage to the territory.

Alvarado resigned of his own accord in January, 1842, and was succeeded by Emanuel Micheltorena, a Mexican general, who was chiefly noted for the infamous gang of cutthroats and adventurers that he brought up with him in the guise of soldiers. They were popularly known as "Micheltorena's Lambo." These creatures became at length intolerable, and a revolution started in the north, with Alvarado at its head, to drive them out of the country. This culminated in another of the bloodless battles, the location being at Cahuenga — for Los Angeles had taken an active part in the final uprising. Micheltorena left the country, by request, in February, 1845, having served as governor three years.

The last of the governors under Mexican rule was Pio Pico of Los Angeles, who held the office until the American occupation. He was involved in constant difficulties with Castro, the commander of the military forces, but no revolution took place during his brief administration, save that of the change of control from Mexico to the United States.

CHAPTER 15. THE RUIN OF THE MISSIONS.

The most important event of the period of the Mexican governors was the destruction of the mission system. This took place in the year 1834, during the administration of Figueroa. The dissipation of the mission properties followed hard upon the overthrow of the system, and by the time of the American occupation the ruin was complete.

In spite of the demands made upon the missions for supplies and money for the army, during the period of the rebellion from Spain, the establishments continued to prosper, and when the Mexican governors cast about them for means to run the territorial government, they could find no better plan than to follow the example of their Spanish predecessors. The Mexican congress was very liberal with its promises and appropriations, but the treasury was always empty. Government by revolution is an expensive luxury. At one time every cent that could be raised was required to put down a rebellion, and a little later, the other side being then in power, the money was all needed to pay off the patriots who had just saved the country. So California was left to look out for itself. There was some revenue from the customs duties, but it fell far short of the sum required to maintain the army and the civil list. The missions made up the deficit, which varied in amount from $30,000 to $50,000 a year.

One would suppose that the authorities, both in California and Mexico, would be disposed to look with extreme leniency upon an institution possessed of such hard-cash virtues; that they would, in other words, hesitate to kill the fowl that laid the golden Q.gg. Thai this view was held by the first governors under the Mexican rule is shown in their treatment of the padres who refused to take the oath of allegiance. When word was sent to Mexico that Sarria, the president of the mission system, had declined the oath, orders came promptly back to send him down to be tried for treason. In one way and another this order was evaded, together with the instructions that came later from the home" government calling for the expatriation of all priests who were not loyal to the Mexican republic. The priests denied that they were disloyal, in the sense of wishing evil to the existing government, but they objected to the oath, on the ground that they were made to promise to bear arms against the enemies of Mexico, which was contrary to their clerical vows. And more than one of them declared that he was tired of taking so many oaths of allegiance to the changing forms of government in Mexico, and that the whole performance seemed frivolous and undignified. In the end several of the padres were sent out of the country, but only those whose opposition to the new order of things was open and vehement.

"We cannot send these priests away," said Echeandia, the second of the Mexican governors, "because we shall then have nobody to manage the missions, which are the basis of our supplies."

But while the padres had this advantage over the local government, that they were needed as producers, the governors had on their part a most effective weapon in the threat of secularization or the seizure of the temporal possessions of the missions. In 1813, when the territory was still under Spanish control, the cortes, or national assembly of the mother country, passed an act declaring that the missions of California should be converted into parish institutions: that is, mere churches for spiritual instruction, with no industrial features. This decree was never carried out, and its legality, after the transfer to Mexico, might be questioned, but it was a suggestion to the padres of what would come to pass if they failed to support the local government.

Arguello, the first of the Mexican governors, complained, in 1825, in a report to the Mexican authorities, that the Indians were practically slaves, and that no progress was being made in bringing them nearer to civilization. This latter statement was probably true. The Indians had been living under the mission system now for about half a century.

While they were an improvement over the original savages from an industrial point of view, as they toiled faithfully under the guidance of the padres, and produced large crops, they were far from being civilized, and had made no progress in the last quarter of a century.

Possibly as a result of Arguello's comments instructions were issued to his successor, Echeandia, to make a careful study of the condition of the Indians, and to report to the home government on the question of secularization.

Echeandia saw fit to exceed his authority, and, not content with a mere report, he drew up and made public in California a plan for the emancipation — as he regarded it — of the Indians. In 1830 he had this plan adopted by the California legislature (diputacion), but as neither that body nor the governor had any authority to carry it out, it was never put into practice. Some of its more important provisions were incorporated in the plan adopted in 1834 by Figueroa, under instructions from the Mexican congress.

The publication of Echeandia's scheme for taking the Indians away from the missions and establishing them in pueblos showed the padres very clearly what they were to expect. Several who were then in trouble over the question of the oath of allegiance hastily left the country, but the majority determined to stay and fight it out. It is charged that even at this early date they began to regulate the affairs of the missions with a view to the property ultimately passing into alien hands — that they sold off stock where they had an opportunity, or converted it into hides and tallow. It is certain that they followed this policy to a considerable extent in the last year or two, before the decree of secularization finally went into effect. They would scarcely have been human had they failed to do so. It is to be recorded to their credit, however, that they made no effort to get the money thus obtained out of the country, but used it either for the purchase of supplies for the Indians, or laid it by against the time they saw was soon coming, when the mission properties would fail to support them and their wards.

Victoria, who succeeded Echeandia, was friendly to the padres and the mission system. He denounced the proposed plan of secularization as a scheme to despoil these useful establishments and dissipate their property.

There is little doubt that when Figueroa was sent to California by the Mexican authorities he understood what was expected of him, and that he was himself a sincere advocate of the plan of secularization. He was an honorable man, however, and, as a rule, clearheaded, and it is safe to say that if he could have foreseen the rascality this plan would bring into play — the destruction of the Indians and the demoralization of the forces of the church — he would never have given it countenance.

The Mexican congress passed the first formal decree of secularization in 1833. The missions were to become parish churches, their property, with the exception of a small tract, 600 feet square, to be divided among the Indians and any other settlers that might choose to take it up. Provision was made for a bishop for the territory. The expense of maintaining these churches and the bishopric was to be met by drafts on the "Pious Fund."

It will be remembered that when the Jesuits founded the missions of Lower California, in the latter part of the seventeenth century, they raised a considerable fund for their maintenance. The investments of this fund passed into the hands of Mexico, with the success of the rebellion from Spain. The annual income of the fund at this time was about $50,000, but no payments had been made to the California missions since about 1810. To draw on a fund originally subscribed for missionary work to pay for parish establishments was evidently illegal, but not more so than the frequent borrowing from this fund by the Mexican government, and its ultimate complete confiscation.

Figueroa transmitted the decree of the Mexican congress to the local legislature with a message in which he declared his belief that the missions were "entrenchments of monastic despotism." The governor had a strong humanitarian sentiment, and was possessed, moreover, of some Indian blood; and the stories he had heard of the harsh treatment of the neophytes by the padres aroused in him a bitter prejudice. He little suspected how much worse a fate he was preparing for the unhappy Indians.

The first decree was found to be incomplete, and a year later the Mexican congress acted again, and the California legislature followed.

Commissioners were appointed for each of the missions, whose duty it was to take an inventory of the stock, utensils and real estate of each, to inform the Indians that they were free, to distribute the land among the neophytes much after the manner in which it was distributed to the settlers of the pueblos, and to appoint in each establishment a major-domo, who should see that the Indians were kept in order, and their rights respected by the padres. Seed corn and farming utensils were to be given to the Indians, and they were to be urged to go to work and support themselves.

The commissioners set out in the month of August, 1834, and, under their stupid, and frequently corrupt, mismanagement, the marvelous mission system of California, which it had taken half a century of industry, self-sacrifice and pious devotion to build up, was, within an incredibly short period of time, thrown down and broken to fragments. It is perhaps questionable whether any plan could have been devised by which the Indians, whose daily life and occupation had been controlled by the padres as though they were children, could have been made independent and self-reliant, but scarcely any policy could have been worse than the one adopted. The commissioners, instead of asking the advice and co-operation of the padres, treated the latter as though they were a band of robbers, whose booty was about to be wrenched away. The Indians were called together, and informed with dramatic gusto that they were free, and might go where they pleased — a privilege which they translated to mean idleness and debauchery. Thousands of them ran away to the mountains and relapsed into savagery. Others wandered about from one mission to another, and finally brought up in the towns or on the ranches, where they worked for small pay, part in cash and part in brandy. The effort to form them into pueblos was an almost complete failure. If land was given them they made haste to sell or mortgage it, and to put the proceeds into liquor. And all this was due not so much to the innate depravity of the race, nor to the teaching of the padres — incomplete and impolitic as that may have been — as it was to the shock of the sudden release from all bonds of restraint, and to the poverty and wretchedness that followed.

The property of the missions, the stock, lands, utensils, and finally the buildings themselves, all melted away through the combined incompetency and corruption of the administrators. The cattle were slaughtered in great numbers, or were driven off to neighboring ranches; the lands were sold at low figures or given out in grants. The industrial buildings were looted, and then left to fall into decay.

The census of the later years of mission rule showed for the twenty-one establishments (San Rafael, 1817, and San Francisco Solano, 1823, are now to be added to the list) a total of 30,000 neophytes, 420,000 cattle, 60,000 horses and mules, 320,000 sheep and hogs, and an annual product of about 40,000 bushels of grain. At San Gabriel, which was one of the richest of the missions, there were nearly 100,000 cattle, and in two years none were left. The plain for miles in every direction was covered with the rotting carcasses, so that a pestilence was feared.

Left to themselves, and utterly dazed at the fall of the establishments in which they had been reared, the Indians planted no crops; and the government, which had come to depend upon the mission supplies, found itself in an awkward case. The commissioners declared that nothing could be done with the Indians except through coercion, and thus presently there came to be a tacit understanding that the major-domos, or overseers, were somehow to bring the neophytes back to their industrious ways. This meant a renewal of the flogging practices at which the authorities had manifested so much horror when the mission system was in force. Then came dreadful stories of Indians beaten to death, and of women and children allowed to starve, of the frequent shooting down of Indians by the white colonists, and of misery and degradation all along the line of the once prosperous establishments.

In 1839 Governor Alvarado appointed William E. P. Hartnell, an American, to make the round of the missions, report on their condition, and advise what should be done. His report is a sorrowful document. Barely one-eighth of the Indians are left, he estimates, living in or about the missions — which means that 25,000 of them had disappeared. While he makes no direct charges of corruption against the commissioners, it is plainly evident that he understands what wholesale robbery had been committed. In the matter of the flogging he suggests that the curates, or resident padres, be allowed to take charge of that — an interesting admission. His investigation finally brought him to such utter discouragement that after a year and a half of service he begged the governor to relieve him from the work.

A few years later, when Pio Pico, the last of the Mexican governors, was beginning his short and troubled term, an order was issued for the sale of the last remnants of the mission properties, to meet, in most cases, the demands of creditors — for, in addition to robbing them of everything that was tangible, the commissioners had actually brought the establishments out in debt — and all the buildings, except those in active use for church purposes, were sold to the highest bidder. With this last melancholy flicker the mission system of California, which was one of the most unique and remarkable institutions ever founded on the American continent, went out in the darkness of utter ruin.

CHAPTER 16. THE FOREIGNER ARRIVES.

The Spanish theory of the colony: that it existed solely for the use and benefit of the mother country, was exemplified in the laws respecting foreigners. Neither China nor Japan, in the years of their greatest exclusiveness, was more tightly closed to outsiders than was California in the years of Spanish rule. This policy did not prevail in Spain itself. Strangers possessed of satisfactory passports from their own countries might travel at will within her boundaries. The dependencies, however, were guarded with a jealous eye, evidently in the fear that they might be enticed from their allegiance to the mother country.

Little difficulty was experienced in maintaining this policy with regard to California during the first forty or fifty years of Spanish occupancy, for the reason that there was no inducement for foreigners to attempt to visit the country. It was entirely out of the regular line of ocean travel, and great deserts and hostile tribes of Indians shut it off from the people of the new republic to the east. At rare intervals an American vessel would be seen along the coast — about once in ten years. Governor Pedro Pages, who succeeded De Neve, the founder of Los Angeles, was greatly disturbed in 1787 by the presence of a boat which he thought was "owned by General Waughengton" — such being his idea of the spelling of our first president's name. English and French explorers, coming with the official recognition of the home government of Spain, were afforded every courtesy, but all traders were warned to keep away from the coast.

This rule of absolute exclusion was broken at last in 1814, when John Gilroy, an Englishman, landed from a trading vessel and announced his intention of remaining. He was little more than a boy, and perhaps for that reason his presence was not regarded with much apprehension. He declared himself a Catholic, and asked to be entered as a citizen of the country. In 1820 his request was formally granted, and he married into a California family. Shortly afterward Philip James, an American, was received under the name of Felipe Santiago; and an Irishman was entered with the very un-Irish name of Juan Maria. In 1816 an American schooner was driven into Santa Barbara, and the captain and five sailors, after a brief period of imprisonment, were received as citizens.

The first American to settle in the vicinity of Los Angeles was Joseph Chapman, whom the native Californians called "Jose el Ingles." He came with Bouchard, the privateer, whose capture of Monterey has been described in an earlier portion of this narrative. He was at first treated as a prisoner of war, but, proving himself useful — for he was a man of extraordinary ingenuity and resource — he was freed and accepted into citizenship. He married Guadalupe Ortega, of the Santa Barbara family, whose ranch house was destroyed by Bouchard. Stephen C. Foster, who was a prominent man in Los Angeles at the time the Americans took possession of California, and who died recently in this city, was accustomed to tell an interesting and romantic story of the capture of Chapman at Santa Barbara, and of his rescue from death by Guadalupe, but this was pure imagination with the person that originated it, for Chapman left the Bouchard party of his own accord at Monterey. Padre Zalvidea of San Gabriel, who was one of the cleverest industrial managers developed by the mission system, early recognized the possibilities of the versatile stranger, and made a friend and co-worker of him. He built for Zalvidea the first successful water power gristmill to be operated in California. Attempts had been made before, but the water wheel always threw moisture all over the grist. The Yankee Chapman introduced the bevel gearing to get around this difficulty. The mill was slow, but it was a great improvement over hand grinding, or the mill which the horse turned.

Chapman and the Indians, working under his direction, prepared most of the timbers that were used in the construction of the Church of Our Lady of the Angels, on the Plaza, and as these same timbers were used in the remodeling of 1861, his work still stands for the service of the present generation. In 1831 Chapman took charge of the construction of a schooner for the padres at San Gabriel, to be used in the business of otter hunting. With the aid of the Indians he prepared various parts and fitted them together in the workshops of the mission. They were then carried down to the ocean at San Pedro, put together again, and the boat was launched amid great rejoicing. While this craft was scarcely suitable in appearance and speed for international racing, perhaps, it served well the purpose for which it was constructed, and was the second boat to be built in California. Chapman died in 1849, after thirty years of active and serviceable life. A descendant of his still resides in this county. The Americans who now occupy this region are entitled to pride themselves on the fact that the first one of their people to come on the ground was a man who exemplified in his energy, skill and integrity, the very best qualities of the national character.

When the republic of Mexico assumed control of California it adopted, without much change, the Spanish rule with regard to foreigners. But a new factor had entered in the shape of foreign trade, which, during the latter years of the revolution, had become a necessity, all Spanish trade having ceased, and there being none from Mexico to take its place. Presently the American trading companies that bought the hides and tallow from the missions found it necessary to establish local agencies at Monterey, the capital; and in the decade from 1820 to 1830 a number of Americans became settlers on this basis, with no one seemingly disposed to object.

During this same period there came into California the first overland travelers — the advance guard of the great army of immigration that was presently to overwhelm and take possession of the country. Although this was only 75 years ago, there was at this time a great strip of country beginning a short distance back from the Pacific coast and running nearly a thousand miles to the east, covering more than one-fourth of the present area of the United States, that was practically unexplored. There were no maps nor charts for the traveler's guidance, and no protection from the attack of warlike savages, save in one's ability to defend himself. On that side the Californians had thought themselves impregnable, and when the first overland parties arrived, the shock of astonishment and anger was to them almost like a presentiment of the inevitable. They had become entirely accustomed to the foreigners entering by the sea. They welcomed them as traders and tolerated them as citizens. But the foreigners creeping in over the mountains were enemies, whose advent was fiercely resented.

The first party consisted of fifteen trappers, under the command of Jedediah S. Smith, who came down the Colorado river from Salt Lake to San Gabriel and Los Angeles in 1826. They were promptly ordered out of the country, but became scattered, and several of them remained, although their leader went back. In 1828 a party of eight, led by Sylvester Pattie, a Kentuckian, and later by his son, James O. Pattie, came into California by way of New Mexico and Arizona, arriving first at San Diego. Three members of the party settled in Los Angeles, Nathaniel Prior, Richard Laughlin and Jesse Furguson. They had passports from the American authorities, but Governor Echeandia received them with great harshness. According to the account given by the younger Pattie, and subsequently published in book form, he tore up the passports and threw the trappers into prison. The elder Pattie died while in confinement, and the younger was liberated after nearly a year in jail, when it was discovered that he knew how to perform vaccination. The other members of the party were also freed. Prior, a silversmith, married one of the Sepulveda family, and was for many years active in Los Angeles affairs. Laughlin, a joiner, owned a vineyard east of Alameda street. Furguson had a store on Main street, near the Plaza, during 1828 and 1829, and then went to Lower California to live.

About this time came George Rice and John Temple. They opened a store for general merchandise on the spot where the Downey block now stands — then the extreme southern limit of the town. Temple was a leading commercial and financial man of Los Angeles — an older brother of F. P. F. Temple of the Temple & Workman bank. His partnership with Rice ceased in 1831, and from that time until 1845 he conducted the store alone. In 1857 he built the southern portion of the Temple block. Two years later he built on the site where the Bullard block now stands a building which he intended for a market house and theater, but which was finally purchased by the county to use as a court house. He died in San Francisco in 1866. John Temple was a native of Massachusetts; he married Dona Rafaela Cota in 1830.

In 1827 came J. D. Leandry, who for a time conducted a store on the south side of the Plaza. He afterwards purchased the "Los Coyotes" ranch, dying in 1842.

The famous Abel Stearns — universally called "Don Abel Stearns" — came in 1828. The title "Don" was bestowed by Americans, as well as Californians, upon a few of the earliest immigrants who had married into the families of the country, and who were so thoroughly identified with the Spanish population as to seem to the later comers to be like natives. Don Abel was a man who would have made his mark at any time and in any community. He began with merchandising in a store located where the Baker block now stands, and where later he erected a home so large and elegant that it was called by the people of the town "the palace of Don Abel Stearns." He had a natural talent for making money, and there was no line of business in which he did not, at one time or another, take a hand. At his death he was the largest individual landowner — not in number of acres, but in valuation — in the southern half of the state. He married Dona Arcadia, daughter of Don Juan Bandini. After the death of Don Abel she married Col. R. S. Baker, who died several years ago. She is still living and in control of large property interests in and around Los Angeles.

On Christmas day, 1828, the American brig Danube was wrecked at San Pedro, and Los Angeles received several settlers from the crew. One of these was Samuel Prentiss, who afterward engaged in otter hunting on Catalina island, and died there in 1856. Another was John Groningen, or Juan Domingo, as he was generally known among Californians who found difficulty with the pronunciation of his German name. He married a Feliz, and acquired a large vineyard at the corner of First and Alameda streets. He purchased from the city the original site of Yang-na, the Indian village, and expelled the few savages that still remained in that vicinity. The place had become a sink-hole of filth and iniquity, and its clearance was a necessity.

As Groningen was the first German, so Louis Bouchette was the first Frenchman. He had a vineyard on Macy street, and a house near the site of the Baker block. Another Frenchman coming at about the same time, 1831, was Jean Vignes, who owned the Aliso vineyard.

William Wolfskill, a Kentucky trapper, arrived in Los Angeles overland in 1831. He married into the Lugo family, and, securing a large tract of land to the southeast of town — since known as the Wolfskill ranch, or Wolfskill tract — he set it out to vines. There were at this time a few orange trees at each of the missions in the southern part of the state, and Wolfskill determined to raise the fruit on a larger scale. He therefore laid out two acres of his ranch in 1841 to oranges, and is entitled to be known as the pioneer American orange grower of California. In 1860 he had over 100 acres in oranges.

James, or Santiago, McKinley, a Scotchman, came in 1831, and engaged in business until 1846. He took a hand in several of the revolutions.

Jonathan Trumbull Warner, known as Juan Jose Warner, arrived in Los Angeles in 1831, overland. He was a native of Connecticut, and for a space of over sixty years he holds an important place in the history of this region, not only because he was active in political and industrial affairs, but also because he was an observant man, and possessed the faculty of recording what he saw and heard.

In 1840 he returned to the east for the purpose of urging the construction of a railway to the Pacific coast. He was one of the earliest advocates of that project. He lived for many years on his ranch in San Diego county, but the latter part of his life was spent at his residence in this city, located on the site of the Burbank theater. He died in 1895.

The pioneers of 1832 were Juan Isaac Williams, a trapper, who married into the Lugo family, and for a long time owned the Chino ranch; and Lemuel Carpenter, who established a soap factory on the road to San Gabriel. Those of 1833 were Santiago Johnson, an Englishman, who conducted a ranch in the vicinity of San Pedro, and Jacob P. Leese, who carried on a merchandise business in Los Angeles for several years and then went north.

In 1834 came Hugo Reid, a Scotchman, who married an Indian woman of the San Gabriel mission. In 1852 he contributed to the Los Angeles Star an important series of articles on Indian manners and customs. In 1835 Henry Melius, who appears in Dana's "Two Years Before the Mast," settled in Los Angeles, whither he was followed, four years later, by his brother Francis. Both were in the firm of Melius, Howard & Co. Henry served as Mayor of Los Angeles in 1860.

In 1835 came Leon I. Prudhomme, a Frenchman, who acquired the Cucamonga ranch. In 1836 John Marsh, a physician, settled in Los Angeles. His letters on the country were published in Missouri and Michigan newspapers, and stimulated immigration. In the same year came John Forster, an Englishman, who married the sister of Pio Pico, and who purchased the ex-mission ranch of San Juan Capistrano. He died in 1884.

In 1841 the first notable immigration party arrived in Los Angeles, starting from Pennsylvania. Among its 40 members were several who were afterward active in local affairs. John Rowland, who settled at Puente; Wm. Workman, B. D. Wilson and D. W. Alexander. F. P. F. Temple came in this same year. From this time on Americans began to come in by the overland routes in considerable numbers.

CHAPTER 17. LOCAL EVENTS
OF MEXICAN RULE.

During this period of its history Los Angeles was generally known as "The Pueblo"— its full title, El Pueblo de Nuestra Senora la Reina de Los Angeles — being used only on official documents. There was a short time during which an effort was made to change the name to Santa Maria, as the theory seems to have prevailed that the name of the saint, as well as her title, was used in the original name of the town — thus. El Pueblo de Nuestra Senora, Santa Maria, la Reina de Los Angeles. There may have been a feeling that the original name was not quite long enough for the dignity to which the place was now attaining as a revolutionary center. In 1827, Los Angeles had a narrow escape from an official change of name, but not to Santa Maria, however. The Mexican authorities complained that the name of the California city was frequently confused with that of the Puebla de Los Angeles, the capital of the Mexican state of Puebla, and the California legislature reported back advising that the name be changed to Villa Victoria de la Reina de Los Angeles, the purpose evidently being to call it Victoria in everyday use. At the same time it was proposed to change the name of the territory from California to Moctezuma. The reason for this does not appear. Fortunately the whole proposition was pigeon-holed in Mexico, and Los Angeles was allowed to hold its unique title. There are plenty of Victorias in the country, but only one Los Angeles. The first American settlers had the habit of calling the place "Angeles" — without the "Los."

Cosme Pena, who served as prefect of the southern district of California during part of the administration of Alvarado, introduced a new variation of the name. He had a great deal of trouble with the residents of the city, who were at that time in a condition of chronic tumult. In his letters to the governor Pena was accustomed to write the name "Los Diablos" instead of Los Angeles.

The period from 1830 to 1840 does not show as rapid a growth of population as the two preceding decades, but there was material improvement in a commercial way, and a promise of future growth in the arrival of active, enterprising men from the country east of the Rockies. In 1833 it was estimated that there were in all about 200 families living in the pueblo. An approximate census for the whole district now included in Los Angeles county, taken in 1833, gives 1675 white and 553 Indians. In 1836 there were said to be 40 foreigners living in the region, of whom 30 were Americans. Thus it will be seen that while the Americans were prominent as a class through their individual activity they did not, as yet, contribute much to the increase of population. There was no longer any colonization from Spain or Mexico, although extensive schemes were broached at times for immigration from the latter country. The elimination of the missions as an industrial factor decreased the local capacity for self-support, and that probably affected the increase of population.

The new-coming Americans seem to have been brought under the same spell of fascination that affects visitors to Southern California even to this day, making residents of those that thought to be merely sojourners. In spite of their isolated position in the world, and the foreign language and customs which they met here, the first Americans in California seem to have been well satisfied with their lot, and to have readily accustomed themselves to the surroundings. Almost without exception they married women of the Spanish-American families, and the marriages proved to be happy for both parties. The California women discovered that the foreigners — particularly those from the republic — made good husbands. It is generally conceded by those that study and compare national characteristics that the American man possesses a fair allowance of what may be called the domestic virtues. He enjoys his home, and wants it to be livable. He takes pride in his wife and children, and sees to it that they have the best his income will provide.

While the original Spanish settlers had been, many of them, men of force and industry, a new generation was growing up' that had enjoyed little opportunity for education, and whose ideas of life had been demoralized by the ease with which a fair competence could be obtained through the labor of the Indians. Instead of devoting their energies to the improvement of their estates — for so the great ranches of the older families may be termed — they wasted their time in frivolous pursuits, and in trifling political intrigues. Amiable, polite and superficially unselfish, they made delightful companions, but for the serious, practical affairs of life — of which matrimony is certainly one — they were not to be compared with the Americans; and the young women of the best families made this discovery early, and took it to heart.

The newcomers were required to swear allegiance to Mexico, and, if they proposed to marry into a California family, to accept Catholicism. These demands were usually fulfilled with cheerful alacrity. The Mexican government was a shadowy affair, which the Americans believed would in time fade away entirely, and be succeeded by the solid reality of their own republic. As for the religion, by the time a man had made his way to this far-off corner of the world, all churches seemed very much alike to him; and it was the Catholic church or none, for no other existed. As a rule, the California fathers and mothers were glad enough to secure American husbands for their daughters, and objection seldom had to be overcome. One interesting, and rather romantic, exception was the case of Henry Fitch and Dona Josefa, daughter of Joaquin Carrillo of San Diego, which, as it has a bearing on the history of the Church of Our Lady at the plaza, may be briefly told here.

Fitch was a dashing young American sailor, who came to California in 1826, and in 1827 became engaged to Dona Josefa. Her parents seem to have been in doubt as to the wisdom of the alliance, but, after two years of waiting, a reluctant consent was granted, and preparations were made for the wedding. At the last moment the uncle of the bride refused to serve as a witness, and interposed such vigorous objection that the officiating padre was afraid to proceed. He showed a very human sympathy for the pair, however, and suggested that there were other countries where no such difficulty would be met. An elopement was planned, in which Pio Pico, a cousin of the bride, assisted. The marriage was performed in South America, and the couple returned to the coast a little more than a year later, accompanied by a third party, to wit, an infant son. An ecclesiastical court was summoned to meet at San Gabriel, and Don Enrique was tried for violating the laws of the church and the territory; and the question of whether he was legally married or not was passed upon. The case awakened a great deal of interest, as may be imagined, and the international marriage question was discussed in every household. The court finally decided that the marriage was valid, but, "considering the great scandal which Don Enrique has caused in this province," he was condemned "to give, as a penance and reparation, a bell of at least fifty pounds weight for the church at Los Angeles, which now has barely a borrowed one." And that is how the church on the plaza secured its first bell. During the last half of the decade — after the year 1835 — Los Angeles enjoyed the empty honor of being the capital of the territory. This was accomplished by Jose Antonio Carrillo, an active citizen of Los Angeles, and an indefatigable plotter, who was serving in the Mexican congress at that time. The announcement of the proposed change brought out a fierce protest from the people of Monterey, in which some very pointed remarks were made. Among other things, it was declared that Monterey was a larger city than Los Angeles — which was certainly not true — and that its people were more moral and better cultured. It was asserted that Monterey had the better climate, and that its soil was more fertile; and in proof of Monterey's general superiority over Los Angeles, it was said that at the former place "women, plants and useful animals are more productive." A much more effective argument than any comparison of the merits of the two cities lay in the fact that Monterey was provided with suitable buildings for the use of the government, whereas Los Angeles had nothing of the kind. On one or two occasions, when a governor had visited the pueblo, great difficulty was experienced in finding a place for him to stay, while he transacted public business. And now, as often as the Los Angeles ayuntamiento demanded to know why the order of the Mexican congress was not obeyed, and the seat of government removed, the territorial authorities always responded with a polite inquiry as to whether Los Angeles had provided the necessary public buildings. With this retort the discussion usually came to an abrupt end, for there were no philanthropists in the pueblo in those days, and the territorial treasury being always empty of funds, the dilemma seemed a hopeless one.

It was not until 1826 that San Pedro was recognized as a port, and provision made for the collection of revenue. Prior to that time all business done between Los Angeles and the ocean was practically smuggling. Even after the port was established, as the collector lived at Los Angeles, more than twenty miles away from the water front, the temptation to evade the payment of duties was very strong. During the years from 1826 to the American occupation, Catalina was a favorite resort for smugglers, and some of the most prominent citizens of Los Angeles were believed to take part in the contraband trade. Don Abel Stearns built a large warehouse at San Pedro in the early thirties, and when his political enemies could find no other convenient method to annoy him, they would bring in a charge of smuggling and demand that the warehouse be torn down. Don Abel managed to hold his own against them, however, and invariably escaped with a verdict of "not proved."

The coming of numerous bands of trappers through by the southwestern route finally resulted in the opening of trade between Los Angeles and Arizona and New Mexico. The blankets made in New Mexico were of a superior quality and much in demand, not only for bedding, but also for personal wear. The serape was the overcoat of the period. The California horses and mules were superior to those raised further east; and the exchange of blankets for stock was advantageous both ways. Presently the Arizonans found it cheaper to steal the stock than to trade for it, and in 1835 the ayuntamiento of Los Angeles passed some resolutions calling upon the local alcaldes along the line between the pueblo and the border to require parties driving horses and mules out of the territory to show a bill of sale. By this method the stealing was diminished but not entirely broken up.

In 1836 the question of titles to town lots was agitated, chiefly for the reason that disputes as to ownership were becoming more common. Up to this time no written titles had been granted except those to the first few settlers, which were of doubtful value, by reason of their limitations. Anyone who wished a piece of land, either for building a house or for cultivation, applied to the ayuntamiento, and received oral permission to go ahead and do whatever he pleased, as long as he did not interfere with his neighbors. Boundaries were vague, and, if no fence or wall had been constructed, were subject to constant dispute. In the year 1836 the ayuntamiento began the practice of giving written titles, and a notice was issued calling upon all who held land in the pueblo to file a claim describing the exact location, and have it accepted and endorsed by the authorities. As the city was thus far entirely without a plan, its streets being undefined, crooked and irregular, great difficulty was experienced in locating and describing the individual boundaries. The people, moreover, were indolent and neglectful, and, after repeated calls, many had failed to respond.

The total of the yearly receipts of the municipality in these days was something under $1000, of which about half came from the tax on liquors, and the remainder from fines. The treasury was always empty, and there were continual complaints that the salary of the city's officers were unpaid. Practically no attempt was made at municipal improvement, except that the irrigation ditch was generally kept in order. Indians were punished for drunkenness by being put to work on the ditch, and the supply of malefactors of this kind was inexhaustible. There was no lighting of streets at night, except that each keeper of a tavern or wine-shop was required to hang a lantern in front of his place. In 1836, the filthiness of the city was so great that crows and other carrion birds were attracted to it in vast numbers, constituting a veritable pest. A voluntary contribution was called for by the ayuntamiento to pay for the expense of killing them off. In this same year a decree was passed that no man should keep more than two dogs, and that both of these should be securely tied. What to do with the superfluous ones was a question. The treasury was as usual; but the second alcalde came forward — limping a little, perhaps — and offered to provide at his own expense the necessary poison.

In 1839, an incident took place which, though trivial in itself, added to the general unpopularity from which the town suffered throughout the territory. Don Cosme Pena had been appointed by Governor Alvarado prefect of the southern district, with headquarters at Los Angeles. There being no other place offered for his use, he had an office in the residence of Don Abel Stearns, and the flag of the Mexican republic fluttered from the top of a pole in front of the house. One Sunday, when Pena was out of the city, a party of fifteen young men pulled down this flag, and then, by way of added insult, slaughtered a calf at the flag pole. The explanation offered by the citizens of the affair was that Stearns was accustomed to use the pole as a hitching post for cattle that were presently to be slaughtered, and that the flag was removed and the calf killed as a mark of their disapproval of Pena's choice of headquarters. In the territory generally it was taken as an insult to the national emblem. Pena resigned in anger, and the governor fined each member of the ayuntamiento $10, and compelled twenty citizens who had signed a letter to him on the subject to pay $5 apiece for their rashness.

CHAPTER 18.
THE PASTORAL AGE IN CALIFORNIA.

The early Californian presents the most picturesque and distinctly unique type that appears in our national history; and his life, prior to its modification by contact with the people of the United States, is extraordinarily romantic and interesting. It is quite probable that the modern American, if suddenly transplanted into the California of 1830, would find much that was disagreeable, and perhaps also some things that would excite his horror and disgust. He would, on the other hand, find not a little to enjoy, and a great deal to wonder at and admire. At the root of it all he would discover a principle so radically different from that on which he endeavors to base his own life policy, that the whole scheme would seem to him an almost hopeless puzzle. Asking himself constantly the question: Why do these people do these foolish things? he would see no wisdom in the answer: Because it is the custom of the country, as it was formerly the custom of our ancestors in Spain.

For example, nothing distressed the first American visitors more than to observe the way the Californians yoked the oxen for work in the fields, or for draft purposes on the road. Instead of the weight being put upon the neck and shoulders, it was thrown directly upon the horns. The poor creatures showed by their lifting and twisting of the head that they were suffering pain, and the limit of their strength and endurance was quickly reached; they were by no means as efficient as they would have been if properly yoked. But when the visitor called attention to the cruelty and the wasted energy in this system, he received always the same answer: That it was so done in Spain.

This admiration of the Mexicans for the mother country, even after they had passed out from under its control, was almost without limit. Though not always expressed in words, it showed in their intense conservatism. They were totally ignorant of the change that had taken place in the relative position of Spain and other European countries, whereby it was no longer a great and powerful empire, but a tottering ruin. That country was to them still the Spain of Ferdinand and Isabella, of Charles V and Philip II. Those who could read were an insignificant fraction of the total, but even for the educated there were no books, newspapers or periodicals. We may go further, and say that had all the means been at hand for enlightenment, it would still have required many generations of knowledge to have removed the hereditary self-complacency — the innocent and almost modest pride, that is an essential part of the Spanish character.

Lacking a word to exactly correspond to our "civilized," the first Spaniards used the phrase, "La gente de razon" — people who can reason — to distinguish them from the Indians, whom they regarded as little else than brutes. There were, at the time of the American occupation, about 4000 native Californians of this order, and about 1500 of these were in Los Angeles or its vicinity. A very small percentage were pure-blooded Spaniards, although few were ready to admit that they were anything else. Cases were rare in which whole families emigrated from Spain, or Spanish soldiers sent back for their wives or sweethearts to come over, and the extremely small number of women from the mother country is the clearest evidence of the mixed character of the population. In the early history of Mexico many negroes were brought into that country, and, as we have seen, there was some element of negro blood among the first settlers of Los Angeles. As a rule, however, the mixture was Spanish and Indian in varying proportions. The combination was not a fortunate one, when to the haughtiness and conservatism of the Spaniard was added the ignorance and indolence of the Indian. That the results were no worse in the composite character is due partly to the favorable influence of the Catholic church, and partly to the natural conditions of the country that made life simple and easy.

The higher class Californian, whose blood was nearly if not entirely Spanish, was generally the owner of a huge ranch, tens of thousands of acres in extent, covered with cattle. The offices of the territory, and most of those of the municipalities, were filled from this class. Their characteristics were the same as we know them today among the few remaining representatives of the old order. They were elegant of manner, dignified, hospitable, generous to a fault, honorable and just, as far as their limited knowledge of the world admitted. It takes a wise man to be a just one. If, for example, at the time of the American occupation, some of the Californians were guilty of questionable transactions in the matter of land titles and government claims, it was rather through their failure to understand the technicalities of our law, and their desire to do as they thought the Americans did, than from any actual wish to defraud. But, on the other hand, the original Californians of the better class were not lacking in faults. They were seldom good business men — one might almost say never — they were utterly unprogressive, they were given to political plotting and scheming, they were vain of their personal appearance, and too often were what in the south is called "trifling" and in New England "shiftless." The last characteristic was on so grand a scale as almost to be invested with a dignity of its own. From the beginning of the American invasion it was only too plainly evident that this class would never be able to hold its own against the superior shrewdness and determination of the Anglo-Saxon.

The lower class Californian forms by no means so pleasing a picture. In numbers he exceeded the others more than ten to one. He had something of the dignity and the generosity of his superior, but lacked his self-control. Indolent, reckless, entirely without education, addicted to drink, and purposeless in his occupations, we can only wonder that his race continued through half a dozen generations, down to its improved condition of the present day.

Although generated from a different set of causes, the conditions in California before the American occupation were not unlike those of the south before the war. The actual labor of the country was performed by the Indians, who were held in servitude, and may be compared to the negro slaves of the southern states. The upper class Spaniards may be compared in an industrial sense to the slaveholders of the south (although they regarded the institution of slavery with abhorrence); and, finally, the lower class Californians may be likened to the poor whites of the slave states, despising labor, as the latter did, and existing somehow on the overflow of the general prosperity. The comparison is hardly fair to the Californian, however, for the poor white was spiritless and weak, whereas the other was full of pride, and was not without energy in certain directions.

Life in California, during this period, is inseparably bound up with the horse. As soon as children could walk, they were taught to ride, and by the time they were grown they were at home not merely in the saddle, but all over the horse, whether he were saddled and bridled, or was naked and wild from the herd. Horses were so cheap as to be practically valueless. At times it was found necessary to kill them off in great numbers. No attempt was made to breed them to any points of excellence, nor were they trained with the skill and good judgment that horsemen now employ. The average Californian had so many animals at his disposal that he paid little attention to any one in particular. They rode their horses recklessly, and were thoughtless about matters of food and drink and care. Fine trappings for the horse were highly esteemed, and one of the few manual industries held in great regard in California, as it had been in Spain, was leather working, an industry that has been handed down in improved form to the present generation.

The industrial pursuits, of these people consisted of agriculture, on a very limited scale, of the manufacture of a few articles in common use, and of the raising of cattle for hides and tallow. The latter was a business that largely took care of itself, and it was practiced on a grand scale. Once a year there was a rodeo, or round-up, when the cattle of a district were gathered together by vaqueros, and new stock was branded with the mark of the owner. Special officers, called "jueces del campo," or judges of the plain, were present at these gatherings to decide all disputes of ownership. This office was continued for a time even under American rule. The rodeos usually took place in the spring or early summer, and were occasions of great merry-making, large feeding and deep drinking, so that even the most indolent were willing to forego their habitual rest to take part and help. In the autumn of the year the annual killing took place. Hides brought an average of $2 apiece, and tallow sold at from 6 to 8 cents a pound. On a large ranch there would be perhaps 1000 cattle ready for the slaughter, which would bring the owner $10,000 to $15,000 in cash or trade — usually in trade, for coin was scarce. It has been estimated that when the pastoral system of California was at its height, there were 1,200,000 cattle on the ranches. The annual exportations of hides and tallow averaged over $250,000. The cattle were of an inferior grade, lean, wild, and of little value for domestic purposes. Butter, cheese, and even milk, were rarities. The beef from these animals was tough, stringy and tasteless.

The sheep were a "scrub" breed, with short, coarse wool, and their flesh was seldom used for food. Hogs were raised in small numbers, but the "gente de razon" disdained the use of pork, except in the form of lard for cooking, and the Indians regarded it with suspicion. The early Californians seem to have devoted very little thought or energy to the pleasures of the table. Travelers among them speak in the highest terms of their hospitality, but are chary of compliments on their cooking. In most places it was left to Indian women, who were everywhere the house servants, and their ideas on the culinary art were decidedly crude. In spite of the monotonous and indigestible fare, good health seems to have been the rule among the Californians, and sickness the exception — which was fortunate, because doctors were practically unknown.

California agriculture consisted in the raising of wheat, corn and grapes — the latter for the making of wine and brandy. Enough grain was raised for local necessities, but none for export. The plow was a clumsy wooden affair, generally shod with a piece of iron. Wheat was threshed by driving mares over it, as it lay heaped upon the ground. The straw was then raked off, and the grains winnowed out by hand. There were good vineyards at the missions and in Los Angeles, but few anywhere else. The missions also had fruit trees and vegetable gardens, but until the Americans came these were not to be found in the towns — to any extent — nor on the ranches.

Very little manufacturing of any sort was carried on outside the missions, and the work at those institutions was only such as could be accomplished by ignorant savages under the training of the padres. Coarse blankets, the simpler articles of leather make (including a poor quality of shoes), a coarse meal, soap, tiles for roofing-, brandy and wine about complete the list. Nearly all articles of wearing apparel, furniture, and even the better grade of leather goods, were imported, at first from Mexico, later from the United States and foreign countries. The only means of conveyance, other than the backs of horses, was the carreta, which was a huge, clumsy creation, with two immensely thick and solid wooden wheels that turned on wooden axles, and were sometimes — but not always — lubricated with soft soap.

The California man was rather vain of his personal appearance, and lavished a great deal of attention and money upon his dress. An outfit such as would be worn by a wealthy rancher on any special occasion was likely to cost anywhere from $500 to $1000. Every article of his dress would be imported, and the Yankee skipper could be depended upon to charge him all that the traffic would bear. The trading business on the coast was expected to pay several hundred per cent on each transaction. The hats were from South America, with a stiff, horizontal brim, and a conical crown. A black silk handkerchief was usually tied around the head, under the hat. This was a Spanish custom, and it still prevails in the mother country. The overcoat was the sarape, a blanket of fine or coarse grade, according as the owner was able to pay. It had a hole near the center, through which the head was inserted. As a rule, this garment was striped with bright colors, and either woven thick like a blanket, or of double cloth. Those made of cloth, and provided with a rich embroidered collar, were called mangas. There was a short jacket of silk, or figured cloth, a white embroidered shirt, tied with a silk handkerchief for a cravat, a vest of silk or damask, and a pair of pantaloons, open from the knee down on the outer seam, which was trimmed with buttons and gold braid. Sometimes short breeches of velvet or velveteen, dark blue or crimson in color, were worn, and below them, long white stockings. The shoes were of buff-colored leather. Around the body was a silk sash of bright hue. When on horseback, the Californian wore leggings, especially if he had on knee breeches, and these were bound with handsome clasps or garters.

The woman's dress was not so elaborate nor gaudy, although as expensive as her husband's purse would stand. It usually consisted of a bodice of silk, with short embroidered sleeves. A bright silk sash was worn loosely about the waist, and the skirt below was elaborately flounced. The shoes were of satin or velvet. Over the shoulders, and frequently over the head as well, the rebozo, a long dark scarf of silk or cotton, was worn, and arranged with a great deal of grace and expression. The hair of the younger women was usually plaited in two long braids fastened together at the ends with ribbon; that of the older women was more often done up with a comb.

The amusements of these people constituted a large and an important part of their life. They came together from great distances to attend fiestas, which were celebrations extending through several days and nights, or fandangos, which were dance parties. Social life was on an informal basis. No invitations were issued to these gatherings, other than a general notice, and almost everyone in the adjoining country was expected to come. One pleasing fact to be set down in this connection is that there were almost none of those distressing feuds, or life-long enmities, that are so often to be found among primitive peoples, and sometimes, we may add, among those of a presumably higher civilization. Dueling was almost unknown, and homicides rare. The faults of the early Californians were not of the savage and brutal order, but were rather the outgrowth of qualities that are not far removed from virtues. It is but a short and easy step from generosity to prodigality, from good humor to shiftlessness, and from sociability to indolence.

CHAPTER 19. THE STARS AND STRIPES.

The history of the United States prior to 1861 is largely a history of the slavery question. Not only were all internal political events affected in some measure by this issue, but even the foreign policy did not escape its baleful influence. When the Missouri compromise set a definite limit, as was supposed, to the spread of slavery to the north, the acquisition of more territory to the south and southwest was necessary to the slave-holding interest, so that it might maintain an equilibrium with its opponents. Our relations with the Mexican republic were controlled, almost from the beginning, by this salient fact, and out of it finally came the war of 1846-8, and the acquisition of California, Arizona and New Mexico. There were, of course, other considerations that entered into the impulse for war, when the time came for its actual declaration. A great majority of the people of the north, as well as of the south, believed that the "Manifest Destiny" of the republic required that it should extend through on even lines from ocean to ocean. In due course of time this sentiment might have led to the purchase of this territory, and would certainly have aroused active and forcible opposition to its seizure by any foreign power; but the Union would scarcely have been drawn into a deliberate war for conquest — which the Mexican war undoubtedly was — on a mere desire for expansion, nor would the opportunity for that war have been provided had not a potent cause existed in the political situation.

The final appeal to arms grew out of the annexation of Texas to the United States. While still a Spanish dependency Texas had been colonized by numerous parties of Americans; and during Mexican rule it filled rapidly with emigrants, chiefly from the southern states. In 1836, when the Mexican republic was in the midst of one of its periodic revolutions, the Texans declared themselves independent, and asked to be admitted to the American Union. The proposition was, of course, declined, as its acceptance would have constituted an act of deliberate and inexcusable aggression; but Mexico contended that the Americans constantly gave aid and comfort to the rebels. Unable to win back its revolted province, Mexico, nevertheless, refused to acknowledge its independence.

In the eight years following, the offer of Texas to come into the American Union stood open, and was discussed at each session of congress. It was well understood, both in the United States and in Mexico, that the acceptance of the offer meant war. There was, it is true, an element in Mexico that favored letting Texas go, because it feared that the outcome of a conflict with the United States would be the loss of California and the neighboring territory, but those holding that view were in the minority.

The continuous strain under which the two countries rested is revealed in the incident of the raising of the American flag at Monterey by Commodore Jones in 1842. This occurred four years before actual war broke out, and while Micheltorena was governor of California. England was believed to have her eye on the province, which was to be taken in exchange for fifty million dollars' worth of Mexican securities held by British citizens. France had been sending numerous exploring parties into the country. The weakness of Mexico made it possible that California might easily be wrested from her grasp, and the European powers were believed to be ready to seize it on the first opportunity. Instructions had been issued to the American naval commanders of the Pacific, that in the event of war breaking out over the Texas difficulty, they were to hasten to Monterey and raise the American flag.

Under this condition of affairs, Commodore Jones was lying in the harbor of Callao, Peru, with the Pacific squadron, when a rumor reached him that hostilities had begun between the two nations. At the same time the British squadron lying in the harbor left in haste, without divulging its course. The American commander jumped at the conclusion that the English were about to seize California, and promptly sailed for the north. October 19th he came into the harbor of Monterey, and although he found no British vessels there he proceeded to carry out his design. Landing a force of 400 sailors and marines, he took possession of the town, no resistance being offered, and raised the Stars and Stripes over the fort. There the flag waved for a day, and then the commodore received information that convinced him he had made a mistake. He promptly withdrew the American ensign, ran up the tricolor in its place, and expressed a willingness to apologize and make suitable reparation.

Governor Micheltorena was at Los Angeles, slowly making his way northward from Mexico with the ragged, thieving army that afterward brought him so much trouble. Thither Commodore Jones repaired, bringing his fleet to San Pedro. When Micheltorena heard of the capture of Monterey, he issued a furious proclamation, in which he declared that he would shed his last drop of blood in defense of his country, but his wrath cooled when he received a letter of apology from Jones, accompanied by an offer of reparation. The governor's idea of what was proper and adequate reparation and the commodore's idea did not coincide exactly. There was a streak of thriftiness in Micheltorena's character that came to light on this occasion. He announced that the wounded feelings of himself and his countrymen could be soothed only by a donation from Jones of 50 uniforms for the army, a set of band instruments and $15,000 in cash. The commodore declined to consider this request, saying that the damages would have to be settled by the respective governments. The two principals to the controversy met on amicable terms at the residence of Don Abel

Stearns, and a grand ball was given in honor of the Americans. Commodore Jones ordered a special salute to be given the Mexican flag at San Pedro, and in this way the incident came to a pleasant ending.

Four years later, when war was imminent, although not yet declared, Captain John C. Fremont, of the U. S. Topographical Engineers, entered California overland, with an exploring party that consisted of 61 men, most of whom were trappers and experienced mountaineers. Fremont was a unique figure on the national stage and his relation to the affairs of California, during the period of conquest, was subsequently made the basis of so much bitter partisan discussion that it is difficult, even at this remote period, to arrive at a just judgment on his conduct. While there were numerous individual acts committed by him that are open to criticism, if tried by modern standards, two material points of defense may be urged in his behalf: First, his youth, imbued with an enthusiastic and aggressive Americanism, and, second, the secret but easily divined instructions under which he worked, coming through his father-in-law, Senator Benton, direct from the administration. Without doubt, President Polk and his cabinet believed that a war with Mexico was inevitable, and they were ready to welcome any reasonable excuse that should start the train. We do not have to assume that Fremont was specifically instructed to pick a quarrel with Mexico in California. It was enough that he should have had conveyed to him, even in vague terms, the administration's willingness to fight; his intense and almost reckless loyalty would do the rest. The censure that seems to be his must, therefore, be passed higher up — it belongs, in fact, with the majority of the American people, whose sentiment at this time Fremont most thoroughly typified.

It was in the month of January of the eventful year 1846 that Fremont entered the state and encamped in the Sacramento valley. He came immediately in person to Monterey, and, accompanied by Thomas O. Larkin, the United States consul, he called on General Castro, the military head of the California government, Pico then being governor with his headquarters at Los Angeles. The negotiation was oral, and its terms afterward a matter of dispute. Fremont explained that his purpose was one of scientific exploration, and Castro seems to have given a kind of consent to his remaining. The commandant was very much astonished a few weeks later to find that Fremont had brought his men over on the coast range, and was encamped near San Juan Bautista mission, only 30 miles from the capital at Monterey.

The party was not molested, however, until there were numerous complaints of horse-stealing, and a charge that several of Fremont's men had behaved in an insulting manner toward the daughter of a prominent Californian in the vicinity. There is no evidence that any of these charges were true, but the commandant believed them, and he ordered Fremont to leave the territory. For answer, the American threw up earthworks around his camp, and raised the Stars and Stripes. This was, in effect, an act of war, and one for which it is quite impossible to find an adequate defense, except on the theory that Fremont had been sent into the country for the deliberate purpose of making trouble. It seems to have occurred to the young captain that perhaps he was going ahead too fast, for when Castro assembled an army of 200 men at San Juan Bautista, Fremont and his backwoodsmen slipped out in the night and made away to the north.

Fremont was accustomed to speak with extreme bitterness of Castro, who, he said, welcomed him to the state and then expelled him by force. Some months later, when Commodore Stockton, U. S. N., was issuing a proclamation to the Californians, announcing the American occupation, and was casting about for a reasonable cause for this policy, the news of the war between the nations not having been received as yet, Fremont suggested that his expulsion from the territory constituted an adequate "casus belli," and Stockton incorporated a savage reference to it in the document. It was indeed a cause of war — but to Mexico and not to the United States. In driving out armed and rebellious foreigners, Castro merely acted as a loyal officer should act; his mistake, if any, was in allowing Fremont and his party to enter at all.

This took place in the month of March, 1846. In April, Lieutenant A. H. Gillespie arrived at Monterey with private dispatches for Fremont, and, learning that he was on his way to Oregon, started off in pursuit. What the nature of these dispatches was has never been made public, but their effect on Fremont was to cause him immediately to return to the Sacramento valley, and establish a camp near the mouth of the Feather river. This confirms the theory that Fremont was sustained, and even urged on, by the administration at Washington.

By this time the policy of insolence and aggression on the part of the Americans had borne its inevitable fruit in a feeling of resentment, suspicion and hatred on the part of the Californians, and a thousand rumors sped over the territory, generated out of these sentiments, and then in turn increasing them. It was said that 10,000 American immigrants were on their way to California with the avowed purpose of taking possession of the country; that the Californians were preparing to rise and massacre the Americans without mercy; that the British were about to seize the territory; and that the home government of Mexico was in a condition of absolute anarchy. In the midst of this confusion, a handful of adventurous spirits, living in and around Sonoma, decided on the impulse of the moment, that the shortest road to order and good government lay in following the example of Texas — for the Americans of the territory to revolt from Mexico, set up a republic of their own, and then ask for annexation to the United States. They were few in number, uncertain of purpose, without a competent leader, and but for the fact that the war between the Union and Mexico happened in the very nick of time to extricate them from their dilemma, they would have paid dearly for their folly; but, despite all this, the Bear Flag incident goes down to history as an important and exciting chapter of the California narrative.

The conspirators presented their plan to Fremont, but while he was perhaps willing enough to see anything done that would widen the breach between the two countries, as an officer in the American army he could not participate in a movement of active rebellion against a nation with which the United States was not yet at war. The leaders in the affair consulted with him from time to time, and when the rebellion was fairly on its feet, he allowed himself to become considerably identified with it. By that time, however, news had reached him that fighting had begun along the Texas frontier between the American and Mexican armies, and that a declaration of war would soon follow.

On the morning of June 14, 1846, the party of revolutionists, 32 in number, entered the little town of Sonoma, took General Vallejo and several others prisoners, and seized the fort, which contained cannon, muskets and other government property. There was no fighting, either then or at any time during the affair, although two Americans were captured and put to death by the Californians, in return for which three Californians were slaughtered by the Americans.

When the Mexican ensign was hauled down from the fort at Sonoma, it was decided that the new republic must have a flag, and the bear was used as the central figure of a hastily constructed design. The name chosen was "The California Republic."

The absence of any one commanding figure soon threw affairs into confusion. Wm. B. Ide, who was nominally the leader, lacked pretty much everything that enables a man to direct the actions of others. Finally, early in July, when the so-called republic had been in existence less than three weeks, the whole party placed themselves in the hands of Fremont, on the understanding that he was to get them out of the difficulty as best he could. Fortunately, just at this time, the news came that Commodore Sloat had entered the harbor of Monterey, and had taken possession of the entire territory in the name of the United States. This brought an abrupt end to the Bear Flag movement, and transformed those whom the Californians regarded as desperate rebels, and who regarded themselves as brave revolutionists, into what history regards as hare-brained enthusiasts.

Actual hostilities between the United States and Mexico broke out in April, 1846, but the news did not reach Washington for nearly three weeks, this being before the days of transcontinental railways and the telegraph. On May 13th war was declared, but no knowledge of that fact reached the Pacific coast until August 12th. Early in June, however. Commodore Sloat, lying in the harbor of Mazatlan, had news of the opening of hostilities from which he knew a declaration of war must come, and, proceeding in accordance with general instructions which he had received some time before, he hurried north to Monterey, entering that port on the 2nd of July. He spent several days inquiring into the condition of affairs in California, where he found no news of the fighting had yet penetrated, and on the 7th of July he made up his mind to go ahead with his plan to seize the country, deeming it better, as he said, to be censured for "doing too much rather than too little."

CHAPTER 20.
THE AMERICANS ENTER LOS ANGELES.

Castro was at Santa Clara at the time of Commodore Sloat's arrival at Monterey, engaged in an effort to raise men to put down the Bear Flag rebellion. The relations between Governor Pico and himself were, at this time, strained almost to the point of civil war. The former was, indeed, assembling a force, ostensibly to assist in maintaining order, but really for the purpose of attacking Castro, whom he charged with usurpation of civil power. The correspondence that passed between the two becomes almost ludicrous, when read in the light of subsequent events, but each took his part with the utmost seriousness, Pico standing upon his dignity as governor of the territory, and demanding that Castro take no step of importance without consulting him, and Castro bombastically vowing to shed his last drop of blood in defense of his country, but wisely keeping out of the way of the Americans with his pitiful force of 200 ill-equipped men. Later in the month the two representatives of Mexican rule came together in the south, and made a feeble effort to rally their forces against the Americans, but as each was suspicious of the other, concert of action was impossible. A generation of habitual plotting and revolutions had rendered the Californians useless to themselves and to one another.

On the 7th of July, 1846, Commodore Sloat landed his men at Monterey, and raised the Stars and Stripes over the fort. The local commandant offered no opposition, merely putting himself on record with the statement that he was overpowered by a superior force. The commodore then issued a proclamation, couched in temperate and conciliatory language, in which he declared that California would henceforth be American territory — although what authority he had to make that statement does not appear — and that the Californians themselves would be the ones most benefited by the change, as they would come under a stable government, where revolutions were unknown and where life, property, and the right to religious freedom would be secure. He assured them that the limitations on commerce would be removed, and that the value of real estate and of all California products would be advanced. He urged all local officers to continue with their duties, until the government of the territory could be definitely arranged and he promised that no private property should be taken for public use without just return.

Within the next few days the flag was raised at Yerba Buena (San Francisco), Sonoma, Sutter's Fort (Sacramento district), Santa Cruz and San Jose. This completed the conquest of the northern part of the state, and no difficulty was experienced either then or later in holding it under American rule. The real war of conquest in California was all in the southern portion, with Los Angeles, which was the capital, as its chief agitator.

About the middle of the month Commodore Stockton arrived; and as Sloat was in bad health and anxious to return to Washington, he placed Stockton in command and sailed to the south. For some reason Stockton seemed to feel that it was incumbent upon him to follow Sloat's example and issue a proclamation, although the latter had said all that was needed on the subject of the relation of the Californians to the new authority. Stockton, however, succeeded in saying a good many things that were better left unsaid; his missive contained a violent attack on Castro, whom he called a usurper that was to be expelled from the country by force. His threatening, ill-humored language was well calculated to stir up disorder rather than to allay discontent.

Fremont's original party had now grown to such proportions that it was mustered into regular service as the "Battalion of California Volunteers," with Fremont as major, and Gillespie as captain. On the 26th day of July, this command was sent to San Diego with instructions to work north to Los Angeles, so as to meet in that vicinity with Stockton's sailors and marines, who would come up from San Pedro. The purpose of this movement was to cut off Castro and his army from escape to the south. Fremont landed at San Diego July 29th, and on the 13th of August met Stockton and his men just outside of Los Angeles.

Meantime, what had been transpiring in the City of the Angels? News of all these great events — the expulsion of Fremont, the Bear Flag rebellion, the capture of Monterey, and the approach of Stockton and the California battalion had been brought to the pueblo, and now last of all came Castro himself with his remnant of an army. Through most of this period the territorial legislature or a piece of it, had been in session. As fast as new disasters were reported, this body would pass resolutions denouncing the authors thereof, and calling upon the people to rise and arm themselves and resist to the last. The governor undertook to do his part by issuing proclamations of the same tenor. But the people did not rise. There was no money in the treasury to provide arms and uniforms, and no army organization worthy of the name. Moreover, there was a large element of the population made up of Americans and their friends, and including also many of the shrewdest and most progressive of the native Californians, who appreciated that the best thing that could happen to the territory was for it to be absorbed by the American republic. While these men hesitated to declare themselves in favor of the invaders, they certainly could not be depended upon to resist them.

Just at this juncture there appeared in Los Angeles a Catholic priest named Eugene McNamara, who had a scheme that he declared would extricate California from all its troubles; and the legislature devoted a week's time to its consideration, clinging to it evidently as a sort of forlorn hope. He claimed to represent an English colonization company that was prepared to send 10,000 Irish emigrants into the territory, provided a land grant of 27,000 square miles be given for their use. The theory on which the scheme rested was that if an English company held a grant of this magnitude — 270 miles by 100 would be a huge slice out of the state — it might result in interference on the part of the British nation with the plans of the Americans. The hope was futile, for McNamara represented nothing but a firm of irresponsible London speculators, who wanted a land grant to serve as a claim against the Americans when the latter should take the country. The deed was given, the land being a large part of what is now known as the San Joaquin valley, but it was not signed until a few days after Sloat raised the flag at Monterey, whereby it was of no value whatever.

In the last days of July a definite plan for the organization of an army was adopted and a call was issued for all men of suitable age to bear arms to assemble in Los Angeles and be enrolled. Only a few responded. The total forces of Pico and Castro probably did not amount to much over 200 men, although the Americans at the time believed them to be six or eight times that number.

On the nth of August, 1846, Stockton and his 400 men started up from San Pedro dragging their cannon by hand. Two days were consumed in making the march. He encamped on the mesa, about three miles southeast of the city, and waited for Fremont. While here a rumor reached him that Castro and Pico had fled to the south, accompanied by a considerable band of horsemen. On the 13th Fremont and the California battalion came up, and the combined forces marched into the city. There was no opposition nor even a manifestation of ill-will. The officers of the territorial government went into hiding, but, with the exception of Castro and Pico, they were either captured or surrendered themselves within the next few days. Castro had fled to Mexico. Pico was concealed at the ranch of his brother-in-law, Don Juan Forster, and he made his way over the border about a month afterward.

Permanent headquarters were established for the American government in an old adobe, where the St. Charles Hotel now stands, on North Main street, and Captain Gillespie and a garrison of fifty men were stationed there.

Stockton remained about two weeks in Los Angeles, during which time he formulated a plan for the civil government of California, and announced his intention of appointing Fremont as governor. He did not actually put the plan in force at this time, however. He wrote a long and rather boastful report of his success in conquering the new territory, and sent it back to the national authorities by Kit Carson, the famous scout, who had accompanied Fremont through the whole of his recent adventurous course — a conspicuous and interesting character of this period. Stockton and his sailors then returned to San Pedro, and sailed for Monterey. Fremont and his battalion went north by land. Both the commanders were entirely confident that there would be no further difficulties, and that California was now safely under the flag of the republic.

They did not appreciate, however, the capacity of the ancient pueblo for making trouble. Revolution had become a habit with its residents, and the quiet of good order was distasteful and fatiguing. It is not improbable that the rule of Captain Gillespie was somewhat lacking in diplomacy and consideration. The failure of the Californians to stand for a conflict had caused them to be rated as cowards by the American soldiers; and Gillespie and his men no doubt showed insolent and unwarranted contempt for the people in their charge. He refused to allow the Californians to gather in friendly reunions, such as they were accustomed to hold, would not allow liquor to be sold except on his special permission; and on slight pretexts — so it is charged — he would order leading citizens to be arrested and brought before him, that he might humiliate them by his arrogance. These statements are no doubt subject to considerable discount, and it may be that no man, however discreet and well-disposed, would have pleased these people as a ruler — for they did not wish to be ruled; but the unanimous testimony of the American residents of Los Angeles, at this time, was that Gillespie made bad business of his authority, and that he was largely to blame for what happened.

There was a band of wild young men in the pueblo, headed by Serbulo Varela, who played at revolution and plotted for sport. They called one of their number "governor," and managed to annoy Gillespie and his men, while they kept discreetly out of reach. On the night of September 22nd this gang, consisting of perhaps twenty youths, surrounded the old adobe where the Americans were, and feigned an attack by beating drums and discharging muskets in the air. The soldiers supposed it was a genuine attack, as perhaps the Californians intended it should be later, and they fired into the crowd, wounding one man in the foot. The next day Gillespie arrested a number of the leading men of the town, none of whom had participated in the affair of the night before, and threw them into prison; whereupon a revolt started in good earnest. Gillespie and his men managed to retreat from their exposed position in the adobe to one of the hills above and to the west of the city, and there they constructed a fort of sandbags. A courier was dispatched to the north to apprise Stockton of the dangerous position in which they were placed; for the number of Californians in arms was increasing daily, and although the Americans had successfully beaten off every attack so far, it was only a matter of a very short time when their supplies would be exhausted.

The courier, who was known as "Juan Flaco," or "Lean John," his true name being John Brown, made the trip to Monterey, 462 miles, in the extraordinary time of fifty-two hours, changing horses at frequent intervals, but taking no sleep by the way. One horse was shot beneath him, as he passed the suburbs of Los Angeles. This ride was long talked of by the early American settlers of the state.

Stockton had, before leaving for the north, organized a local militia company of twenty Americans under the command of B. D. Wilson. They had been scouring the country in search of Castro, but failing to find him they were now in the San Bernardino mountains, hunting for bears. Gillespie sent word to them to come to his aid, but the Californians, anticipating the plan, met them at the Chino ranch, and a fight ensued which is called the "Battle of Chino," although little more than a skirmish. Three of the Americans were wounded, and one of the Californians, a popular young man of good family, was killed. Varela, the originator of the revolt, led the Californians, and he gave his word to Wilson that if he would surrender he and his men should not be harmed. The Americans thereupon gave themselves up, but so great was the anger of the Californians over the death of their compatriot that they were restrained only with the utmost difficulty from slaughtering Wilson and the whole company.

The capture of these men discouraged Gillespie, for there was no hope of succor from Stockton within two or three weeks. When General Flores, who had now taken charge of the military operations of the Californians, proposed that he leave the city with all the honors of war, Gillespie gladly accepted the terms, and on the 30th of September he made his way to San Pedro.

There was an understanding that he should be allowed to carry his field pieces as far as the water front, but that there he was to surrender them to the Californians. Gillespie violated the spirit of this understanding, for he spiked the guns, knocked off their breech knobs and flung them into the water at low tide. Several years later these cannon were rescued by B. D. Wilson, and hauled back to Los Angeles. Wilson at that time had a large store at the corner of Main and Commercial streets, where the Farmers and Merchants' bank now stands; he put the cannon in the ground at the corner, as mementoes of his narrow escape from death in the war. Two of them are still there, and the other two are now to be seen in front of the Broadway entrance of the courthouse.

Gillespie was about to start north on an American merchant ship that was lying in the harbor, when Captain Mervine arrived, most opportunely as it seemed, with the frigate Savannah. On the 7th of October 350 men from the frigate, together with Gillespie's detachment, undertook to get up from San Pedro to Los Angeles, and the battle of Dominguez ranch took place, on the evening of that day and the morning of the next. The Californians

102

were not numerous, but they were all mounted, and they had a fieldpiece, which they used with good effect. When the Americans charged and attempted to capture it, the Californians galloped off, dragging it after them with their reatas. At length when six of the Americans had been slain, and a number wounded they gave up the fight and retired to San Pedro. The men slain in the battle were buried on Dead Man's Island, at the mouth of San Pedro harbor.

CHAPTER 21.
THE LAST REVOLUTION IN LOS ANGELES.

The rebellion had now gained a good headway, and had spread all over the southern portion of California, with Los Angeles, the ancient home of revolutionary movements, for its headquarters. At Santa Barbara the American force consisted of nine men under Lieutenant Talbot. Manuel Garfias was sent up from the pueblo to drive them out, but they, learning of his approach, contrived to escape into the Santa Inez mountains, in order to evade parole. The Californians set fire to the brush to dislodge them, but they escaped over the ridge, and, striking out across the desert, came down finally into the San Joaquin valley. By this roundabout way, suffering terrible hardships, and with many exciting adventures, they came through to Monterey. One of these men was Elijah Moulton, who still lives, and has a residence in East Los Angeles. San Diego was also taken by the Californians, but they held it for a short time only.

The sentiment throughout the southern country in favor of the revolt was practically unanimous, although a few natives, like. Juan Bandini of San Diego, and his brother-in-law, Arguello, favored the Americans, because they represented a strong government; and all the resident Americans were doubtless hopeful that California would become part of the Union, however wary they may have been of expressing their sentiments. An army was mustered, which was at no time larger than 500, the great difficulty being not so much to secure men as to arm them. The country was raked over for weapons of every kind. There were a few old muskets and pistols, and one ancient four-pounder cannon that had formerly stood in front of the guardhouse on the plaza to be used in firing salutes. When Stockton took Los Angeles, in August, this gun had been hauled to the garden of Dona Inocencia Reyes, on Alameda street, and by her it was ordered buried. While the men were lamenting the fact that they had no artillery. Dona Inocencia produced this cannon, and they in their gratitude named it the "Woman's Gun." It is now in the National Museum at Washington.

But the worst difficulty with which the revolutionists had to contend was the lack of powder. There was a small amount of good powder stored in Los Angeles, of which they immediately possessed themselves. The padres at San Gabriel had been accustomed to manufacture the article, and a knowledge of the method was supposed to be held there yet. A quantity of powder was ordered from the San Gabriel factory, but whether the formula had been forgotten or whether some one of the makers was friendly to the Americans and doctored the compound, is not known, but it was a failure in the field. Guns that were loaded with it were altogether too deliberate about going off.

In the battle of Dominguez ranch, which was described in the last chapter, the Californians had just enough good powder for one charge in the gun that they hauled about with reatas — the "Woman's Gun." They maneuvered for the most favorable opportunity, and then put in the charge, that shot doing almost the entire execution that was accomplished during the battle.

Jose Maria Flores was elected governor and chief of command, with Jose Antonio Carrillo, an habitual revolutionist, second, and Andres Pico, the late governor's brother, as third. The legislative body was called together, and such officers of the old government as remained on the ground were reinstated in their former positions. All of the principal men — Flores, Carrillo, Pico and others, had been admitted to parole, and hence were in danger of being shot if captured. Their justification, as they claimed, lay in the fact that Gillespie had thrown them all into prison, which absolved them from their allegiance and nullified the parole.

The Flores regime lasted from the middle of September until the following January — less than four months — but even that short period could not be passed without an attempt at a revolution — a wheel within a wheel — and this, too, at the time when the Americans were closing in on the city. In December Flores was seized, deposed from power, and thrown into jail as a traitor. The difficulty arose out of his threat to send the Americans captured on the Chino ranch to Mexico for safe-keeping. Several of them, particularly B. D. Wilson, had powerful friends through marriage connections. From the interior of the jail Flores saw things somewhat differently, and declared his entire willingness to have the Chino prisoners remain in the country.

A day or two after the affair at the Dominguez ranch, Commodore Stockton arrived at San Pedro with about 800 men. Had he then made a quick dash for Los Angeles he could easily have taken it, there being few to oppose, and they so badly equipped. The Californians, however, led by Carrillo, moved their cavalry about over the adjoining hills with a rapidity that gave an impression of great numbers, and this effect was heightened by the droves of loose horses they urged before them. In his reports Stockton speaks of the enemy as having 800 cavalry. Through the whole rebellion the Americans proceeded under the idea that the Californians had at least 2000 men in arms. Before the occupation the Americans had been taught to believe that the Californians were cowardly, and that they could not be induced to fight. The recent experiences in and around Los Angeles had opened their eyes to some dangerous qualities in the native cavalry, and they were presently to have a much severer lesson in the battle of San Pasqual. After waiting several days at San Pedro, with no improvement of the outlook, Stockton sailed away for San Diego, intending to begin his attack from that place.

The commodore had left Fremont in Monterey, under instructions to follow as soon as possible, with such recruits as he had secured. Fremont started south by water, but, learning that no horses were to be had at San Pedro, and that the entire country was up in arms, he thought best to return to Monterey, increase the size of his command, and go south by land, taking with him ample supplies and plenty of animals. This consumed time, and it was not until the middle of November that he left Monterey, and he arrived at Los Angeles too late to be of service in the active part of the campaign. On his way south he captured Jesus Pico, a cousin of the late governor, who had taken the parole, but was discovered in arms. Fremont ordered him to be put to death, but finally pardoned him, on the tearful implorations of his wife and children. This act of clemency did a good deal to restore better feeling between the Californians and the Americans.

In the meantime a detachment of the American army was making its way across the continent under General Stephen W. Kearny, who had left Fort Leavenworth, Kansas, with 1600 men, and a full equipment of animals and supplies, in the month of June, 1846. As he came through Arizona and New Mexico Kearny raised the Stars and Stripes at every place of importance that he passed, and left a number of garrisons. On his way he had fallen in with Kit Carson, the famous scout who had been with Fremont's party, and was now on his mission to carry the news to Washington. From him Kearny learned that Stockton had taken complete possession of California, the rebellion having broken out since his departure. Acting on this information, Kearny did not hesitate to distribute his force along the line as he came through, until he had only 121 left in the command. He induced Carson to commit his dispatches to some one else, and turn back with him. This was a fortunate move on Kearny's part, for Carson's services were presently to be in great demand.

Early in December the party crossed the Colorado river, and presently was met by a detachment of twenty men under Captain Gillespie, whom Stockton had sent out to act as an escort into San Diego. As they came to a stream called the San Bernardo they learned that General Andres Pico was encamped near the Indian village of San Pasqual. By this time the soldiers had heard of the rebellion, of the driving out of the Los Angeles garrison, and the defeat at Dominguez, and all were eager for a chance to meet the enemy. Carson had assured them that the Californians were cowards and would not stand against a determined attack, and there was probably a disposition among Kearny's men to show Gillespie and his following that the rebels would cut a sorry figure when the regulars fell upon them.

Early in the morning of December 5, 1846, as the Americans were riding along in the bed of the San Bernardo, near the village of San Pasqual, which is thirty-eight miles northeast of San Diego, they suddenly came upon Pico and about eighty Californians, all mounted and armed with lances. The lance used by the Californians was about eight feet long, light, strong and furnished with a sharp blade at the point. It was a very effective weapon for a short-range combat.

The Americans were badly strung out, and in no condition for a fight. Their guns and pistols were wet with the morning dew, and refused to discharge. The mounts were tired and ill-fed, many of them mules that had recently been pressed into service and were hard to manage. There was every reason why the force, if its commander had used average military intelligence, should have been kept out of a battle, and by a little maneuvering it might easily have been avoided. The moment the Californians came in sight, however. Captain Johnson, who led the van, seemed to have lost all control over himself, and he dashed forward with a yell, followed by the small party of a dozen men, who were in advance of the main body of the Americans.

A moment later Johnson lay on the ground, shot through the head, and several of his men were wounded. The Americans fell back in confusion, until the next detachment came up, which consisted of about fifty dragoons under Captain Moore. Then the Californians wheeled and galloped away.

Instantly the whole party of Americans started in pursuit, and the race lasted for half a mile of running. By this time the Americans were scattered and spread out, owing to the unevenness of the ground, and to the fact that those mounted on mules could not keep up with those mounted on horses. Looking back and discovering the state of things, Pico halted his men, turned them about, and the real battle began.

It proved very serious for the Americans, and although generally recorded as a victory for that side, by reason of their holding the field, while the others finally retreated, it was in effect a defeat, and a bad one. In an incredibly short space of time eighteen Americans lay dead, stabbed by lances, and as many more were severely wounded. Of the enemy few were hurt, and none were killed. The extraordinary percentage of Americans killed and wounded, out of the number engaged, makes the battle unique in the country's history. Surgeon John S. Griffin, whose account of the affair was that of an intelligent eyewitness, declares that not more than fifty of the Americans ever saw the enemy, and certainly not more than that number were actually engaged in the fight, and yet thirty-seven were either killed or wounded.

Toward the close of the affair an effort was made to get one of the howitzers into action, but the mules attached to it became frightened and ran away, and the piece fell into the hands of the enemy.

Captain Moore, who led the second charge, was killed, and General Kearny and Captain Gillespie were both severely cut with lances. The wounded were in the care of Dr. Griffin, who afterward became a citizen of Los Angeles, and was for more than a quarter of a century its leading physician. He was also a large land owner, controlling at one time most of the present site of Pasadena and of East Los Angeles, and he was one of the founders of the present water system of the city.

The effect of this engagement was to badly demoralize the forces of General Kearny. Their opinion of the valor and the fighting qualities of the Californians underwent an entire change, and although the number of men still ready for service probably exceeded those of the command of Pico, they did not venture out of the camp which they had hastily thrown up. It was cold and wet, and the provisions were giving out. Then it was that Kit Carson came to the front. Accompanied by Lieutenant Beale of the regular army, and an Indian, he crept past the enemy by night and succeeded in getting to San Diego.

Stockton immediately sent reinforcements to Kearny, consisting of 200 marines, and with this escort the overland company managed to get through to the coast.

Stockton had come to San Diego, after his brief stay at San Pedro, in the last days of October. He experienced considerable difficulty in getting into the bay with his flagship, the Congress, and at one time very nearly had it aground, but finally managed to get over the bar into the harbor. Although the Americans still held nominal control of San Diego, the condition of affairs on shore was not very promising. The Californian men had all escaped into the interior, taking with them the horses and cattle, and leaving the women and children for the Americans to support or to let starve. Numerous foraging parties were at once dispatched into the country, to bring in stock, for horses were necessary to Stockton's plan for an expedition to the north by land. Some of these were successful, and brought in not only a plentiful supply of fresh meat, but also horses enough to fit out a cavalry company made up of sailors. The efforts of the latter to ride without putting both arms around the horses' necks afforded the camp plenty of amusement.

It was on one of these raids after stock that the Bandini flag incident took place. Captain Hensley, who had been sent down into Lower California, was returning in triumph with 500 cattle and 140 horses and mules, which he had obtained from Juan Bandini, an enthusiastic sympathizer with the American cause. He was accompanied by Bandini and his family, who were making their way to San Diego. The American officer was expressing his regret that he had no flag with which to march into camp with his booty in proper style, when Juan Bandini's wife, who was the daughter of the former governor, Arguello, offered to construct one. Three of her children were playing about, one dressed in white, one in blue, and one in red. Ordering these dresses changed for others, she hastily cut out and stitched together the red and white stripes and the white stars on the blue field. Two of these children afterwards became residents of Los Angeles, and many members of the Bandini family in the next generation now live in and about this city. The story is a pretty one, and as it is vouched for by credible eye-witnesses, we may believe it to be true. This was the first American flag ever made in California.

CHAPTER 22. LOS ANGELES REGAINED.

The American force which set out from San Diego to capture Los Angeles consisted of about 500 men, nine tenths of whom were Stockton's sailors and marines, and the remainder Kearny's dragoons. The commission under which Kearny had been sent to California made him military governor of the territory, thus superseding Stockton, as well as Fremont, whom Stockton had proposed to make civil governor. The commodore seems to have understood that Kearny's authority went beyond his own, for he offered, as soon as Kearny came into camp from San Pasqual, to turn over the control of affairs to him. The latter was, however, suffering from a wound, or he may have thought it only courtesy to allow Stockton to continue with the work of preparation.

At all events he certainly declined the command at that time. But when the expedition was ready to start, December 29, 1846, Kearny asked who was to take charge, and, on being told by Commodore Stockton that Lieutenant Rowan had been appointed, he announced that he would prefer to occupy that position himself. Stockton thereupon appointed him to the command. ,

This was the beginning of an undignified controversy between the two commanders, which presently involved many of the officers stationed in Los Angeles, and at last brought Fremont to a court-martial in Washington. There is no doubt that of the two principals to this affair, Stockton's behavior was the more reprehensible, for the military governorship certainly lay with Kearny, and not with the commodore; but, on the other hand, there was a lamentable lack of judgment shown by Kearny in all his acts, and a seeming desire to make trouble rather than to smooth over difficulties.

When the party had been on the march a few days they were met by Julian Workman and Charles Flugge of Los Angeles, who had been sent out by the Californians to negotiate for a temporary cessation of hostilities. They bore a letter from Flores, in which he asserted that news had been received from Mexico that the war with the United States was at an end, and that satisfactory terms of settlement were now being negotiated. He suggested that under the circumstances it might be well to wait and see whether bloodshed in California could not be averted.

When Stockton read this letter — he seems to have ignored Kearny in the matter, although the latter was theoretically in command — he returned answer orally that he had released Flores on a parole of honor, in spite of which he was now in arms; therefore if he caught him he would shoot him, but would have no further dealings with him.

On the 8th of January, eleven days having been consumed on the march, the party came to the San Gabriel river, and prepared to cross, just north of the place where the bridge of the Santa Fe railroad to Orange now spans the stream. At this spot, which is situated about ten miles southeast of Los Angeles, the battle of San Gabriel was fought. The Californians had mustered all their forces — a total of 500 mounted men — and with four pieces of artillery were posted in an advantageous position on high ground, a quarter of a mile back from the river. The Americans sent forward their artillery, and were about to drag it across the stream, when some one warned Kearny that there was quicksand in the river, and that the cannon would be lost. There was a momentary halt, and some confusion, for the roar of the enemy's guns was already heard. Stockton rode up, and was told by Kearny what was the matter. "Damn the quicksand," shouted Stockton, *T)ring up those guns." Kearny fell back, and allowed Stockton to direct affairs. The cannon were hurried across, and no quicksand was encountered.

A heavy cannonading was begun by the Americans, under cover of which the troops waded the river, and, climbing up on the higher ground, formed into squares to resist the attack of cavalry. The Californians charged, but were unable to stand the fire, and fell back. Presently the whole line of the enemy began to give way in a slow and orderly retreat. They continued to fire their cannon at intervals as they fell back, until they were entirely out of range.

The engagement lasted only about an hour and a half. The Americans lost two killed and eight wounded. The loss of the Californians was about the same. Had the latter possessed powder of any value the American loss would undoubtedly have been much greater. The Americans advanced, with their band playing "Hail Columbia," and took up the ground that Flores had occupied before the battle opened, and here encamped for the day and the following night.

On the morning of January 9, 1847, the Americans advanced toward Los Angeles and came upon the enemy about noon, three miles south of the city. There was a long-range artillery duel, in which neither side effected much damage on the other. The Americans formed a large hollow square, with the baggage in the center, and advanced slowly for about four hours, driving the enemy before them. Three times Flores ordered his cavalry to charge, but when they came within a few hundred feet of the American line they encountered a fire so severe that they were compelled to withdraw. Stockton had five men wounded, but none killed. At about 4 o'clock the enemy gave up the struggle and retreated. The Americans crossed the Los Angeles river, and encamped for the night within sight of the pueblo.

Next morning, January 10th, a small delegation of citizens waited on Stockton and informed him that the Californian army had fled, and that the people were prepared to surrender the city without resistance, if they could have an agreement that their lives and property would be respected. They were evidently in fear that the place was to be sacked. Stockton assured them that no injury would be done peaceable citizens, and they went away. In spite of these friendly advances on the part of the rebellious city, the Americans proceeded slowly and with great caution. About noon they came to the plaza. The streets were filled with people, some few of whom showed their disapproval by curses and shaking of fists. The hills above were crowded with horsemen, who fled at the approach of soldiers sent to dislodge them.

The band played its repertoire of national and popular airs, and the Californians forgot their anger and crowded to listen. Gillespie led the way to the old adobe on Main street, which he had formerly occupied as headquarters, and asked permission himself to run up the colors which he had been compelled to haul down some four months before. The permission was granted him, and the men cheered lustily as they saw the flag restored to its accustomed spot. Los Angeles was once more an American city, and this time it was destined permanently to remain so.

A strong detachment of artillery was placed on the hill directly above the city, and the chief topographical engineer of General Kearny's division was instructed to prepare plans for a fort in that location. Before this work had advanced very far Kearny left the city, and Lieutenant J. W. Davidson of the First United States Dragoons was ordered to enlarge the plan and begin the work. This was finally completed by July 4th of that year, 1847, and was named Fort Moore. It was on the hill above the present Broadway tunnel.

Looking about for a place in which to establish his headquarters, as he entered the town, Stockton discovered a large, well-furnished house, with its doors open and apparently quite unoccupied. It was the residence of Dona Encarnacion Abila, at 14, 16, 18 Olivera street. This building is still to be seen standing (1901), although now in very bad repair. Olivera is a small street running out from the plaza, north of Marchessault. Fearing lest the vengeance of the American soldiery might fall upon the inhabitants of the pueblo, the Senora Abila had left the house in charge of a young man, and escaped into the country; and he, attracted by the playing of the band, had left it unguarded and standing open. Here Stockton made his headquarters during his stay, to the great discomfiture, no doubt, of the loyalist owner of the property. General Fremont secured for his use, and that of the civil government which he established, a series of low adobes that occupied the space where the engine-house now stands, on the southeast corner of the plaza. Adjoining these to the west was the residence of J. A. Carrillo, pretentious for its day, on the spot where the Pico house, now called the National hotel, was afterward constructed.

112

On the day that Stockton and Kearny entered Los Angeles, Fremont, coming down from the north, encamped at San Fernando. He had made the march slowly, acting on repeated messages from the commodore, who advised the utmost caution. Santa Barbara was retaken as he passed, and garrisoned against further attack. Learning that the Californian army was encamped on the Verdugo Ranch, Fremont sent out Jesus Pico, the man whose life he had spared, to confer with the rebels.

After the battle on the mesa, on the 9th of January, the Californians scattered, many of them laying down their arms and returning to their homes. Flores, mindful of the threat of Stockton that he would put him to death if captured, took a small escort and escaped over the border into Mexico. The command was transferred to Andres Pico, with J. A. Carrillo second in authority, and they were advised by the escaping leader to yield on the best terms possible. Two days later Jesus Pico came into the rebel camp and announced that Fremont was at hand with a large force; and he urged the Californians to surrender to him, rather than to Stockton, in the hope that they might secure better conditions.

On the 13th of January, 1847, articles of capitulation were ratified between the Californians and Fremont, at the Cahuenga ranch house, only a few miles out of Los Angeles. It was agreed that the Californians should surrender their artillery and "public arms," and should take the parole not to assist in carrying on war against the United States. Such as preferred to go out of the territory into Mexico would be allowed to depart, and those that remained were to be pardoned for their participation in the rebellion, irrespective of whether they had been under parole or not. Until a treaty of peace should be signed between the United States and Mexico, no resident of California was to be compelled to take the oath of allegiance. The "public arms" thus secured amounted to a handsome total of six muskets, and two diminutive cannon — the "Woman's Gun" and one other.

The evidence is clear that Fremont knew of the occupation of Los Angeles by Stockton at the time he entered into this agreement with the Californians; and it was afterwards charged by his enemies — of which he had always a flourishing crop — that he overstepped the bounds of his authority in making terms with the belligerents almost in the very presence of his superior. It was an infraction of military etiquette, to say the least, but it did not displease Stockton, who was, on the contrary, rather relieved to have the matter thus taken out of his hands. He had repeatedly threatened to put to death Flores and others who had broken their parole, and such severity, if actually carried out, would have made the complete pacification of the country difficult, if not impossible. Fremont had provided him a way out of an awkward dilemma.

There may have been another reason why Stockton was well satisfied with Fremont's course in this matter. The tendency toward disagreement and mutual suspicion that had always been rife among the Californians, and which was indigenous to the southern pueblo, seems by this time to have thoroughly infected the Americans, and the row between Stockton and Kearny was assuming serious proportions. The former may have been the more ready to overlook any seeming irregularity in Fremont's conduct in the hope of obtaining his support in the controversy.

On the day of the surrender at Cahuenga, Fremont sent on his second in command to Los Angeles, with instructions to find out which of the two — Stockton or Kearny — was ill authority. He found that each claimed to be the civil and military governor of the state, although they each admitted privately that as soon as peace was restored in the territory they intended to make Fremont civil governor. Kearny based his claim on the fact that he had been commissioned by the national government to take entire charge of affairs, his instructions bearing a later date than any held by Stockton. As a matter of fact, this claim was entirely valid, and Stockton's position was untenable. The latter held that Kearny's instructions were based on a theory that a state of war existed in California, and that the country was in alien hands, whereas, before Kearny had come to the state the Americans had secured complete control, and a civil government was practically in operation. To this he added the argument that when Kearny had first arrived at San Diego and was offered the reins of authority by Stockton he had declined to accept them.

Fremont's emissary dodged the whole question by making his report to both claimants, and when Fremont himself came into the pueblo the next day he made an official call upon each of them, and waited for developments.

On the 16th of January the matter came to a direct issue upon Kearny's sending instructions to Stockton to proceed no further in the formation of a civil government for the territory. Stockton refused to obey, and issued an order removing Kearny from command of the troops. For the purpose of putting Fremont on record, Kearny sent word to him not to make certain contemplated changes in his battalion. He then sent for Fremont, and urged him to come over to his side, assuring him that he would make him governor in return. But Fremont was loyal to Stockton, to whom he felt himself indebted, and he refused to be led away by a bribe. He sent a formal communication to Kearny to the effect that until the latter and Stockton settled their differences as to their respective authority he would be compelled to take his orders, as before, from Commodore Stockton.

A day or two later, finding himself utterly ignored in the plans of Stockton and Fremont for the governing of the territory, Kearny addressed a note to the commodore, in which he said that to avoid further discussion and disagreement, which would bring scandal upon the powers they represented, he would withdraw for the present to San Diego, and await further instructions from Washington. On January 18th he left Los Angeles with his dragoons and marched south.

January 19th Stockton issued to Fremont his commission as civil governor of the state, a position which he held about fifty days, although his technical right to it is open to question. Stockton offered the place of secretary of state to Gillespie, but the latter preferred to be major of the battalion. An order was issued, convening a legislative council, which was to contain, among others, ex-governor Alvarado, Juan Bandini and his brother-in-law, Santiago Arguello, and Thomas O. Larkin, the American consul, who had been captured early in the rebellion, and was held as a prisoner in Los Angeles through the whole affair. But this gathering never came together, for early in March Colonel Richard B. Mason arrived with new instructions from the national government that left no doubt as to the pre-eminence of Kearny's military and civil authority. Stockton was no longer in command on the coast, having been succeeded by Commodore Shubrick, and the latter at once recognized Kearny as governor of the state. Fremont came up to Monterey, whither Kearny had repaired, and he also admitted the authority of Kearny. About this time Fremont and Colonel Mason, who was Kearny's chief of staff, and who was subsequently appointed governor, became involved in a quarrel, out of which came a challenge to a duel. The affair of honor never took place, owing to the intervention of General Kearny. Fremont was ordered to Washington, where he was tried before a court-martial for disobedience and conduct prejudicial to good order and military discipline. After a long and tempestuous trial he was found technically guilty, and recommended to the clemency of the president. But Fremont declined to accept the verdict as a just one and resigned from the army.

CHAPTER 23. THE PUEBLO IS MADE AMERICAN

Los Angeles was under military rule from January of 1847, when the Americans took possession of the city for the second time, to August, 1848 — a period of nineteen months. During the time of his quasi-governorship, Fremont kept his headquarters at Los Angeles, because it had been the capital under the Mexican administration, but as soon as General Kearny came to be recognized as governor, he sent for the archives and had" them brought up to Monterey. This put a final quietus on the long-cherished ambition of the southern city.

On the first of March Kearny sent instructions to Fremont to muster out his battalion, and report in person at Monterey. Colonel P. St. George Cooke, who was in command of a battalion of Mormon volunteers from Missouri, was appointed to succeed Fremont in charge of affairs at Los Angeles. Through the disbanding of the California Battalion, a regiment which Fremont had gathered in California, Los Angeles gained a number of settlers. The Mormon command came up from San Luis Rey, in San Diego county, where it had been stationed, and encamped in Los Angeles. These were the men that did most of the work on the fort. They had it nearly completed when they were summoned to Monterey, to be mustered out. Colonel Cooke was succeeded in the month of May by Colonel J. B. Stevenson, of the New York regiment of volunteers. This regiment, like the Mormon battalion, had been enlisted on the understanding that when the war came to an end, the men were to be paid off in California, and allowed to remain there. Thus the conflict between the United States and Mexico brought many settlers to California.

The presence of so large a body of soldiers in Los Angeles, varying from 300 to 1000, had the effect not only of finally demolishing all plans for rebellion against the new authority, but also of rapidly initiating the Spanish city into American manners and customs. The upper class Californians, those whose blood was largely or entirely Spanish, and who had education and a property interest, adapted themselves in dignified fashion to the new order. When the state constitutional convention met in 1849, J. A. Carrillo and Manuel Dominguez were elected delegates from Los Angeles, as representing the progressive Spanish-American element. W. M. Gwin, who was afterward United States senator, happening to remark, in the course of his argument on some point, that the constitution of the state was not framed so much for the original inhabitants of the territory as for the newcomers of American birth, Carrillo was on his feet in an instant, declaring that he considered himself and his fellow-Californians just as true and patriotic Americans as any members of that body; and the remark brought out long and enthusiastic applause. But in the lower class of

Californians the same adaptability to new conditions did not develop. There were no rebellions, although rumors to that effect were incessant; but the presence of the Americans, or "gringos," as they came now to be called, was more and more resented, and, in the end, acting upon a bad example set by the Americans them selves, a great amount of lawlessness sprang up among this class.

Colonel Stevenson found his position by no means an easy one, although his difficulties were identical with those of the governor and all others in authority in the state, who were attempting to apply American ideas of justice and civic improvement, through the awkward medium of old Spanish laws. Mason's instructions to his subordinates had been to interfere as little as possible with the civil affairs. They were to keep order and assist in the administration of the laws as they existed. This was by no means as easy as it sounds. Questions were constantly coming up, as between the military and civil authorities, and on several occasions things came to a complete deadlock.

In the year 1847, an ayuntamiento had been chosen in Los Angeles that was made up entirely of native-born Californians. They were informed by Colonel Stevenson that they might go on with the government of the city, just as before, with the one limitation that they were not to give away or sell any of the pueblo real estate. The "Very Illustrious" body continued to hold meetings, after its ancient custom, observing its traditional formalities with all the more pomp and circumstance by reason of the fact that the Americans were looking on. In the month of June of that year the records show that one of the regidores, or councilmen, was fined $10 for impoliteness toward another member. A month or two later the second alcalde caused the arrest of Varela, the same who had raised the tumult and driven out Gillespie and started the rebellion a year before. Colonel Stevenson, for some reason, set him free; whereupon the alcalde resigned, and the ayuntamiento left his place vacant as a standing protest.

This experience and several others of a similar character led Stevenson to suggest to the governor that he appoint at least one American in the next ayuntamiento, and he, acting upon this advice, notified the people of Los Angeles that Stephen C. Foster, who had come to the coast with the New York regiment as their interpreter, and who for nearly half a century was destined to play an active part in the city affairs, was to be alcalde. This was, of course, an assumption of authority on the party of the governor to which he could lay no legal claim. It was, in fact, a war measure, and it seems to have been seriously resented by the citizens of native birth. The out-going alcalde refused to comply with custom and swear in his successor, Foster, and Stevenson cut the Gordian knot by swearing him in himself. The other members of the ayuntamiento all resigned, and Foster and Don Abel

Stearns, who had been elected sindico, or city attorney and tax collector, ran the government for a time.

They seem to have conducted the city's affairs very successfully. A chain gang was established and put to work on the dam, or headworks on the river, and on the irrigating ditch, both of which had fallen into disrepair. Several small Indian settlements within the pueblo, which were haunts of vice and filth, were demolished, and their inhabitants driven out — a harsh but probably salutary measure. Vagrants were brought to time, and some regulation of the liquor traffic was attempted.

In December of 1848, notice was issued for an election of a new ayuntamiento, but the people paid no attention to it; whereupon the governor announced that the present officers would continue to hold until the voters of Los Angeles made up their minds to elect successors for them. In May of the following year, 1849, the governor learned that the fit of sulks was over, and he issued another order for an election. This time a considerable vote was cast. The ayuntamiento chosen was made up of Californians, except that John Temple was elected sindico. By 1850 the prejudice against admitting Americans to a share of the local government seems to have died out, for Abel Stearns was chosen first alcalde that year, with D. W. Alexander and B. D. Wilson also members of the ayuntamiento. Although the Americans continued for many years to be in the minority at the polls, they were always, after this, admitted to more than their proportion of the local offices.

In the year 1847, Los Angeles being still a military post and full of soldiers, a great celebration was held of the Fourth of July. This was the first recognition of Independence Day in the old Spanish pueblo. Col. Stevenson issued a proclamation, in which he called for a celebration of the day, to be combined with the dedication of the fort, now nearly completed. The troops under his command were instructed to make ready for the affair, and to put up the best showing that was possible. "Circumstances over which we have no control," says Col. Stevenson in his proclamation, "have prevented the command at this post being completely uniformed, but each officer will appear on the Fourth with the perfect equipments of his corps, as far as he has them; and most perfect cleanliness as well in arms and accoutrements as in person will be required of all."

At sunrise the national salute was fired and the colors displayed for the first time at the fort. At 10 o'clock the soldiers marched through the town and up to the summit of the hill, where they formed a hollow square and listened to the reading of the Declaration of Independence. This was translated into Spanish by Stephen C. Foster, for the benefit of the large crowd of Californians who had gathered to witness the celebration. Prof. J. M. Guinn of the Los Angeles Historical Society, who has written an entertaining description of the event, suggests that possibly, as the

Californians sat on their horses and listened to the fierce denunciation of King George in the famous document, though they were not able to comprehend quite what it was all about, they could recognize a pronunciamento when they heard it, and they knew from experience that a revolution must follow, and they smiled, no doubt, at the thought that they would soon behold the gringos falling upon one another in a row among themselves.

The fort, or "field works," as the proclamation calls it, was then dedicated and named in honor of Captain Benjamin D. Moore of the First United States Dragoons, who fell in the battle of San Pasqual. Stevenson speaks of him as "a perfect specimen of an American officer, whose character for every virtue and accomplishment that adorns a gentleman was only equaled by the reputation he had acquired in the field for his gallantry as an officer and a soldier." The honor of raising the flag for the first time over the fort was granted to Lieutenant Davidson, who had taken charge of the work almost from the beginning. During the Civil War he attained to the rank of major general. The flagpole consisted of two tree trunks brought down from the San Bernardino mountains by a special expedition sent out for that purpose, and spliced together, making a shaft of about 150 feet in length. The colors flying from this, on the top of the high hill, could be seen for miles in every direction. All traces of the fort and the famous old flagpole have long since disappeared.

Through the whole of the year 1847 there were frequent rumors of intended attacks by the Mexicans as well as of rebellious plottings on the part of Californians, but these do not appear to have had any substantial basis. Mexico had its hands full with the Americans on its own soil, and the appeals of Flores and Pico received little attention. The native Californians were accustomed to whisper among themselves about the return of Flores, leading a great army, and the flight of the Americans; but they never seriously contemplated rebellion on their own account. Nevertheless, Colonel Stevenson, as was perhaps natural from his lack of acquaintance with the Spanish character, and his ignorance of the true state of affairs in Mexico, gave ear to these rumors, and, like a careful soldier, was never off his guard. The construction of Fort Moore was really due to a fear of attack from Mexico.

On the night of December 7, 1847, a frightful disaster occurred as an indirect consequence of these persistent rumors. On the afternoon of that day an old woman resident of Los Angeles called at the headquarters of Colonel Stevenson, which were located on the spot where the Ferguson livery stable now stands, nearly opposite the Baker block, and informed him that there was a plot on foot to attack the guardhouse that night and capture the city, slaying or driving out all Americans. If there was any plot of that description, and if the whole affair was not a fabric of the old woman's imagination, it certainly did not involve any number of people nor any citizens of responsibility. However, Colonel Stevenson thought best to take no chances. He doubled the sentries at the guardhouse, which was on the west side of New High street, in the rear of the St. Elmo site. The men were all nervous and on the alert, and when, about midnight, one of them saw a cow off in the darkness he mistook it for a horseman and fired. The guard turned out, and everything was put in readiness for an attack. When the mistake was discovered, arms were restored to the racks, and the men were preparing to return to their beds. Then an artilleryman, who had lighted a fuse ready to discharge a fieldpiece, if that should be necessary, threw it, only half extinguished, into an ammunition chest. The explosion that followed shook the entire city and brought the population all out of their homes. The guardhouse was blown to fragments, some of the loof timbers landing clear over into Main street. Four men were killed outright, and twelve were seriously injured. The guardhouse was immediately rebuilt of adobe.

The first American legislature of California, which met late in the year 1849, and continued in session until April of 1850, divided the state into twenty-seven counties, one of which was named Los Angeles. Its boundaries included part of Kern, all of San Bernardino, part of Riverside, and all of Los Angeles and Orange. Roughly speaking, it included all north of the old limits of San Diego county to the Tehachapi range, from the ocean to the Colorado river, except that the modern counties of Santa Barbara and Ventura then formed the county of Santa Barbara. The first election in this county took place April I, 1850. Three hundred and seventy-five votes were cast. Augustin Olivera was elected county judge. He was originally a resident of the City of Mexico, but he had been living in California since 1834. B. D. Wilson was elected county clerk; Benjamin Hayes, attorney; J. R. Conway, surveyor; Manuel Garfias, treasurer; Antonio F. Coronel, assessor; Ignacio Del Valle, father of R. F. Del Valle of Los Angeles, county recorder; George T. Burrill, sheriff; Charles B. Cullen, coroner. The preponderance of Americans will be noted by the reader.

The first assessment taken in this huge district showed that it contained real estate to a total value of $748,606; improvements, $301,947; and personal property valued at $1,183,898. The disproportionate size of the last item is explained by the fact that land was considered of small value, and stock, with which the county was at this time fairly well filled, was, of course, included in the personal property.

CHAPTER 24. CALIFORNIA ENTERS THE UNION

Thus far the history of Los Angeles city has been so intimately connected with the history of the whole territory of California that the narrative has, of necessity, often strayed outside the local limits. Los Angeles was not only the largest and most prosperous city of Spanish and Mexican California, but it was also the most considerable political factor of the territory, a leader in all plots and rebellions, and for a time the capital. But now, under American rule, the relation of the city to the state undergoes a change. Los Angeles presently ceases to be the largest center of population in the territory. The little town of Yerba Buena, which had recently been rechristened San Francisco, and which at the time of the American occupation contained perhaps a thousand people, is suddenly flooded with a great wave of immigration, as a result of the discovery of gold, so that Los Angeles becomes little more than a village in comparison. Other towns besides San Francisco spring up in the northern part of the state, rivaling the southern city in size, and surpassing it, for the time being, in business activity. The political center of the state shifts to the north, where is the largest body of voters and the greatest property interest. Under the American system, moreover, the city, as such, has no longer any status in the political affairs of the territory. Its residents have votes as individuals, but the municipality exercises no power save in its own local limits.

But before leaving the wide field of the state for the narrower one of the city, it may not be amiss to complete the narration in brief form, down to California's admission into the Union. Upon the departure of Kearny, as told in the preceding chapter, Colonel Richard B. Mason acted as military and civil governor of the territory, his term extending from May 31, 1847, to April 12, 1849 — a period of about two years. He made his headquarters at Monterey, the ancient capital. The war in Mexico, which had begun in 1846, by Taylor's invasion over the border from Texas, continued through 1847, with Scott's march from Vera Cruz across to the City of Mexico, which he took and occupied on the 14th of September of that year. This ended the conflict, the republic of Mexico acknowledging its hopeless defeat. A treaty of peace was entered into at Guadalupe-Hidalgo, a little town near the Mexican capital, on February 2, 1848, which finally went into effect May 30th of that year. In this treaty all of Alta California, New Mexico and Texas were ceded to the United States, for the sum of $15,000,000, to be paid in annual installments of $3,000,000 each. By the payment of this money the United States undertook to palliate, in some degree, its offense in waging war of aggression. The sum paid was, of course, quite inadequate to the value of the territory even as computed at that time.

The boundaries of Alta California had never been accurately defined, either as to the east, where it touched the other Mexican territory, called New Mexico, or to the north and northeast, where it touched the domain of the American Union. It included, however, the whole of the present state of California, Nevada and Utah, the territory of Arizona, and fragments of Colorado and Wyoming. Its status, until such time as congress should organize it under some form of government, or until it should be accepted as a state, with a government of its own making, was that of a conquered province under military rule.

The admission of California to statehood marks an important milestone in the history of the nation. It constituted the grand crisis — the turning point in the struggle between the slave power and its opponents. Thus far, through a series of compromises engineered chiefly by Henry Clay, the number of slave states taken into the Union exactly equaled the number of free states. They had come in as pairs, one from the north and one from the south, and thus an equilibrium was maintained, in the senate, at least. The controversy was growing more bitter with each new phase, and like the ghost of Banquo, to which it was constantly compared, it would not "down." To admit California as a free state, with no territory at hand out of which to construct a slave state meant a serious disturbance of the existing arrangement. Every move in connection with the territorial government was, therefore, closely watched by both factions at Washington, for as the territory was bent so was the state likely to be inclined.

When congress met in December, 1848, President Polk called attention, in his annual message, to the fact that no form of government had yet been provided for California, which was particularly unfortunate in view of the rapid increase of population following the discovery of gold. The question had come up in the previous session, soon after the ratification of the treaty of Guadalupe Hidalgo, and the acquisition of the territory. It had arisen through a resolution introduced into the house by David Wilmot of Pennsylvania, and known in American history as the "Wilmot Proviso." It was an effort to attach to the bill appropriating the first installment of the $15,000,000 purchase money, a provision that none of the territory thus obtained should be open to slave holding. A fierce struggle had been precipitated. The provision passed the house and failed in the senate, but the expression of public sentiment called out by the controversy showed the slave-holding element in congress that California, if admitted, would be a free state. The south, therefore, resisted the effort to give it a territorial government, hoping to postpone the day of its entrance to the Union.

President Polk's recommendation of statehood immediately reopened the old quarrel, and it continued with great bitterness through the session. As March 4th drew near, marking the end of the administration, the factions became positively hysterical. Regret was frequently expressed that

California had ever been obtained from Mexico, and the suggestion was made in genuine earnest that it be given back. The finding of gold, which made a territorial government necessary, was characterized as a misfortune. Secession was threatened by the south, and was received with contemptuous taunts by the north. But in the end nothing was done for California, and the military rule continued.

Mason proved to be an excellent governor for the territory, through these troublous and difficult times. He was firm, just, kindly and discreet. Although possessed of a keen sense of order, he managed to endure the confusion and anarchy with philosophic calmness, for the space of two years. But when the gold excitement was thrown in, as a wild and fearful climax to it all, he begged to be recalled. There were, of course, no general laws, no state government, and no local institutions save those of the Spanish-Mexican regime. Hostilities having ceased, military rule in the towns was not practical. It was neither best for the people, nor likely to insure their good will. The alcaldes and ayuntamientos were therefore ordered to continue the administration of justice and of local affairs under the old Spanish law. As the Americans began to arrive in larger numbers, these offices were frequently filled from their ranks, and the newcomers found great difficulty in conducting affairs under the Mexican laws. Up to this time there had been no such thing in California as a trial by jury. There was no warrant for the institution under Spanish or Mexican law; but as soon as the Americans took possession, they demanded that this constitutional right be recognized, and it was recognized in most cases. On the other hand, when a certain priest, who was sued for breach of contract, took refuge behind the Spanish law, which gave him special privilege as an ecclesiastic, Governor Mason refused to admit his claim. The governor's theory of the situation seems to have been that while the Spanish laws were to hold in the main, until the national government should act, the people could not be deprived of inherent rights they enjoyed under the constitution of the United States. Although himself a military man, he would not allow interference by the soldiers with the local governments. On one occasion Colonel Stevenson, who was in command at Los Angeles, undertook to forbid the carrying out of a decision of the alcalde; but Mason ordered him to withdraw from his position, and allow the city authorities to arrange their own affairs.

In July, 1848, Pio Pico returned to California. Although the treaty of Guadalupe-Hidalgo had been ratified two months before, no news of the fact had yet reached the coast, except that it was known the document was under consideration. Pico came to Los Angeles, and Stevenson immediately wrote to Mason that the former governor was still claiming authority, and asked what was to be done. Pico also wrote to Mason, saying that "as the Mexican governor of the territory," he would be glad to co-operate with

Mason m establishing harmonious relations between the Californians and the Americans. It is quite probable that his use of the expression "as Mexican governor'" was merely an awkward way of describing his former status. It is certain that he had neither expectation nor desire to make trouble. There were frequent rumors at this time of contemplated rebellions, and the language of the ex-governor was unfortunate. Stevenson was ordered to arrest and imprison Pico, but within a few days came news of the final acceptance by both countries of the treaty, and on his making suitable explanations and apologies, Don Pio was set free.

In January of 1848 an event took place in California which ranks in our national history in the same class of importance with the signing of the Declaration of Independence and the firing on Fort Sumter — and that was the discovery of gold at Coloma, on the American river, near Sacramento. The stream of wealth that presently began to pour out of the state enriched and built up the north, whose free enterprises naturally absorbed most of it, until that section was ready, ten years later, to enter upon a long and frightfully expensive war for the maintenance of the Union, and extermination of slavery. This is a great economic fact that serves as a cornerstone to the unique fame of California.

The presence of gold in California had been known for half a century, and the metal had been obtained in commercial quantities in the southern part of the state. In 1842 a Californian named Lopez found some fragments of the precious metal, when digging for wild onions in the San Francisquito canyon, about thirty-five miles northwest of Los Angeles. A small furore of placer mining then broke out in Los Angeles, and numbers of claims were staked out; Don Abel Stearns estimated that $6000 to $8000 was secured annually for four years. After that the work was intermittent, and finally was abandoned almost entirely.

The real discovery of gold in California was accomplished by James W. Marshall, a carpenter in the employ of John A. Sutter. The latter was a Swiss, who had acquired considerable land in the Sacramento valley, and owned a store and several mills in that region. He was constructing a saw mill on the American river, and Marshall, who was something of a millwright, was in charge of the work. In the tailrace of this mill, Marshall found some small fragments of a bright yellow metal, which he believed to be gold. He showed them to Sutter, who begged him to keep it a secret until the mill was finished. The story of the discovery soon leaked out, however, and spread to San Francisco. People began to flock to the American river, but finding that the Feather, Yuba, Bear and other streams were quite rich, they spread out over the Sacramento valley, finding gold almost everywhere. By the summer of 1848 San Francisco was very nearly deserted, and Los Angeles had lost much of its American population, and some of its Californian. Ten million dollars' worth of the precious substance was taken out in the first year.

In 1849 came the great wave of immigration from the eastern states, carrying over 80,000 people, and bringing the total population of the state up to and beyond the hundred thousand mark. Of these a little more than half came by land, the remainder by the ocean. In that year $40,000,000 of gold was taken out, and the next year, 1850, $50,000,000; then came two years of $60,000,000 each, and the next year, greatest of all, $65,000,000.

The failure of congress to provide any form of territorial government for California, and the evidence showing in the debates.hat statehood was not to be gained without a hard struggle, roused the people of American birth who had come to live in the region to the necessity of acting for themselves. It was decided to take the unusual but emphatic course of forming a state constitution, electing officers and starting off the whole machinery of government, exactly as though the state had been admitted, and then demanding of congress that it be allowed a place in the Union. As early as December, 1848, before the second failure of congress to act, meetings were held in San Jose and San Francisco, to agitate this plan, and when General Bennett Riley, who had been appointed by President Polk to succeed Colonel Mason as governor, arrived in Monterey, in April of 1849, the people were ready to act. He wisely determined to make the movement an official one, and on June 3rd issued a proclamation for an election to be held on the first of August, for delegates to a constitutional convention. This gathering came together in Monterey September 1st. Los Angeles was represented by four delegates, San Francisco by eight, and other places in proportion, to a total of seventy-three delegates. The Los Angeles men were Abel Stearns, J. A. Carrillo, Stephen C. Foster, and Manuel Dominguez. Hugo Reid came from San Gabriel. A state constitution was adopted, made up of elements of the constitutions of several eastern states welded together. The provision that slavery should not exist in the state passed unanimously, without discussion, thus destroying the last hope that the slave-holding element in congress had of establishing that peculiar institution in California.

An election to ratify this constitution, and for the choice of national and state officers under its provisions, was called for November 13, 1849. At this election Peter H. Burnett was chosen governor and Edward Gilbert and Geo. Wright representatives. On the 15th of December the legislature met and chose John C. Fremont and Wm. M. Gwin United States senators.

These quasi-representatives and senators started immediately for Washington, where congress was in session, and where they found that the admission of California was the chief topic of discussion. Henry Clay was endeavoring to make it the basis of a new series of compromises. Calhoun was demanding that the territory be cut in two, and the lower half kept for slavery. All understood that to admit California as a free state, without a slave state to accompany it, meant a disturbance of the equilibrium so carefully built up in half a century of compromising, and each faction braced itself for a terrible struggle. The fight was bitter, fierce and determined. The slave-holding element finally went down, though not without a formal protest, in which the threat of secession was made and attempted to be entered upon the record of the senate. The bill admitting California finally passed, was signed by the president and became a law September 9, 1850. News of the event reached California October 18th, and was received with great rejoicing.

CHAPTER 25. THE CITY TAKES SHAPE.

An important point of difference between the Spanish made-to-order city and the American accidental city is that the former possesses all of its site on a communal basis, while the latter has no land of its own except such as it may purchase. The pueblo of Los Angeles under De Neve's regulations was to own all the land about the plaza for a distance of three miles in each direction, making a square six miles to the side, or thirty-six square miles in the whole area. The original settlers were given each a small building lot and a tract of fourteen acres for cultivation, and the few additional settlers that came during the first year were held to be entitled to the same privilege. Several hundred acres were given out in this way — scarcely more than one per cent of the 23,040 acres of the whole tract. The remainder belonged to the city, to dispose of as it saw fit.

Contrast this situation with that of the average American city which has its beginning in the natural drawing together of population in some spot that is favorable for local business. The people own the land on which they build their homes, acquiring by purchase from those who had formerly held it for farming or other purposes. The city owns nothing until it has attained a size that makes the purchase of land for municipal use a necessity; and then as a rule it buys sparingly, for although the price of land may be low, the city's finances will not admit of heavy investment. Thus it happens that many cities of the eastern states have been compelled to use a large element of the revenue raised by taxation in the purchase of land for school, park and other municipal purposes, and are, nevertheless, always cramped for room. There are some instances, particularly among cities in the middle west, where far-sighted officials have urged the municipality, early in its career, into the acquirement of large tracts of land, of which later generations have reaped the benefit. A notable example of this type is Chicago, which not only owns a chain of parks running through the city, but also has large tracts of so-called "school land," some of which is in the very heart of the business district, and is occupied by valuable buildings on a 99-year leasehold. If that city's affairs were always administered on an honest and equitable basis, if its government were made a matter of plain business, after the English method, instead of a political amusement, after the American, Chicago would be the city that enjoys the lowest taxes and the highest municipal privileges of any in the Union.

But to return to Los Angeles and its magnificent patrimony of broad acres. After the original settlers had received all that their contracts called for — given them not by the pueblo, but by the governor — then the city began giving away building sites to all that asked them for actual use, and small tracts, rarely exceeding ten acres, to those that wished to carry on agriculture. No written title passed, nor was there any definite marking of limits. Probably no record was kept of these transactions — certainly none has descended to us. A man's title to his property lay in his occupancy of it, either by actual residence or by tilling. If he moved off, or ceased to cultivate it, any one could take possession by "denunciation." This prevented the holding of land for mere speculative purposes, and tended to concentrate the city in a limited area. The outlying districts were left intact in the hands of the city. The time came presently when the necessity for definite boundaries and written titles to ownership dawned on the people of Los Angeles, and, as has been related earlier in this work, the ayuntamiento required all owners to present their claims for ratification by that body. This was the beginning of modern land titles in Los Angeles, for the titles granted to the original settlers by the governor had all been lost by this time, and the ownership of the ill-defined building lots and agricultural fields had passed into other hands, either by inheritance or through the process of denunciation. The only case in which a written title had been given by the ayuntamiento was that of J. A. Carrillo, in 1821, who petitioned for "a parcel of land containing forty varas (111 feet) front and sixty (166 feet) deep, bounded with Dona Encarnacion Urquidez, Don Francisco Sepulveda, and near the new church which is now in course of erection." The tract referred to is the one where the Pico house (National hotel) now stands, near the plaza. Note the vague character of the description. No consideration is mentioned in the deed. The regular practice of granting titles by the ayuntamiento did not begin until more than ten years later, and by that time property began to have some money value — but not much. For ordinary building lots — such as those along Main street or Aliso, the price charged by the ayuntamiento was "dos reales per front vara." A real was 12 1-2 cents and a vara 33 1-3 inches, which would make the value of the property about 8 cents a front foot. A building site usually had about 100 feet of frontage, and it would not be difficult to locate many pieces that sold in the '40s for $8, and are now worth more than $100,000.

The phraseology used in defining the city in the original regulation was a little vague, as to whether it was to be four leagues square or four square leagues. The former meant twelve by twelve miles, or 144 square miles, the latter six by six, or thirty-six square miles. Up to the time of the American occupation, no one had raised the question of the exact boundary, but it came up' now at the same time with the general question of land titles all over the territory. The Americans were not satisfied with the hap-hazard forms of title customary among the easy-going Californians. They foresaw the time when land would have a definite and an increasing value. No survey of the state had ever been made by the Spanish or Mexican authorities, although all grants of land, outside the pueblos, were supposed

128

to emanate from the governor. When a Californian had obtained his grant of land he went to the alcalde nearest the tract, who, on the payment of a small fee, provided a man who called himself a surveyor, but whose only tools were a rope 50 varas long (140 feet) and a couple of pins which could be stuck in the ground without dismounting from horseback. The rope sagged and stretched, and was given direction merely by a careless sighting. The deed required that landmarks should be set up, but that formality was often waived. When the measurement was completed, the alcalde signed the deed, and the title was then regarded as complete.

In 1851 an act passed the congress of the United States, providing for a board of three commissioners, with a secretary and a law agent, the latter skilled in Spanish, to pass on all matters of title in the new acquisitions. The board began its sessions in San Francisco December, 1851, and continued for five years. It held one brief session in Los Angeles, in the autumn of 1852. Of the 813 claims presented to this body, 591 were finally confirmed and 203 rejected. The board did not complete the work of settling ail land claims, but it settled a large number of them, and it gathered the material by which they could be finally settled in the district courts.

It will be readily understood that the work of this board could not be carried on without arousing a considerable amount of resentment among the Californians, who found themselves dispossessed of property to which they believed they had a perfectly valid claim. But the situation was one that called for a day of judgment some time, and the inevitable consequence of long-continued carelessness in business matters is that the innocent must suffer as well as the guilty. There had been no little fraud in the granting of land under the Mexican regime, and an incredible amount of inaccuracy. The verdict of history seems to be that the commissioners were honest men, who performed a very difficult task with shrewdness and painstaking care. More than that; it does not appear that they allowed themselves to be governed by too great a devotion to technicality, but endeavored in each case to get at the real intention of the authority granting the land, and judge the issue on its merits in equity. This, however, is not the estimate of the commission that was formed by most of the Californians. They and their descendants, even to this day, will maintain that the whole proceeding was a deliberate plot to rob them of their lands, to take back into the public domain hundreds of thousands of acres that were owned by individual Californians, many of whom were stripped of their holdings by the commission.

The pueblo of Los Angeles followed the example of many of the ranch owners, and proceeded to make its claims as wide as possible in the hope of getting the more in the final settlement. Its demand was put in with the commission for four leagues square, or 144 square miles. The case of Los Angeles, like many others, did not receive final settlement before the board, but when it was at last passed upon by the courts the area was fixed at four square leagues or thirty-six square miles.

At the time of the American occupation, and even down to 1853, more than 80 per cent of all this great expanse belonged to the city itself. Private ownership covered merely the area in the immediate vicinity of the plaza, and along the foothills In a narrow strip from Buena Vista street bridge to First street, and east as far as the river. Today all that remains in the possession of the city is a few hundred acres along the river, known as Elysian park, and some arroyo and river wash land — tracts that were considered of so little value that they were somehow "left over." Even the pieces that the city has devoted to parks, like Westlake and Eastlake and others, were either purchased by the city or were benefactions — one of the latter being the enormous tract of Griffith park, which lies a little way beyond the city's limits to the west. The land in use for school purposes and for public buildings has, with one or two small exceptions, been acquired by purchase. All the great expanse, where lie now ten thousand homes, and many blocks of business buildings was once city property, and was sold for trifling amounts, and much of it actually given away in large tracts — and this outrage was committed not during the administration of the careless Californians, but after the occupation by thrifty Americans.

It is an almost heart-breaking thought — the "what-might-have-been." Great foresight was not required, for the land did not need to be purchased. It was already owned by the city. All that was needed was a small fraction of intelligence in the sale of it — the withholding of pieces here and there, of every other lot in favorable tracts, and of occasional ten-acre divisions for parks. Had this policy been pursued, Los Angeles might be today the richest municipality of its size in the Union. That such folly could have been committed as to save practically nothing out of the whole area is almost incredible, but it is true.

The first survey of the city, and the making of a plan of its streets, was accomplished by Lieutenant E. O. C. Ord (afterward, during the Civil War, raised to the rank of a major general) in August of 1849. Before the Americans came to Los Angeles the need for a survey to lay out streets for future growth was frequently discussed, and the crookedness and irregularity of the city, as far as it had extended, was spoken of with regret. Reforms were attempted at various times, and people were urged to move back from the plaza, and to cease stopping up the embryo streets. But these good efforts came to naught. There were no competent surveyors in the territory, and the citizen who had once gained possession of a prominent place for his house was 10th to move back and surrender it to public use.

The ayuntamiento of 1849, which contained several Americans, proposed to Governor Mason that he should send down an army engineer to survey the pueblo, in order that the titles might be perfected and descriptions made clear before the land commission should begin its work, for by that time the plan for a land commission had been bruited about. Ord was offered $3000 in cash, or his choice of building sites to the number of ten, and about 160 acres of land in the farming districts of the city. He took the cash. The land would now probably be worth several millions of dollars. The area covered in his "Plan de la Ciudad de Los Angeles" is now bounded by Pico street on the south, by Pearl street and the hills on the west, by the river on the east, and by the San Fernando street depot on the north. He seems to have assumed without question that the natural growth of the city would be in a southwesterly direction, as the hills shut it off to the west and north, and the river and low lands interfered to the east. Doubtless the older residents explained to him how, prior to 1825, the river had flowed through Alameda street.

The two most ancient streets of the city that are now in existence are Aliso and Spring. The former was the ending of the road from San Gabriel, and originally led out into the Plaza, but was stopped at Los Angeles street by the enterprising house builders early in the century. Spring street was the road into the Cahuenga and to the north, although it did not follow the route of the present Spring street beyond First. At the junction by the Nadeau it started across lots, passing Fourth and Hill, and skirting the foothills until it reached modern Ninth street, where it turned to the west, and then to the north to Cahuenga pass. The line of the old road is sketched upon Ord's map. The part which we now call North Spring was originally called Charity street, because, being far out of town, it was occupied by poor people, dependent upon others for support. Ord transferred this name to Grand avenue, and that street continued with this title until 1886, when the City Council listened to the plaint of many people who were tired of the incessant joke about their "living on charity," and the name was finally banished from the city's streets.

Broadway was named Fort street, after the fort built the year before Ord's survey, which looked down the street from the hill to the north. The change of name was made in 1889. Figueroa street appears as the Street of the Grasshoppers. Buena Vista is Eternity street, because of the cemetery. Castelar is the Street of the Bull, for that is where the bullfights were formerly held. What we call Yale was then the Street of the Hornets.

The names are given on the Ord plan both in Spanish and English, and the name Spring is put into Spanish as Primavera, showing that it was for the season, and not for any spring of water. Temple street was not cut through at this time, and, indeed, there was no public thoroughfare running west out of Main and Spring, all the way from the Plaza to Franklin street.

Note to Chapter XXV. — The exact area of the city as determined by the appeal from the settlement of the commission was 17,172.37 acres. The Spanish league on which the city's claim was based was a variable quantity (as was also the vara) ranging with the locality from 2.634 miles to 4.214 miles. The square league was generally figured at 4428.4 acres. The author does not attempt to go into the complications of these varying forms of measurement, and the figures given in the text are merely approximations.

CHAPTER 26. THE BEGINNING OF THINGS.

NEW city was now coming into existence in Los Angeles — an American growth grafted upon a Spanish stock. Had it been located in an accessible part of the nation, the change from the old order to the new would have been rapid, for the region presented then, as it does now, many natural advantages to attract a desirable population. The climate was just as favorable in 1850 as it is today, and the soil just as productive; but between Los Angeles and the eastern states was a great gulf of distance and danger, that only the most intrepid would venture to cross. The discovery of gold, which brought 80,000 people to the northern part of the state in one year, affected the southern part only in a reflex way. In the decade from 1850 to 1860, several thousand of the Argonauts drifted down from San Francisco, some of them with a little capital acquired in the diggings, but more of them penniless; and some of both kinds located permanently in Los Angeles. Then there were also those who left the eastern states in the expectation of mining for gold, but were dissuaded by the bitter stories of failure that came to their ears, and they turned their course to the south, where they were told men grew rich quickly in raising stock.

But the total number of all that made their way into this far-off corner of the new territory was not large, and of those who came many returned soon to the east, for they found their hopes of sudden wealth were idle. On a superficial view, the region had but little to offer the new-comer. A small amount of commerce had sprung up between Los Angeles and Arizona, and later there was trade with the mining camps of Nevada and Utah, and across the mountains to the San Joaquin valley, and over the desert to Inyo county. The old pueblo was a station on the route from Texas and the southern states into California, and not a few of the gold-seekers came through that way. Except for these small sources of revenue, whatever means the people of Los Angeles enjoyed came out of the territory that immediately surrounded them. The extraordinary producing capacity of the soil under the favoring semi-tropic climate had not yet been discovered. It was known to the padres and a few others, but rather as a theory than as a practical fact. The first Americans found that the Californians grew almost nothing, and they assumed that the reason must lie in the natural deficiency of the country. It was fit for nothing but the raising of stock, they thought — for that was the only use to which the Californians had put it. Now the raising of stock would not employ great numbers of people, nor would it support a considerable population. Hence during the next thirty years of its existence, from 1850 to 1880, the growth of Los Angeles was slow. This meant that it remained, during most of that period, a Spanish-American rather than an American city.

The first American census, taken in 1850, showed the population of the city to be 1610, and of the county 3530. The number was, no doubt, abnormally small, owing to the prevalence of the gold excitement, which drew hundreds of men away to the mines. But for that, the census would probably have shown over 3000 in the city. The next enumeration by the government, that of 1860, showed 4399 in the city and 11,333 in the county. The gain was made for the most part in the first years of the decade, when the mining excitement had died down, and the gold-seekers came south in search of homes. In the next decade, from 1860 to 1870, there was very little increase. The census of 1870 gave the city a population of 5614, and the county 15,309. This small growth was not due to the Civil War, which added rather than subtracted from the population. There was but little enlistment from Los Angeles on either side in the great conflict, so the loss was not great; and on the other hand, at the close of the war, many ex-Confederates whose homes had been destroyed made their way to the Pacific coast, that they might begin life anew in happier surroundings. The failure to advance was due to the apparent inability of the country to support a larger population. By this time the Central and Union Pacific rail connection with the east had been established, but the line was not as yet extended to the southern portion of the state. A regular system of steamers plied between Los Angeles and San Francisco, giving the southern city a part of the advantage of the new opening to the east. Still it did not grow. Twenty years after the American occupation it was in spirit and customs and even in population largely a Mexican town. It is now a thoroughly American city, with a few faint traces of Spanish origin. The change began in the latter '70s, and was completed within ten years.

In the first period of transition, from 1848 to 1855, many of the institutions that make up the foundation of our American life came into being in Los Angeles — unknown before that time. Of trial by jury, and the equality of all before the law, we have already spoken, as being decreed by the authorities of the state. Schools, newspapers, churches and municipal improvements were purely local matters, for the people of Los Angeles to settle for themselves. The newcomers attacked them with the traditional energy of Americans; but whether it was due to certain qualities of the climate that it pleases people to term "enervating," or to the doubtful example set them by their predecessors, it must be admitted that the good beginning was but languidly followed up, through the period next intervening.

Schools were not unknown during the Mexican regime in Los Angeles, but in the sixty-six years from the founding of the city to the American occupation, there was a total of about ten years of school. These years were scattered along at irregular intervals, the longest stretch of continuous instruction being the school maintained from 1838 to 1844 by Don Ignacio

Coronel, the father of Mayor Antonio F. Coronel. The teacher usually received a small salary from the ayuntamiento, averaging about $15 a month, and in addition was entitled to whatever fees the pupils were willing to pay for tuition. Most of the teachers were poorly educated, and their schools attracted few pupils. The teacher was occasionally summoned before the ayuntamiento, to explain why there had been no school for the past week or so, and his answer usually was that the pupils had all run away. Don Ignacio Coronel was a well educated man of excellent family, and his school accomplished good work. His daughter, Soledad, assisted him at times. The location of this school was at the Coronel residence on Los Angeles street, near Arcadia, part of the time, and later at one of the plaza church buildings.

In 1844 a school was opened under the patronage of Governor Micheltorena, who promised $500 from the state funds to its aid. It was in charge of Ensign Guadalupe Medina, an officer of the Mexican army, who was said to be expert in the latest educational methods. He introduced a plan by which the older pupils were to teach the younger, and in this way the membership of the school was brought up to over 100, with only one regular this school.

In 1850, after some Americans came into the ayuntamiento, a school committee was appointed out of the membership of that body, but great difficulty was experienced in finding any suitable teacher. This was at the time when the city was in the throes of the gold fever, and men were scarce. Hugh Owens finally agreed to establish a school for $50 a month, on the understanding that not more than six boys were to be sent free by the city. This school continued a few months. In November of 1850 Rev. Henry Weeks proposed to the city council that he be assisted in establishing a school for both boys and girls by a subsidy of $150 a month. In return for this sum he agreed to give his own and his wife's services, and to provide the necessary school accommodations. This school opened in January, 1851, and lasted under that arrangement until 1853, when all subsidies ceased, and schools were made free. In August, 1852, a tax of 10 cents per $10 of valuation was levied for school purposes, and the next year three commissioners of public schools were selected by the council, one of whom, the chairman, was made ex-officio superintendent of schools. In 1855 there were 753 children of school age in the city, but the average daily attendance was only fifty-two. Most of the children of American parentage were sent, but the native Californians either disapproved of the school because it was an American institution, or they were utterly indifferent to the advantages of education.

Stephen C. Foster who was elected mayor in 1854, was a graduate of Yale college, and took a lively interest in the education of the youth. He urged that permanent school buildings be erected, and that a regular system, similar to that used in Eastern cities, be adopted. The council met this suggestion by making him superintendent of schools, as well as mayor, and with his administration the modern educational system of Los Angeles had its beginning. The first schoolhouse was erected in 1855, on the corner of Spring and Second, where the Bryson block now stands. It cost about $6000. The second was on Bath street, a thoroughfare which was afterwards absorbed by the opening of Main street north from the plaza.

When the Americans took possession of Monterey in 1846 they found a font of type which had been used occasionally by the California authorities to print official documents. Although one letter was lacking in the alphabet of the Spaniard the Americans, nothing daunted, seized upon the type and began the publication of a newspaper which they called "The Californian." It was maintained throughout the earlier period of the occupation. The missing letter, W, was produced by putting two V's together.

The first newspaper in Los Angeles was called "La Estrella," "The Star," the first number of which, printed in both Spanish and English, appeared May 17, 1851. In the preceding October Theodore Foster had applied to the city council for a piece of ground suitable for a newspaper office, and had suggested a location near the city jail, on Main street. He seems to have had a presentiment that a large amount of news was likely to originate in that vicinity. The matter of a donation of a piece of land for such a purpose aroused a good deal of debate. Few of the Californians had ever seen a newspaper, and the description supplied by their American neighbors who had enjoyed some experience with the institution in Eastern states was not entirely reassuring. Finally the donation was agreed to, but the words "for this once only" were attached to the resolution, and the site selected by Mr. Foster was denied him. He was given instead a piece no feet square fronting the zanja on Los Angeles street, between Commercial and Arcadia, on the spot where the Foy harness shop now stands. Here a two-story adobe building was erected and a four-page, five-column weekly paper began to appear, bearing the names of John A. Lewis and John McElroy as publishers. Its subscription price was $10 a year. The press was a Washington Hoe, which had been brought around the Horn in the first days of the gold excitement. This machine was sold to Phineas Banning in 1864, who took it to Wilmington to start a paper there. In 1870 it was sold to the "Anaheim Gazette," and that paper, which is still enjoying a prosperous career, was printed from it until 1878, when a fire ended the story of the Star press. The Spanish portion of the "Star" was presently segregated from the English and given the name of "El Clamor Publico." In 1851 William H. Rand became a partner in the "Star," and remained with it for several years. He subsequently returned East, became the foreman in the "Chicago Tribune" printing office and, in company with Andrew McNally, founded the famous publishing house that bears their names.

Changes too place from time to time in the firm publishing the "Star"; J. S. Waite and William A. Wallace entered and departed, and the paper finally came to be owned by Henry Hamilton, an able and practical newspaper man, who conducted it from 1856 to 1864. He was an ardent sympathizer with the Confederate cause, and refusing to moderate his utterances in spite of frequent warnings from the authorities, he was at last ordered to cease editorial connection with the paper. In 1868 he returned to the work and continued in charge, with one or two intermissions, until 1873. In that year the "Star" passed into the hands of Major Ben C. Truman, who had been secretary to President Johnson, and who is now living in Los Angeles. Hamilton was a man of scientific tastes and made considerable study of the botany of the country. At his solicitation Hugo Reid, who had lived among the Californian Indians, contributed a series of articles to the "Star" on the latter's habits and customs, containing information of considerable value. The "Star" continued under Truman's management until 1877, becoming a daily in 1873. It finally came into the hands of the Rev. A. M. Campbell, who was succeeded by the sheriff, and in 1879 the paper passed out of existence.

"El Clamor Publico" ceased publication in 1859. No other Spanish paper was attempted until 1872.

In 1854 the "Southern Californian" appeared. Don Andres Pico was one of the owners, and its demise, which took place before it was two years old, is said to have left him $10,000 poorer in money, whatever gain he may have made in other directions. The plant was taken by J. J. Warner to be used in publishing the "Southern Vineyard," which began in 1858 and ran two years, merging into the "Los Angeles News." The "News" was changed to a daily in 1867, and continued until 1873, when it gave up the ghost. Of the more modern journals, those that are now on the ground, an account will be given later in this work.

CHAPTER 27. LOS ANGELES AT ITS WORST.

The people of Los Angeles seem, from the very beginning, to have adopted the principle that whatever they undertook to do they must do thoroughly. During the Spanish regime their chief purpose was to avoid work; and indolence was practiced until it became almost an art. Probably there was at that time no city within the boundaries of the Union where more work was permanently left undone than at Los Angeles. In the quarter of a century of Mexican rule the pueblo leads as the great rallying point for revolutions. Here again a comparison with other cities of the United States need not be feared. When California was brought under American rule, however, revolutions became dangerous and impracticable. If the city was to continue to be pre-eminent, it must be for some other characteristic than political turbulence.

This brings us to the darkest chapter in the history of Los Angeles; for, during the period from 1850 to 1870, it was undoubtedly the toughest town of the entire nation. During most of this time it contained a larger percentage of bad characters than any other city, and for its size had the greatest number of fights, murders, lynchings and robberies. This long era of violence and contempt for law had its culmination in 1871, in the brutal slaughter of nineteen Chinamen and the looting of Chinatown by a mob of 500 men. The number of lynchings during this period (not including the Chinamen) is estimated at thirty-five, which is more than four times the number credited to the famous vigilance committees of San Francisco. In addition to the executions that were done in the name of order, if not of law, there were legal hangings about twice a year. As to the number of killings, it is impossible to make an estimate, as no record was kept. There is no complete file of the earliest volumes of the newspapers, all having been destroyed in a fire in 1880, but such copies as are still in existence contain here and there brief items, two or three lines in length, that show by the very absence of comment what the state of things was. A murder which in these days would be given half a page of newspaper space, with pictures of the victim and all his family, and a lurid diagram of the spot and its surroundings, was dismissed with a few short sentences, accompanied by no comment. The Los Angeles News of March 2, 1866, contains these three items, for example:

"The verdict of the coroner's jury on the body of Seferino Ochoa returned that he came to his death by the discharge of a gun loaded with powder and balls."

"A party of Salt Lake and Montana teamsters had a lively row in the Monte on Monday night; several shots were fired, from the effects of which one man died."

"A shooting affray occurred recently between Mr. T. Baldwin and Mr. Adam Linn. Mr. Baldwin was shot through the heart, but unloaded his pistol before he expired, dying without speaking. Mr. Linn was uninjured."

The Southern Californian of March 7, 1855, remarks:

"Last Sunday night was a brisk night for killing. Four men were shot and killed and several wounded in shooting affrays."

This lawlessness had its beginning in the years that California was without a regular government — the interregnum between Mexican and American authority. The semi-military government that prevailed through part of this time served to hold things in check, but it was withdrawn before the new authority was firmly in its seat. The changed order brought inevitable confusion in the effort to accommodate Spanish law to American customs and Spanish customs to American law, and this confusion was suddenly confounded by the arrival of a hundred thousand newcomers in the state — the gold hunters. In such a vast number, coming for such a purpose, it was to be expected that representatives of the criminal and desperate classes should be included. When the vigilance committees of San Francisco and the northern mining camps began to drive these bad characters out, many of them drifted south to Los Angeles, and the latter city soon took on the character of a frontier town of the toughest type.

The situation was more complicated in Los Angeles than in most other portions of the state, because of the presence in that city of many hundred native Californians of the lowest class. These were idle, shiftless and addicted to drink, but up to the time of the American occupation they had not shown contempt for the law, nor were they given to crimes of violence. The change of government seemed to bring a radical change in the character of many of these men. It may have been that they were merely imitative, and that they were undertaking to do as they saw the American frontier outlaws doing; or it may have been that having lost their country and — many of them — their vague claims to land, they became desperate, and defied all authority; at all events, a large percentage of the killings recorded for this period, particularly the murders done for money, are to be charged to the native Californians, and many of the fiercest and most reckless highwaymen were of this class.

Another element in the population that rendered the maintaining of order difficult was the Indian. About two thousand natives who had either been brought up at the missions or had sometime been under their influence, so that they were not wholly wild, were living in and around Los Angeles. During the week they worked on the ranches and vineyards and on Saturday, having secured their pay, much of it in brandy, they repaired to the city to indulge in a frantic carouse. Their favorite rendezvous was a small street between Arcadia and the plaza, where Los Angeles street now is. "Nigger alley" — as it was called — was surrounded by low drinking

139

places, and was the home of crime and disorder. The Indians fought incessantly among themselves, and without much interference on the part of the authorities; but they seldom raised their hands against the whites, or if they did they were shot down without mercy. When they were all drunk, which happened usually within twelve hours after their discharge from the ranches, they were gathered into a corral back of the present location of the Downey block. On Monday morning they were sold off, like so many slaves, the employer agreeing to pay the fine in return for the next period of service. The Indian received only a dollar or two for his week's work, part of that in brandy. This condition of affairs lasted until the Indians were all dead, and they went out rapidly under such a hideous system.

The city was run on the so-called "wide open" plan, no attempt being made to control the liquor traffic, and gambling accepted as a matter of course. A law-abiding. God-fearing element existed, and at times exerted itself aggressively, but the supply of desperate characters seemed to be inexhaustible; when one lot was run out of the place, a new detachment appeared, and permanent reform was deemed hopeless. The police force of the city was in charge of an officer known as the city marshal, who had several regular deputies that were entitled to fees, but in times of special difficulty he called on the citizens generally to aid him. When the Star printing establishment came into existence, its first job of printing was to prepare for the use of the marshal one hundred white ribbon badges, bearing in Spanish and English the legend "City Police: Organized by the Council of Los Angeles, July 12, 1851," which were to be used on a law and order Committee of One Hundred. Two of the marshals of this period were killed in office, and those who ventured to do their duty had plenty of interesting experiences. Companies of armed vigilantes were formed from time to time, generally under the name of "Rangers." The authorities shut their eyes to the lynchings, few of which were unjustifiable. On one occasion the mayor, Stephen C. Foster, resigned to head a lynching party. This was the extreme case of a murderer, whose guilt was without question and who was likely to be freed by a technicality by the supreme court.

The county was represented in the work of maintaining order by its sheriff; and three of these officers were killed during this period. The circumstances connected with the slaying of Sheriff Barton show what a deplorable condition of affairs existed at the time, although his death led to a temporary improvement. A number of the worst characters in the city had been driven out by a vigilance committee, but they remained in the neighborhood, robbing travelers and committing murder if they met with resistance. In January, 1857, Sheriff Barton gathered a posse of five men, and went to the Sepulveda ranch in search of these bandits. The gang proved to be much larger than he had supposed, most of them native Californians, and all well armed and mounted. There was a fight, in which the sheriff and three of the posse were killed, the other two escaping back to the city. This brought matters to a crisis, and the law and order people of Los Angeles rose in a body to make a thorough job of clearing the country of the bad element. They began by hunting through the city for all suspicious characters, and about fifty were arrested and thrown into jail. The country was then scoured in search of the gang that had killed Barton; General Andres Pico led the posse. The robbers scattered, and some of them took to the mountains, but they were nearly all captured. Over fifty were lodged in jail, and eleven were hung, some by the committee and others through due process of law. This cleared the atmosphere for a time.

The most terrible page in this dark chapter of the city's history is that on which is recorded the massacre of the Chinamen. The Los Angeles of today is so far removed from anything like mob sentiment, its population, 90 per cent of which comes from the older eastern states, is so thoroughly conservative and law-abiding, that it is hard to understand how, only thirty years ago, such a horrible outrage came to be committed in the city. As a mere exhibition of mob rule, however, it was no worse than has been seen since that period in various eastern cities, notably Cincinnati, Pittsburg, Kansas City and St. Louis. If the number of lives taken was greater than in any of these latter instances, that may be accounted for by the fact that in those days nearly everyone in Los Angeles was accustomed to go armed, and knew how to shoot to kill, and by the further fact that public sentiment at the time placed a very low estimate on the value of the life of a Chinaman. This is not offered in extenuation of the crime, but merely to help explain something that seems at first sight difficult of comprehension.

The affair took place on the 24th of October, 1871, and succeeded the great Chicago fire as a topic of news most under discussion throughout the country. This was for many thousand eastern people their first introduction to Los Angeles, and the incongruity of the name as the location for such an awful deed was frequently commented upon. The riot grew out of a war between rival Chinese societies — or "tongs" — that had been in progress for several days, one faction shooting across "Nigger alley" at the other from time to time. A city policeman attempting to make an arrest met with resistance, and summoned to his aid a well-known citizen, named Robert Thompson. Some Chinamen concealed in a building on the corner of Arcadia street and "Nigger alley" shot through the door and mortally wounded Thompson. He was carried to an adjoining drug store, and died within an hour.

The fatal shot had been fired just at dusk. By night time a great crowd of angry men had gathered in the alley and surrounded the building. Several of the Chinamen undertook to escape, but were shot down or captured and hung. The mob finally broke open the building, which the Chinamen had barricaded on the inside, and dragged eight Chinamen out into the street, where they were beaten and kicked and pulled about with ropes tied around their necks, and finally taken over to a corral on New High street back of the Downey block and hanged to a high cross-bar above its gate. This was about 9 o'clock in the evening.

In the meantime a gang of thieves and toughs who had joined the mob for purposes of plunder made the most of the confusion to break open several stores belonging to Chinamen who could not be supposed to have had any part in the murder of Thompson. Some seized the goods and began to carry them off, while others wrecked the buildings and the store fixtures. All Chinamen that came into the hands of the mob were dragged out into "Nigger alley" and hung or shot to death. The crowd was beside itself with rage against the race, and spared neither youth nor old age. Two of the victims were very young boys, and one, an old physician, a man of good education, who begged for his life and offered over $2000 in money to those who had captured him. The money was taken, but he was hanged with the rest. The amount of cash taken by the mob was estimated at $40,000.

There were in all nineteen Chinamen put to death, some with great cruelty. The affair lasted only about an hour. News of what was going on had by this time spread over the town, and a party of brave and law-abiding citizens, accompanied by the sheriff, went down into Chinatown and compelled the mob to desist. A few arrests were made, and when the grand jury met, indictments were found against 150 persons for participation in the massacre. Only six of these were convicted in the trial that followed, and they, after a short imprisonment, were given their freedom on a technicality. The jury severely censured the officers of the city and county for neglecting their duty. From the evidence taken afterward it was established that only one of the nineteen Chinamen killed was concerned in the original conflict between the "tongs." The guilty parties had all made their escape before the mob came on the scene.

CHAPTER 28. BETWEEN OLD AND NEW

The Story of Los Angeles from 1850 to 1880 is largely one of slow industrial development, and a narration of that order is best handled in epochs. A division into decades may be an arbitrary one, but it is convenient and will be employed through the next three chapters of this work.

Many of the principal events of the period from 1850 to 1860 have already been narrated, for the epoch is one of considerable local importance in marking the commencement of the new order of things. There were also sundry happenings of minor note, that have to be recorded as part of the city's history, although their number and variety may make this narrative somewhat disjointed in places.

The year 1850 saw the beginning of the Protestant church in Los Angeles. The Rev. J. W. Brier, a Methodist minister, who was passing through the city on his way to the northern part of the state, held the first Protestant services that ever took place in Los Angeles, on a Sunday in June, 1850. It was in a private residence located where the Bullard block now stands, and where for many years afterward the county court house stood. In 1853 the Rev. Adam Bland was sent to Los Angeles by the California conference of the Methodist Episcopal church to organize a church. He made use of an adobe building on Main street near the Baker block. There he preached for two years, and his wife taught a girls' school in the same building. Others succeeded him, but in 1858 the field was abandoned for eight years.

The next Protestant sect to come to Los Angeles was that of the Presbyterians. In November, 1854, Rev. James Woods of that faith, held services in a little carpenter shop' near the corner of Main street and the plaza. A year later a regular church was organized with Mr. Woods as pastor, and services were held in the first court house, which stood where the People's store now is, on Spring and Franklin — a building that was for many years after 1860 used as the city jail. In 1856 the moral development of Los Angeles was abandoned by the Presbyterians as hopeless, and was not taken up again until 1859, when a movement started to have Protestant services of a general character, there not being enough of any one sect to maintain a church. The Rev. W. E. Boardman acted as pastor. It was decided to erect a church structure, and a lot was secured at the southwest corner of Temple and New High, where the steps now lead up to the court house. A brick building was begun, but before it was finished Mr. Boardman left the city, and the meetings were abandoned. The building was finally turned over to the Rev. Elias Birdsall, an Episcopal clergyman, who had been officiating for a small body of that faith that met in Odd Fellows hall in the Downey block. Episcopal services were first held in the city in 1857, and a parish was organized in that year, but it continued only a short time.

The Baptist church began in the year 1861, although occasional services were held during the '50s, the first being by a Mr. Freeman in 1853. The first Jewish services were held in 1854. The first congregation was organized by Rabbi A. W. Edelman, whose long term of service lasted until 1886.

The abandonment of this field by the clergymen of the various Protestant sects during the later '50s, while it may not be entirely creditable to their devotion to the service, gives some indication, nevertheless, of the moral darkness that hung over the city at that time. The Catholic church continued its ministrations, of course, but few of the Americans attended its services. The "Star" commented upon the departure of the Presbyterian preacher in these terms: "To preach week after week to empty benches is certainly not encouraging, but if, in addition to that, a minister has to contend against a torrent of vice and immorality which obliterates all traces of the Christian Sabbath — to be compelled to endure blasphemous denunciations of his divine Master, to live where society is disorganized, religion scoffed at, where violence runs riot, and even life itself is unsafe — such a condition of affairs may suit some men, but it is not calculated for the peaceful labors of one who follows unobtrusively the footsteps of the meek and lowly Savior."

The Masonic order came into existence in Los Angeles in 1854 with Los Angeles Lodge, No. 42. The next year came the Odd Fellows, Los Angeles Lodge, No. 35. The Hebrew Benevolent Society was organized in 1854; the French Benevolent Society in 1860. The Teutonia Concordia, afterward Turnverein, was started in 1859. In that same year there was a series of lectures given by the Los Angeles Mechanics Institute; the Library Association started a small reading-room at the corner of Court and North Spring street, and an agricultural society came into existence. These three organizations perished when the Civil War broke out.

The first hospital for the sick was opened in 1858 in a private house by some Sisters of Charity from Maryland. This was the beginning of the "Sisters' Hospital," which now occupies a large building on Bellevue avenue. The Catholic Orphan Asylum was founded in 1856. St. Vincent's college for boys began in 1855. The decade was one of considerable development in the local Catholic church.

Los Angeles was incorporated as a city in 1851. During this decade the mayors were elected annually, and the list runs as follows:

A. P. Hodges, 1850; B. D. Wilson, 1851; J. G. Nichols, 1852; A. F. Coronel, 1853; Stephen C. Foster, 1854; Thos. Foster, 1855; Stephen C.

Foster, 1856, four months; J. G. Nichols, 1856-7-8; D. Marchessault, 1859; Henry Melius, 1860.

In 1852 the city began to give away the land in the southwestern section of the city in 35-acre tracts to all who would agree to make improvements. In 1855 the land south of Pico street to the western and southern boundaries of the city was surveyed in 35-acre pieces by Henry Hancock. Two years later A. Waldemar made a similar survey for the portion north of Pico to the western boundary.

In 1848, of 103 proprietors of farms in the city, only eight were "gringos," i.e., not native Californians. Three years later, of the thirteen principal property owners in the county, six were Americans and they owned 135,000 out of 500,000 acres, and $306,000 out of $500,000 of personal property. In 1858, out of forty-five principal property owners in the county, twenty-five were American and twenty Californian. The two largest individual taxpayers were Abel Stearns, $186,000, and John Temple, $89,000. During most of the 50's interest was 5 per cent a month, and the Californians were easy borrowers. In 1856 the city's real estate was assessed at $187,582, and the improvements at $457,535

The average annual income to the people of the county from the sale of cattle during this period was between $250,000 and $500,000, the latter figure being reached only one year, 1856. Next to cattle raising, the production of grapes was the most lucrative form of industry. In 1849 and 1850 grapes sold for 12 ½ c a pound on the vine, to be shipped to San Francisco, where they retailed at any price. In 1858 there were 1010 acres in vines, and a few years later 3000. In 1851 about a thousand gallons of wine were shipped from Los Angeles. Soon after this the northern counties began to grow grapes and make wine, so the shipments to San Francisco diminished; but in 1855 exportation to the eastern market began. In 1857, 21,000 boxes of grapes, or nearly a million pounds, and 250,000 gallons of wine were shipped out. By 1860 the shipments of wine had increased to 66,000 cases.

In 1856 the yield of oranges was estimated at 400 boxes, or a little more than one carload. Wm. Wolfskill, who had the principal orchard, declared that he had received $100 apiece income from several of his trees. By 1860 it was estimated that there were 2500 trees in the state, of which three-fourths were in and around Los Angeles.

Iron working and wagon making began in Los Angeles with John Goller, who arrived in the city by way of Salt Lake in 1849. The charge for shoeing a horse at that time was $16. There was a great scarcity of iron, and Goller sent out on the roads traveled by the emigrants for old abandoned tires, and worked them up into horseshoes. When he finally managed, after many difficulties, to construct a wagon, he kept it a long time before he found a purchaser. Compared with the carreta it looked insubstantial, and was regarded with suspicion by the Californians.

The making of brick was begun by J. D. Hunter in 1852, and the first structure built of them was at Third and Main; the second was a jail building. In 1858 over two million brick were sold for a number of improvements that were either under way or were projected, such as the Temple market house, afterward taken over by the county for $40,000, to be used as a court house, the southern portion of the Temple block, the brick flouring mill of Stearns h Scott, now the Capitol Milling Co., and the Arcadia block on Arcadia and Los Angeles.

In 1854 the first brewing establishment was set up in Los Angeles, and a tannery started. In 1855 the first flouring mill began operations, and in that same year the culture of bees was undertaken by O. W. Childs, who is said to have paid $100 for one hive and swarm brought down from San Francisco. In 1850 the first drug store was established by Dr. Osborne, who came to Los Angeles from New York. He was presently succeeded in the business by John G. Downey, who afterwards became one of the wealthiest men of the region and served as governor of the state.

April 15, 1851, the first child of American parentage on both sides was born in Los Angeles: John Gregg Nichols, whose father, a year later, was elected to the mayoralty.

In 1855 came the Kern river gold excitement. There was a great rush from the northern diggings and from Los Angeles city into Tulare county, where it was reported that vast quantities of gold had been discovered. There was, however, very little gold to be obtained in the San Joaquin valley, and many of the disappointed miners and adventurers drifted down to Los Angeles, where they contributed a new element to the prevailing lawlessness of the time. Partly as a result of the Kern river excitement a new interest sprang up in the San Gabriel mines, and at one time Los Angeles bid fair to have a gold furore of its own.

In 1852 the "Sea Bird" began making regular trips three times a month between San Francisco and San Pedro, and in that same year D. W. Alexander and Phineas Banning put in a stage line from the coast to the city. In 1851 Alexander had brought in from Salt Lake ten heavy freight wagons, the first ever seen in Los Angeles. In 1853 a train of fourteen wagons and sixty-eight mules were brought in from Chihuahua at a cost of $23,000. J. L. Tomlinson put in an opposition line to that of Alexander & Banning in 1853, and for many years there was active competition in freight and passenger business, and the teams raced against each other on the way to the city.

The passenger fare from San Francisco to San Pedro in the early 50's was $45, and freight was $25 a ton. The fare from San Pedro to Los Angeles was $10, but competition finally brought it down to $2.50, and even below that for a short time. Freight from San Pedro was from 50 cents to $1 a hundredweight — about what is now charged from New York to Los Angeles. In 1855 freighting began between Los Angeles and Salt Lake, which had increased by 1859 to a considerable business. This ceased, of course, when the railroad connection was established between the Mormon city and San Francisco. In 1858 some experiments were carried on by the national government in the use of camels for freighting between Los Angeles and Arizona, but the plan was not a success.

In 1850 the Bella Union, now the St. Charles, on North Main street, was the only hotel. In 1856 the United States (not the modern building) was constructed on Main and Requena streets. Shortly afterwards the Lafayette opened in a building that was the predecessor of the modern St. Elmo. In 1856 Ramon Alexander, an eccentric French sailor, began the construction of the "Round House," a peculiar affair built in imitation of a residence he had seen in South Africa. It was located at the corner of Third and Main streets, and in the later 50's was transformed into a saloon, with a garden to the rear of it, running through to Spring street.

The vote of Los Angeles in 1856 was 522 for Fremont, the Republican candidate, against 722 for Buchanan, Democrat. Much of the vote that went to Fremont was influenced by personal consideration. His residence in Los Angeles and on the coast had given him many friends in the vicinity. Four years later Lincoln received only 356 votes, against 703 for Breckenridge, 494 for Douglas (total Democratic 1 197), and 201 for Bell.

In 1849, a special water department of the city government was organized, for at that time the city owned and operated its own water system. In 1857 Wm. Dryden was given a franchise to supply water drawn from the springs located on the land in the vicinity of the old Southern Pacific depot on San Fernando street, which was raised by means of a water wheel in the zanja. A brick reservoir was constructed in the plaza and some iron pipe was laid along Main and Los Angeles streets. This system was maintained until 1861.

CHAPTER 29. IN WAR TIME

During the period from 1860 to 1870 Los Angeles fell back into its Spanish-American habit of standing still. Some progress was made; the city was a little larger, and perhaps a little better behaved at the end of the period than at the beginning, but the advance was not to be compared with that of the preceding ten years, nor with what is usually achieved in such a length of time in an American city. The population was increased by about a thousand people, but the percentage of gain was scarcely that of the average throughout the country, showing that there was not much immigration from the east. The assessment roll doubled, rising to a total of over $2,000,000 in 1870, and there was some enlargement of the city's resources in the adding of new industries. On the other hand, that which had been from the beginning of the Spanish occupation of the territory the chief pursuit of the people — cattle-raising — received a severe setback by droughts, and, in fact, very nearly ceased to exist.

California was, before the war, a Democratic state, and it contained a very considerable southern element that favored slavery and upheld the doctrine of state rights to its farthest limit. One of the senators of the state, Mr. Gwin, made the assertion in Washington that if the South seceded California would go with it. When called to account for this utterance he modified it to the extent of saying that if the Union came to be split up, California would start a Pacific coast republic of its own. After the war had begun this man left the state to enter the diplomatic service of the Confederacy. When things came to a straight-out issue, it was discovered that the Union men. Democrats and Republicans together, were strongly in the majority in the state; but during the years 1859, 1860 and 1861 there was room for doubt as to which side California would espouse. The southern element was particularly strong in the lower end of the state, as will be seen from the fact that Los Angeles county gave Breckinridge twice as many votes as it gave Lincoln, and nearly twice as many as it gave Douglas, who represented the northern or Union democracy.

Just before the war an effort was made to cut the state in two at the line north of San Luis Obispo and Kern counties, evidently with the design of securing another piece of slave territory. The state legislature of 1859 passed an act authorizing an election to be held in the southern counties, to vote on the question of separating from, the rest of the state and forming a territorial government of their own, under the name "Colorado." The election was held, and more than two-thirds of the vote was in favor of separation. Up to this time no state in the Union had ever suffered a division, and when the plan was broached in Washington it was found to involve a number of legal and political complications. Before the separation

148

could be consummated the war broke out and the matter was laid aside, and presently forgotten.

In 1861 the man who afterwards became famous as Major General W. S. Hancock was sent to Los Angeles by the national government to see that the stores and arms which had been gathered there met with no misfortunes. The dutiful sons of southern states were constantly passing through Los Angeles at this time, on their way to join the Confederate army, and on account of the turbulence that had always prevailed in that city there were grave fears that the rebellious element might get the upper hand. Upon his arrival in Los Angeles Hancock called upon the Los Angeles Guards, a local organization of loyal young men, to protect the government property, and they responded in a way to set at rest all question of how Los Angeles would stand during the contest. The flag was hoisted over the court house, Hancock made a stirring speech to the assembled people, and in the evening of that day a public banquet was held, at which patriotic toasts were delivered.

There were occasional expressions of disloyalty during the progress of the war, that the local representatives of the government found it necessary to rebuke, although extreme measures were never employed. At one time the order was issued forbidding soldiers to enter the Bella Union and the United States hotels, because of the attitude of their proprietors toward the Union cause. In 1863 the authorities became suspicious that the alleged working of mines on Catalina island was merely a scheme to establish headquarters there for Confederate privateers, and the island was closed to the public for a time. There is no evidence, however, that this theory rested on any substantial basis. It was a period of false mining "booms" — that of Catalina with the rest. In 1860 and 1861 considerable mining development was undertaken in the mountains north of Los Angeles, and for a year or two Wells-Fargo was shipping out nearly $12,000 a month in gold.

The telegraph line which had been constructed between San Francisco and the east was extended to Los Angeles in 1860, and $100 a month was subscribed by citizens for daily dispatches that should keep them posted on the events of the war. The principal papers of this period were the "Star" and the "News," the latter becoming a daily in 1869, and continuing publication till 1873, when it suspended. Both were Democratic in politics, the "Star" decidedly on the "copperhead" order. The Republican party made considerable gains, however, voting 555 for Lincoln in 1864, as against 744 for McClellan, Four years later the vote in the county was 748 for Grant against 1236 for Seymour.

The mayors of this period were: D. Marchessault, 1861 to 1864, and again in 1867; Jose Mascarel, 1865; C. Aguilar, 1866, 1868 to 1869, and Joel Turner, 1869 to 1871. The term was now lengthened to two years. An important change in the school system was effected in 1866, when the

149

office of superintendent was made appointive instead of elective. In 1869 the position was filled for the first time by a professional and experienced teacher. In 1865 the census showed 1009 children of school age, but of these only 331 attended the public institutions. The remainder were divided about equally between the private schools and the streets.

The industrial development of this epoch was affected in a considerable degree by the erratic behavior of the rainfall. In 1862 the year opened with one of the greatest floods California has ever known, which carried away all the water service erected by the city and by private individuals, and damaged many hundred acres of orchard and farms. The period was, as a whole, however, one of under-average rainfall. The total for the ten years was only a little over ninety inches, or an average of nine per annum. In the season 1862-63 only four inches fell, and that was badly distributed, and in the following year there was little more than a trace. Cattle were slaughtered by the thousand, and died of starvation by the tens of thousands. Vast herds were auctioned off at 37 1/2 cents a head to be killed. The cattle industry received a blow from which it never recovered, and during the first years after the drought there was nothing to take its place as a producer of revenue for the country. Governor Downey advocated the raising of sheep, and as the grade of the flocks had been improved since the American occupation of the country, wool presently became a staple.

In 1868 there was another great flood. Again all the apparatus for city water service was carried away. The San Gabriel river changed its course from the old to the new bed, and a great area of good farming country was utterly ruined. In the seasons 1869-70 and 1870-71 there was very little rainfall — a total of only ten inches for the whole period. This succession of floods and of dry times gave very little encouragement to those who were experimenting in horticulture, and small progress was made. In 1867 there were about 9000 orange trees in bearing. By 1870 the assessment showed 34,000 fruit and nut trees of all kinds in the county. A considerable planting of walnut trees began during the latter years of this decade.

About 1865 a movement began among the owners of large grants to cut them up into small farming tracts and place them on the market. In 1868-69 there was considerable activity in real estate transactions in and around Los Angeles. The price of good farming land, which had been from $3 to $5 an acre, began to rise a little. After the death of John Temple, in 1866, a number of real estate transactions took place in closing up his estate which will give some idea of values at the time. The Cerritos ranch was sold to the Bixbys for $125,000, 27,000 acres, including the present site of Long Beach. Twenty-two lots, 50 feet each, on Spring street, scattered along from First street to Fourth, sold for $50 apiece. The Temple block property, including the southern part of the building, brought $10,000. In 1863 over 2000 acres, forming the best part of what is now called East Los Angeles, was sold by the city authorities for $1014.75, or 50 cents an acre, to Dr. John S. Griffin.

In 1868 George Hansen made a survey for the city of the tract now called Boyle Heights, cutting it up into thirty-five-acre tracts. In the same year the district along the river now covered by Elysian park and the adjoining lands was surveyed by Mr. Hansen. A year later the section lying to the south of the Elysian hills and west of the Ord survey was surveyed and prepared for occupation.

In 1869 a considerable amount of building was under way. Up to that time there were no three-story buildings in the town, and the only two-story structures were the Bella Union, the United States Hotel, the Lafayette (now St. Elmo), Bell's block (or Melius row), Stearns' block (the Arcadia, which is still standing), the old court house, a portion of the Temple block, and several stores on Los Angeles and Main streets. The Pico house was begun in 1869 on the site of the old Carrillo residence. J. A. Carrillo, the famous politician and man of affairs, had passed away in 1862. Work began on the Roman Catholic cathedral in 1869 at the location which was first selected on Main street between Fifth and Sixth. It was afterwards changed to Main street near Second, and the present structure was begun there in 1871. St. Vincent's college building on Broadway and Sixth was begun in 1866.

The first bank in Los Angeles was opened in 1868 under the title of Alvinza Hayward & Co., with a capital of $100,000. John G. Downey was one of the partners. In the same year the banking house of Hellman, Temple & Co. was organized, with a capital of $125,000. In 1871 these two institutions united, forming the Farmers and Merchants bank of today. The Temple & Workman bank came into existence in 1872.

In 1867 the manufacture of gas was begun.

Agitation in favor of the construction of a railroad from San Pedro to Los Angeles commenced early in this decade, and the purpose was finally achieved, and the railway started into operation, in the fall of 1869.

The leader in this movement was Phineas Banning, who owned the stage and freighting line between Los Angeles and the seashore, and was largely interested in Wilmington and the land surrounding that place. He served as member of the California senate from 1865 to 1868. In 1863 a bill passed the legislature authorizing the county of Los Angeles to issue bonds to the amount of $100,000, and the city to issue to the amount of $50,000, the proceeds to be used in subscriptions to the stock of the proposed railway line. It took about five years of active missionary work to arouse public sentiment to a point where there was any prospect of carrying such an issue of bonds, and by that time it had been decided that the amount proposed was insufficient. In 1868 a new bill passed the legislature raising the figures to $150,000 for the county and $75,000 for the city, or a total of

$225,000. The unprogressive element of the community, including, as is usual in such cases, some of the heaviest taxpayers, fought the scheme with great persistence, declaring that it would bankrupt the county, and that about two trains a month would carry all the freight the railroad would ever secure. The issue turned on whether the road could be made to pay expenses, or would prove a constant drain on the county. Within a few years after the opening of the road it was running fifty cars of freight and passengers a day in and out of Los Angeles. The vote on the bonds stood 397 for and 245 against. The railway went into operation in November, 1869. Its freight schedule was simple enough, the principle items being: Dry goods, $6 per ton; groceries, $5 per ton; empty pipes, $1 each. Passengers were charged $1.50 from the vessel to Wilmington and $1 additional to the city. The road was profitable from the very beginning.

The frequent floods of this period, with the consequent destruction of the various city water systems, served to discourage the authorities from attempting permanent municipal operation of the water supply, and propositions of all kinds looking to private control of this utility were offered and considered during the decade. In 1861 water "script" — an easily negotiable form of municipal obligation — was issued to the amount of $15,000, and a year later the city petitioned the legislature to be allowed to issue bonds to the amount of $25,000 to construct a water system. In 1862 a contract was let to Jean L. Sainsevain to build a dam, flume and other works for $18,000. In 1865 the city leased this system to D. W. Alexander for four years at a rental of $1000 a year. He transferred the lease to Sainsevain, who continued the work for three years, during which time he put down wooden service pipes as far as Third street. These were not a success, as they rotted and leaked at the joints. In 1868 Sainsevain sold out to Dr. John S. Griffin, Prudent Beaudry and Solomon Lazard, and they made a proposition to the council to lease the whole system for fifty years, which was presently changed to a plan to buy the whole plant for $10,000, on the understanding that they were to expend $200,000 in betterments, in return for which they were to have a perpetual franchise to take ten inches of water from the river to be sold to the citizens. This proposition came within one vote of carrying the council, in spite of great opposition from the people, who were unwilling that the last hope of a public water system should be destroyed.

Finally in 1868 bids were received on a thirty-years contract to provide the city with water; and Griffin and his associates offered $1500 a year for the privilege, agreeing also to effect the necessary betterments, to which was added the construction of an ornamental fountain in the plaza. At the end of the period the plant was to be bought by the city at a price to be fixed by arbitrators. There were several other bids, but this one was the most advantageous to the city. Had the matter ever been presented to the people, it would probably have been refused acceptance, as two councilmen, elected just at that time to fill vacancies, were both avowed opponents of the plan. It was carried through the council and went into effect July 22, 1868. The $1500 a year rental to the city was presently cut to $400 a year by a compliant council. This contract expired in 1898, and after much litigation the city purchased the plant for $2,000,000 — a figure which was doubtless far beyond the wildest imagination of the council of 1868.

CHAPTER 30. THE COMING OF THE RAILWAY.

The long period of slow growth and of stagnation for Los Angeles was now at an end. It had taken ninety years to accumulate a population of 5000, and in the next succeeding score of years a marvelous transformation was to take place. The changes of the first decade, that from 1870 to 1880, were not entirely unexpected. Those of the second, from 1880 to 1890, exceeded the wildest prophecies. That the building of a railway into Los Angeles connecting it with the eastern states should cause its population to increase 100 per cent was not surprising; but that the building of a second road should cause the increased number to multiply 500 per cent — a total advance from 5000 to 50,000 in twenty years, or from 5000 to over 100,000 in thirty years — that was a marvel that no one could be expected to foresee.

The immediate success that was achieved by the railroad from Wilmington to the city, not only in the freight and passengers it carried, but also in the impetus it gave to numerous lines of industry in the county, encouraged the people of this region to cast about for further opportunities of the same kind. The famous railway operator, Thomas A. Scott, who was pushing out into the southwest across Texas, had projected a line through California from Yuma to San Diego. He proposed to bring this north along the coast, if suitable inducements were offered by Los Angeles. At the same time the owners of the Central Pacific were building southward, and by 1872 were well down into the San Joaquin valley. That region of the state already contained a number of settlements or towns, some of which numbered from 500 to 1000 people. As the road drew near these it demanded a free right of way and, in most cases, a bonus of some description. Where this was refused the line was run some distance from the town, and a new population center established. Most of the towns thus abandoned were ruined, or were compelled to move bodily to the new location. Two exceptions to the rule were Bakersfield and Visalia, which have managed to hold their own in spite of the snub. It must not be supposed that the policy of the road in this matter contained any element of malevolence. The issue was one of business; the question for the town to determine being whether it needed the road, and for the road whether it needed the town.

The people of Los Angeles had the object lesson of the San Joaquin valley towns before them, when the railroad reached the mountains at the southern end of that region and paused to ask what the ancient pueblo would do. Did the people of Los Angeles desire the railway connection with San Francisco and the east sufficiently to be willing to pay 5 per cent of the assessed valuation of all land and improvements in their county, or

154

would they prefer to see the new road turn to the east along the mountains and pass Los Angeles by on the other side?

Five per cent on the assessed valuation of $12,000,000 would be $600,000. There was also an item of sixty acres to be given for depot purposes at some advantageous location within the city limits. As with the road to the waterfront, there was again great divergence of opinion. The Texas Pacific scheme of Scott was in the air, but had not been presented as yet in the form of a definite proposition. The Southern Pacific, on the other hand, was ready to begin work immediately. An understanding was reached between representatives of the railroad and the city that, if the people would vote to ratify the plan, the city and county would give the stock that they held in the San Pedro line, and donate the necessary sixty acres, and also issue 7 per cent twenty-year bonds in the sum of $377,000, making a total of $610,000 of subsidy; and in return for this the railroad was to build down through the Soledad canyon into the city and out to the east to San Bernardino, to connect ultimately with the Texas Pacific at Yuma. To win the concurrence of the people of the southeastern part of the county, the region since set off to make Orange county, it was agreed that a branch line should be constructed to Anaheim.

The matter was put to a vote, after a year's active discussion, in November, 1872, and it carried by a good majority. There were many intelligent men and large taxpayers who declared that the county was hazarding all its future in this enormous obligation, but the dismal alternative of being left out of the railway development of the state compelled them to vote in favor of the bonds. Before half the period for which the securities were to run had elapsed, the county assessment had increased from $12,000,000 to $35,000,000, and at the end of the twenty years the valuation was nearly $100,000,000. The burden, therefore, did not prove to be very serious.

The construction of a railway over the great Tehachapi pass, and through the mountains of San Fernando was a slow and laborious undertaking, and it was not until four years after the proposition carried that the trains began running between San Francisco and Los Angeles. The ceremony of driving the golden spike was held at Soledad, September 6, 1876. Three hundred and fifty citizens of Los Angeles went up from the pueblo to meet fifty residents of San Francisco, who came down to celebrate the union of the two cities. San Francisco was than a little larger than Los Angeles is at present, while Los Angeles was about the size of Pomona. There were speeches full of hope and good fellowship, and then the whole party repaired to Los Angeles, where a banquet was given at Union hall in the Jones block, at which a considerable amount of wine was consumed. The old Spanish pueblo was at last in touch with the great American system of progress and activity.

Scarcely was one road out into the world completed, when agitation was begun for a second. This was to be known as the Los Angeles and Independence railroad, with one terminus at Santa Monica, where it was believed a good harbor could be constructed, and the other at the town of Independence in Inyo county, the center of a district which was then believed to be of great promise, but which has never attained the expected development because of a lack of transportation facilities. It was confidently hoped that after this much of the road was built, it would go on to Salt Lake City. The largest stockholder was J. P. Jones, who afterwards became United States senator from Nevada. Local capital was interested to some extent The line from Santa Monica was constructed in 1875, and a substantial wharf was built at its ocean terminus. The hard times that swept over the country after the failure of Jay Cooke and the Black Friday episode made it impossible to secure funds to carry out the extension to the north, and the plan was abandoned. The Santa Monica branch was sold in 1878 to the Southern Pacific company, which proceeded to take down the wharf, as it interfered with business at San Pedro.

The immediate effect of all this railway projection and construction, from the San Pedro line in 1869 through to the Southern Pacific connections and the Santa Monica line in 1875 and 1876, was to produce considerable activity in all forms of industrial development. As is usual in such cases, anticipation ran rather ahead of the actual event and was followed by depression when the extravagant hopes were not realized. The dry years and the unfavorable money conditions in the east helped to complicate matters. By the year 1875, the bank panic which had been spreading across the country struck Los Angeles. One of the banks — the Temple & Workman — was in an unsound condition, owing to the reckless and extravagant policy of its chief owner, F. P. F. Temple, who was a younger brother of John Temple. The other two were on a solid basis, but as the railway connection to San Francisco had not been established, and as it would take about a week to get word to the city and bring money back, it was agreed that all three should close their doors for a time. For two of the banks this suspension was of brief duration, but for the Temple & Workman bank it was permanent, and the loss of the depositors was complete. This bad failure wrought serious demoralization to the development that was just beginning in Los Angeles, turning confidence and hope into doubt and discouragement. Nearly half a score of years passed before the evil effects of the disaster were entirely dispelled.

There was some agricultural advance during the decade, for the growing of wheat began on a considerable scale in the San Fernando, and the acreage in corn increased greatly. There was some planting of fruit trees, but the mistaken idea still prevailed that enormous quantities of water must be applied to the tree to make it bear in the dry climate, and only those nearest to the streams ventured into horticulture. In 1877 J. De Barth Shorb declared that he had sold his orange crop from seven acres for $7000. These went chiefly to the San Francisco market. In 1877, Wm. Wolfskill shipped the first carload of oranges to the eastern market. They were landed in St. Louis in good condition after a month in transit. The carrying charge was $500. The chief product of the region was now wine, of which 1,329,000 gallons were shipped in 1875. In 1874 fruit drying began on a small scale. In 1878 a pavilion for the holding of horticultural fairs was built on Temple street.

The growing confidence in the future of the city showed in the establishment in 1873 of a chamber of commerce. The first meeting was held in the courthouse August 1, with Governor Downey presiding and J. M. Griffith acting as secretary. One hundred names were enrolled. Among the first directors chosen was M. J. Newmark, who recently served a term as president of the modern chamber of commerce. The organization started out briskly, but was discouraged by the bank failure and the dry years, and about 1877 it gave up the ghost. One piece of work to which it particularly applied itself during its existence was the securing of the first appropriation for the improvement of San Pedro harbor — the sum of $150,000 — which was used toward a project devised by Col. G. H. Mendell of the United States army engineering corps. The indefatigable Banning included the building of a harbor at San Pedro among the labors he had allotted to himself to accomplish for Los Angeles, and by long agitation had succeeded in getting the matter in shape to be acted upon in congress. The project called for a total expenditure of $425,000, and contemplated getting about fifteen feet of water at low tide on the bar. The appropriation was afterward doubled, and a total of sixteen feet gained. Toward the end of this decade the harbor began to be serviceable for vessels of light draft. The subdivision of the large Mexican land grants in the vicinity of Los Angeles continued actively, and hundreds of small ranches from forty to two hundred acres in extent were established in the county. Settlements began to spring up. One of the most notable of these was the Indiana colony, which came to be known as Pasadena a year or two after its founding. Another was Pomona, which, as its name indicates, was designed as a fruit growing colony. The popularity of Santa Monica as an ocean resort began shortly after the building of the Los Angeles and Independence road. The population of the county as a whole increased from 15,309 to 33,881 in the ten years from 1870 to 1880, which was even a larger rate of growth than was shown by the city. Its assessed valuation went up from $7,000,000 to $18,000,000.

The doubling of population in the city led to the developing of new residence districts, and the increase of business brought some activity in building. In 1873 East Los Angeles was laid out and a year or two later was placed on the market and settled up with homes. In 1876 a similar

157

development began in Boyle Heights. Small bridges were built down in the river bottom, one at Downey avenue, opposite East Los Angeles, and one at Aliso street, opposite Boyle Heights. During this decade Prudent Beaudry and J. W, Potts spent nearly $175,000 in improving the western hill section, grading streets and putting in an extensive water system. The district they improved was chiefly along Temple and Second streets, and is now given up for the most part to oil derricks, but it was, during the '70s and '80s, one of the best residence districts of the city. In 1874 the first city railroad was built, the "Sixth and Spring street" line, about two and a half miles in length. A year later the Main street line was constructed, and that was followed presently by the line to East Los Angeles.

The assessment of the city's property increased from $2,000,000 to $7,000,000 during this period. In 1871 the Downey block was built, and in 1872 the northern portion of the Temple block, to be used as the Temple and Workman bank. It was afterward used by the Los Angeles County bank. In 1874 about $300,000 was expended for business buildings. In 1876 the Baker block was built, the most elegant structure of its time not only for Los Angeles, but for all the state outside of San Francisco. This was a period of frequent fires, but an efficient fire department was finally organized, with a good steam fire engine.

The newspapers of the city that now exist began publication during this epoch, the Evening Express in 1871, with Ben C. Truman and H. C. Austin as its earliest editors, and the Herald in 1873, under the management of C. A. Storke, who now lives in Santa Barbara. Both of these papers presently came to be owned and edited by J. D. Lynch, with whom J. J. Ayres was afterwards associated as a partner. In 1875 the Mirror, which was the weekly edition of the Times daily, was founded. The Times came into existence in 1881.

The mayors of this period were C. Aguilar, 1871-72; J. R. Toberman, 1873-74, 1879-82; P. Beaudry, 1875-76; A. F. McDougal, 187778. The county continued to be democratic in politics, giving, in 1872, Greeley 1227 and O'Connor 650 against Grant 1312. In 1876 the vote stood Tilden 3616 to Hayes 3040.

In 1873 the high school building was constructed on the hill where the courthouse now stands. The first teachers' institute was held in 1870. The percentage of school attendance, which was only 6 per cent in 1865, and only 20 per cent in 1870, rose to 37 per cent in 1880. In 1890 it was 63. In 1873 the Library association raised, by subscription, funds enough to open a small library and reading room in the Downey block, which was supported in its running expenses by a small city tax. Books were either donated or were purchased with funds from entertainments and other semi-public sources of revenue.

A considerable moral improvement took place during this epoch, influenced to some extent by a reaction after the wild excesses that culminated in the Chinese riot in 1871. In 1870 there were no drinking places in the city — to 5000 population. Now, thirty-five years later, there are 200 drinking places to over 100,000 population. This was the time of the greatness of Vasquez, California's most famous bandit, who ranged the state with his band from 1863 to 1874, making his headquarters generally in the southern region. His record of murders and robberies exceeds that of Jack Shepard or Dick Turpin. He was captured in the Cahuenga in 1874 and hanged the next year.

CHAPTER 31. THE EPOCH OF THE BOOM.

The word "boom" is a convenient bit of slang that arrived at the opportune moment to supply a lack in the language, and, having proved its usefulness, it is likely to win a permanent position — just as many other expressions of similar origin have done, whose dignified place in the language is now above question. The word was first used to imitate the sound of an explosion, then it came to mean an explosion, and in the later 70's it began to be used to describe any state of sudden and extraordinary activity in a business or, more often, in a town. It superseded the word "bubble," which had done service since the days of John Law.

While there is no other expression in the language that is available to describe the peculiar phenomenon that took place in Los Angeles and Southern California in the years from 1885 to 1888, still there is a secondary meaning to "boom" that does not apply to the case of Los Angeles city. The word carries with it inevitably a conception of some form of utter collapse that must follow. An explosion is supposed to leave ruin in its wake. No such catastrophe occurred in the case of Los Angeles. There was a cessation of the unnatural activity, but no general disaster and no permanent injury to the city. Eastern people frequently ask the question: "Has Los Angeles recovered from its boom yet?" as though the event had been something in the nature of a misfortune or a disease. There were many residents of the city who, during the boom and immediately afterward, were disposed to take this same view of it; but now, fourteen years after the close of the affair, they are able to see it in a better perspective, balancing the small amount of evil it wrought against the large amount of good, and they generally admit that the violent shaking up was just what was needed to bring the old pueblo out of its natural lethargy, and to recognize it as a vigorous, progressive and thoroughly American city.

There were two distinct phases of the boom — the first a development and the second a craze. The whole movement had its origin in a sudden influx of population brought on by a railway war. The arrival of great numbers of people of a good, industrial class, most of them provided with some money for investment, naturally led to a rapid increase in real estate values, and stimulated building and the general development of the resources of the country. Thus far the activity was legitimate and wholly beneficial. Had the changes been proportioned on a moderate scale, or had they come with reasonable speed, all might have gone well to the very end, without even individual misfortune to cloud the record. But the change was neither moderate nor gradual — it was enormous, and it came with lightning rapidity. Men became dazed and staggered at the sight and many of them completely lost their bearings. They saw improbable things happening, and they went on to expect the impossible. A few of the older residents of the town were bitten with the madness, but it affected, for the most part, only the newcomers. While few men of real wealth or of large business experience were seriously attacked, it took entire possession of many that were of small or imaginary means. This was the secondary phase of the boom — its most interesting and picturesque chapter, perhaps, but not the one that bears on the real history of the city.

When the Southern Pacific railway was completed into Los Angeles, that city had its first transcontinental line to the eastern states; when the Southern Pacific was completed through to Yuma, where it met the Texas Pacific, Los Angeles had its second line to the east. Trains over this new connection began running in 1883, and great things were expected to follow. There was a feeling that the southern line belonged to Los Angeles, as the northern belonged to San Francisco; and that one would develop the southern city as the other had the northern. During the first year of the decade of the 80's there was some increase of population and considerable development of the farming country tributary to Los Angeles, but the rate of increase was no greater than it had been in the preceding decade. The Nadeau was built in 1882, the tallest and most pretentious structure in the city, but its location on First and Spring was considered too far out of town to make it desirable for hotel purposes, and it was rented for offices and apartments. In 1883 the stores began to creep along Spring street to Second, and a few went beyond, among the residences. By 1884 business had become fairly brisk, but there was no such influx of new people as had been expected from the building of the second railway. The passenger fare one way from the Mississippi river country was still in the vicinity of $100, with the round trip at $150. In 1885 the round-trip' fell to $125, and early in 1886 to $100. The "personally conducted" excursion began to be popular — trainloads made up in eastern cities and taken through Los Angeles, San Diego, San Francisco and the northern points of interest.

In November of 1885 the Atchison, Topeka and Santa Fe company completed its line through the Cajon, and began to operate independently of the Southern Pacific. This is the date usually given for the beginning of the boom. The Santa Fe road began to advertise their new territory, and the Southern Pacific, which thus far had not given it special attention, presently followed suit. The display of Southern California oranges at the Cotton Exposition in New Orleans in 1884 took the premium over Florida fruit, which was an eye-opener to many Californians, as well as to easterners, and a great planting of citrus trees began. In 1886 the shipments of fruit to the east amounted to 150,000 boxes, which would be a little over 400 cars, as oranges are now measured, or 500 carloads in those days.

Through the winter of 1885-86 the country was filled with tourists as it had never been before, and among them were many who decided to remain

161

and make their homes in Los Angeles. This was the beginning of a new element in the population of the city, and one that was destined to play an important part in its sudden advance. These people had come heretofore as isolated specimens, so to speak, but now they came as a class — people of means, who sought a place to live where they could be free from the incessant struggle with the elements. Frequently there was some member of the family who was in feeble health, or who showed a tendency to consumption. These newcomers bought property on the hills, or to the southwest of the city, paying prices which seemed preposterous to the old-timers who had seen those dry acres go a-begging; and they built pretty homes and planted shade trees and rose gardens and lawns.

The possibilities of Southern California as a health resort had been heralded by many newspaper correspondents and magazine writers who had visited the country; and a book published by the Harpers early in the 70's, written by Charles Nordhoff, set forth in glowing terms the benefit that the mild climate wrought in cases of consumption. This volume had a wide circulation all through the Eastern states, and many thousand people afflicted with that disease were brought to Los Angeles, Santa Barbara and San Diego in consequence. Most of these were far advanced toward death. The country was ill-provided with hospitals, and its hotels were crude affairs, without heated rooms or other comforts. The invalids who were too far gone for recovery died, but those with whom the disease had merely secured a foothold were, as a rule, saved, and they wrote home advising others situated as they had been to come to Southern California.

In constructing its various lines through Southern California the Santa Fe company had come into the ownership of considerable land, and it was interested — and so were some of its leading officials — in many town sites and development enterprises along the route. It was therefore desirous of bringing immigrants into the country. The settlement of the vacant lands was needed to produce freight along the line, where there was as yet almost no business to be had. The policy of the company was to put passenger rates as low as practicable, and war between it and the Southern Pacific was not long in beginning. Through 1886 the rates fell constantly, until they reached $25 for one way, around which figure they hovered for nearly a year, and for a short time they went down to $5, and for one day to $1. In 1887 they began to go up again, and in 1888 the war gradually died out, and the modern rates were established.

In the months when the low rates prevailed, a great flood of people poured through Southern California. The passenger capacity of the railroads was stretched to the utmost, regular trains being divided into numerous sections, and special excursions running in at the rate of three to five a day. Hotels and boarding houses filled to overflowing, and the demand for houses to rent was far in advance of the supply. Los Angeles was the center

162

of this new activity, and the price of city property began to go up with great swiftness. Prior to the boom the best business property was not valued over $300 per front foot. A good residence lot could be had for from $400 to $600, although in a few favored sections it might cost $1000. Within a space of three years there was an average permanent advance of about 300 per cent. Many blocks changed suddenly from residence to business, and others adjoining them began to have a speculative value as future business property. Thousands of acres of farms within the city limits were laid out in residence tracts, and sold off to people that proposed to make Los Angeles their home. In the beginning such lots were to be had at $200 to $300, which yielded a handsome profit to the owner, as he got five city lots out of an acre of ground that cost him originally perhaps $50. The possibilities involved in the subdivision of farming land into residence lots presently began to dawn on the owners of the outer city property, but, although large tracts were thrown on the market, the increase of population was so rapid that the prices steadily advanced.

In addition to the tourists and settlers, the cheap excursions brought another class, to wit, the speculators. Some of these were genuine real estate operators, who had the capital to make improvements in their purchases, always, however, with a view to retailing at a profit; others — and they constituted the greater number — were entirely impecunious, but possessed of unlimited assurance, and they had acquired more or less experience through the booming of other towns. Many of these came from Kansas and Iowa, where booms had been in progress for several years; and the tactics that had been used with success in the middle west were now employed on the Pacific coast. These were the men who committed, or were the cause of, most of the follies and the frauds of the boom. Few of them achieved any permanent success. The great majority left the city when the episode was over, and are now utterly lost to view.

The opportunity for speculation within the city limits was limited, and there was too much that was solid and tangible in the actual advance of values to make the field attractive to the imaginative promoter. The real absurdities of the boom were not perpetrated in Los Angeles city property, which advanced for the most part in a steady, even ratio and did not fall back perceptibly when the influx of new people was checked. One evidence of this shows in the assessment of the years during and after the boom. In 1886, before the advance had well begun, the city was assessed at $18,000,000. In 1887 it rose to $28,000,000. In 1888 it was $39,000,000, in 1889, $46,000,000. By this time the boom was at an end, but the next year the city showed $49,000,000. In 1891 it was $46,000,000. A variation of 6 per cent, which is all that shows between the heights of the boom and the lowest year following it, may safely be attributed to a change of assessors.

Such variations frequently occur. The advance of values halted for a few years, but there was no "reaction" or falling back.

But the county outside of the city shows a different side to the story. Here, and in Southern California generally, was where the professional operator and the crazy, irresponsible "boomer" held full sway. Farm property which had been worth $20 or $30 an acre, and which under favorable conditions of improved railway connection and a larger home market might be worth $100 an acre, was exploited as orange land that would yield $1000 an acre per annum in that fruit, and was sold at from $300 to $500. Some of it was cut up into "choice villa" tracts, and, with some trifling improvements, and a good deal of boasting about its "view," was sold at $800 to $1000 an acre. But the promoter's swiftest road to fortune lay in the town site. From Los Angeles city to the San Bernardino county line is thirty— six miles, and in this distance twenty-five town sites were laid out. As they averaged over a mile square, it may be said that the entire distance was one continuous town site. It was much the same with other roads, and branches of roads, and projected roads. A few of these towns were bona fide railway stations, or farming district centers, where there was a bare possibility of a moderate growth with some small value to the inside lots, but in the great majority of cases they were mere paper towns whose lots possessed no value whatever. The assessment figures for the county outside the city show what was happening in those years of folly. In 1836, $32,000,000; in 1887 it nearly doubled, $62,000,000; the next year $63,000,000. Then came the awakening; in 1889 it was $47,000,000, and in 1890 it fell clear back to a figure below that with which the boom had started, $20,000,000. Here was where the only reaction from the boom was to be found.

The money lost in this change of values — which was not as much as it might seem from these figures — came chiefly from inexperienced people of limited means, of whom some had just come to the country to settle, and were talked into foolish investments, and others were merely passing through the region as tourists, and thought to profit in a little speculation. Incredible as it may seem, the lots in the silly towns were nearly all sold. One scoundrel disposed of $50,000 worth of lots in towns located on the top of the mountains where in all probability no human foot will ever tread. Many Los Angeles people were tempted into unwise speculations, but few of them were permanently injured in the affair. Enormous amounts of money changed hands. The recorded real estate transfers of 1887 aggregated $100,000,000, and probably not more than half the operations of the year were ever entered up. There is no real estate boom in history that is to be compared with this, either in gross magnitude or in sudden contrasts of values. We have noted in various other instances that when Los Angeles has undertaken to accomplish a thing, it has done the work very thoroughly.

CHAPTER 32. THE REORGANIZATION.

The boom folly touched high-water mark in the summer of 1887, and it came to a sudden end late in the fall of that same year. Some of the real estate brokers of that period claim to be able to locate the exact day and almost the hour when the tide turned, and eagerness to buy was suddenly replaced by a wild frenzy to sell at any price. There was, however, no single event that formed the dividing line between the rise and the fall. During the latter months of the boom time, the banks of Los Angeles, which had — let it be recorded to their credit — exercised great caution through the whole episode, began to refuse to loan money on property outside the city, no matter what its supposed value, and to use as their basis of valuation for city property its price before the boom. Presently it became almost impossible to obtain money from the banks for real estate transactions of any kind. There was no combination among them, but the leading financier of the city, Mr. I. W. Hellman, marked out an ultra conservative policy for the bank over which he presided, and the others were entirely willing to follow his lead. Perhaps this of itself and alone might not have sufficed to smash the boom; but as the winter months approached, and the crowd of easterners that was expected failed to appear, the courage of those who had been holding up the market began to ebb, and they started out quietly to unload. In a short time everybody was unloading, and then there was no more boom.

The non-appearance of the eastern tourists, who had for three years filled the hotels to overflowing, was a matter of profound astonishment to the Southern Californians. The latter had made great preparation for the entertainment of their guests by constructing a number of huge wooden hotels in inaccessible places all over the region. Finally it began to dawn on the people of Los Angeles that climate alone would not permanently attract people of the tourist class. The entertainment of guests is a business that must be practiced with shrewdness and diligence. The first essential is good hotels, of which Southern California had none at that time. Other essentials are facilities for pleasant traveling about and opportunity for sport and entertainment. Now Southern California at the time of the boom was not a pleasant place to visit, although the boom itself was a curiosity well worth seeing. The climate was on its best behavior during the winters of 1886-87 and 188788, and the weather was perfect, but that was about all there was to be said in favor of the country. Tourists are, for the most part, people of wealth, and it is their happy privilege to indulge in fads, which they may change as often as they choose. Southern California was for two seasons a fad. The moment it became common, and "everybody" was going there, it was dropped and forgotten. Not until nearly ten years later did the tourists begin to come again in large crowds. At the present time their number is probably several times as great as that of the liveliest year of the boom. There were, however, others besides tourists who had been coming to Los Angeles. These were the people that proposed to make their homes in Southern California. The failure of the real estate boom was not a matter that concerned them very deeply. They were attracted by the climate or by the horticultural possibilities of the region. The southern counties had a population of 64,000 in 1880, which by 1890 had increased to 201,000. Here were 137,000 new people, mostly from the states of the middle west, full of energy and courage, and entirely equal to the task of conquering the arid wilderness. Irrigation systems were established, and hundreds of thousands of fertile acres set to trees. By 1890 the citrus fruit crop had grown to nearly a million boxes, yielding the growers over a dollar a box on the tree. Deciduous fruits, nuts, olives, wine and raisin grapes were planted, the area in wheat and barley increased greatly, small fruits were grown and canneries started up, and presently a beet sugar factory began operations on a large scale. Of all this farming country, Los Angeles was the commercial center and the chief depot of supplies.

Los Angeles had now suddenly changed from a very old city to a very young one. Its population in 1880 was 11,000 and in 1890 was 50,000. Of this latter number, it may safely be estimated that more than three-fourths had not been living in the city more than four years. People who had come to Los Angeles in the 70's, and had been accustomed to regard themselves as new-comers, suddenly discovered that they were in the class of old settlers, and that they and others of earlier epochs had shrunk to an insignificant minority. Just as the Spaniards had wrenched the country away from the aboriginal tribes, and as the first Americans had succeeded in shouldering the Californians out of the control of affairs, so now this overwhelming horde of new arrivals took possession of the land, and proceeded to make things over to their own tastes. There was some confusion at first, but in a surprisingly short space of time a readjustment was effected, with the new-comers very completely in the saddle. Their purchases of business and residence property were largely to the southwest of the center of the city, and a great building activity began in that direction. When the boom was coming to an end, the paving of streets was begun; for up to that time the business portion was deep in mud through the winter months and in dust through the summer. There had been a small sewer system which did not extend beyond Fifth street. It was first extended piece by piece over the business district, and out to Tenth street, and then by a huge bond issue it was made to take in nearly the whole of the residence section as well. The new city hall on Broadway and the courthouse on the hill were both begun just at the close of the boom, and a few years later the federal building was constructed.

Up to 1888 the street car system of the city consisted of a few decrepit horse cars on rather rickety tramways. In that year a consolidation of most of the independent systems was effected, and work was begun on the construction of a cable plant with three large power houses. In 1890 an electric system was built, which was finally consolidated with the cable and all put under electricity. The last horse car disappeared from the city in 1897, when the Main street line, which had not been part of the consolidation, adopted the new power. In 1898 the syndicate that controls the street car systems of San Francisco purchased the Los Angeles lines, with the exception of the system owned by W. S. Hook and the Temple street line, and made many improvements. The city at present enjoys the privilege of genuine street car competition, and its residence section is thoroughly covered with branch lines, both systems being admirably managed.

In 1888 the people of Los Angeles became much elated at the prospect of securing a new transcontinental line to the east through Salt Lake City. A franchise was secured for a railway to run along the east bank of the river, which, it was announced, was to provide the Union Pacific with terminal facilities, it being the intention of that road to build across Nevada to Los Angeles. The line from Salt Lake City was begun and carried through Utah, but a change occurring in the management and policy of the Union Pacific, the plan was abandoned and the hope of a Salt Lake connection was deferred for twelve years. The franchise for a road along the east bank was taken up by a party of St. Louis capitalists, who built a system running from Pasadena and Glendale through the city to San Pedro, which they called the Terminal. This system was sold in 1900 to Senator W. A. Clark, who is now constructing the line from Salt Lake to Los Angeles. It is believed that the connection will be established within two years of the present writing (1901).

During and immediately after the time of the boom, numerous branch lines were constructed by the Santa Fe and Southern Pacific throughout the whole region of Southern California. Most important of these were the direct line to San Diego along the coast, which was completed by the Santa Fe in 1891, and the line to Santa Barbara of the Southern Pacific, which was built in 1887. The latter has since been made part of a through line by the coast connecting San Francisco and Los Angeles. Both these two transcontinental systems' which, before the boom, were housed in Los Angeles in wretched little sheds, are now provided with large, well built depots; that of the Southern Pacific was built in 1888, and that of the Santa Fe m 1893.

Thus the material welfare of the city, from whatever point it is examined, will be found to have greatly benefited through the boom. On the social and moral side, however, there was at first the appearance of a

167

decided loss. Among the new people who came to the city during the height of the boom, the speculative and adventurous class, while not in the majority perhaps as far as numbers went, were always the most conspicuous. They lost no time in asserting themselves in all public and social matters, and for a time something like anarchy prevailed. Here were 40,000 or 50,000 people suddenly gathered together from all parts of the Union, in utter ignorance of one another's previous history. A great amount of money was passing rapidly from hand to hand, and a great city was in embryo. It was the golden opportunity of the fakir and humbug and the man with the past that he wanted forgotten. The native Californian and the early pioneer were hospitable, large hearted and unsuspicious. They were for a time easy prey, but having been repeatedly imposed upon, they became doubtful of all new-comers. Commercial and social life in Los Angeles during the later 8o's was full of startling uncertainties. The man with whom you were doing business every day might be an ex-convict — or he might be one whom the stripes were destined to ornament some time in the future. The people who had bought the house across the street might be married — or they might have neglected that formality, owing to the existence of prior partnerships "back east." A man who came within one vote of being elected chief of police is now in the California penitentiary for life. Another, who was concerned in many of the largest boom enterprises, has since served two penitentiary terms in other states. Another who was a bank president and the owner of a daily paper, recently fled out of the Union with the police at his heels. One who occupied a popular pulpit in Los Angeles during the boom has since become famous as a professional polygamist — confiding widows with money being his specialty. The list of swindlers, embezzlers and confidence men of that period would be a long one, if anybody should undertake to set it forth in full.

Immediately at the close of the boom the sifting out process began. The professional scalawags left of their own accord when the field was found to be worked out. The unprofessional ones were easily detected and disposed of. The adventurers and adventuresses and the people with the scaly records met the usual fate of their kind — they betrayed themselves and were found out. Gradually a new society was formed, a little colder and more discriminating, perhaps, than that of the first pioneers, but felicitous in its combination of the old and new elements. The morals of the city which had gone back a few degrees during the confusion of the boom were brought up to the standard of the best American cities. In 1889 the gambling houses were all closed, and a couple of years later a Sunday closing ordinance for saloons went into effect. Poker dens, where strangers were taken in and fleeced, continued for some years, but they are now so thoroughly under the ban that they are operated only with great secrecy and on a small scale. The Sunday closing law was evaded for a time, but at present it is very thoroughly enforced. During the boom, when the city had a population of 50,000, the county jail averaged 250 to 300 occupants. Ten years later, with a population twice as large, the jail averaged less than 100 occupants — a most remarkable contrast.

In the early 8o's the subject of state division was agitated anew, chiefly because the laws that dealt with riparian rights were suited to the needs of the miners of the north rather than to the irrigationists of the south. It was contended that the interests of the two sections of the state were so radically different that a separation must be effected. In 1881 a mass meeting was held in Los Angeles at which a report was drawn up in the shape or a series of questions addressed to the leading attorneys of the city, asking them what steps were necessary to bring about the division. The reply, signed by eight attorneys, was to the effect that the action taken by the legislature in 1859, followed as it was by the favorable vote of the southern counties, was still in effect, and that the new territory could proceed to organize and ask for admission to the Union. A circular was then issued calling for delegates from each county to meet in convention at Los Angeles, September 8, 1881. This gathering came together on the appointed date, all of the counties being represented. Resolutions were passed favoring state division, but it was decided to take no active steps until the population of the new district was large enough to insure its reception as a state. In 1888 the subject was again called up in a mass meeting at Hazard's pavilion in Los Angeles, and General Vandever, who represented the -Sixth district in congress, introduced a bill attempting a division of the state. The meeting was slimly attended, and little enthusiasm was shown. The Vandever bill was never reported back from committee.

September 5, 1881, the founding of the city was celebrated with a great procession which circled the plaza, much as the procession of De Neve had done 100 years before. The 5th was taken instead of the 4th through the errors of a local historian.

The mayors of the period from 1880 to 1890 were: J. R. Toberman, 1879-1882; C. E. Thorn, 1883-4; E. F. Spence, 1885-6; W. H. Workman, 1887-8; John Bryson, four months in 1889; H. T. Hazard, 1889-1892.

CHAPTER 33. THE MODERN CITY.

The decade from 1890 to 1900 was one of steady, even growth and development for Los Angeles, the population increasing from 50.000 to 102,000, and the assessed valuation of property advancing from $50,000,000 to $70,000,000. The wave of hard times which swept over the Union in 1893-6 did not pass by Los Angeles, but its ravages were not serious. One advantage that the city derives from its somewhat isolated position is that of comparative independence in its commercial interests. Hard times affected the market value of some Southern California products and diminished the amount of tourist travel; four banks in the city closed their doors in the panic of 1893, one of which failed disgracefully; another retired from business with honor and credit, and the other two soon resumed with new strength. There were several mercantile failures, none of them of any considerable size. For a time the city was worried by the presence of a number of unemployed men, chiefly in the building trades. In 1895, in spite of the hard times, the building permits had aggregated $5,000,000, and great numbers of workmen were attracted to the only city in the Union that seemed to be holding its own. The next year the permits fell to $2,700,000 and in 1898 they were only $2,100,000. As times were still bad all over the country, the men thus thrown out of employment were unable to get away, and provision had to be made for them. Funds were raised by public subscription, and the men w(re put to work on the parks. Business generally, however, held its own fairly well through this troublous time. In 1892, before the panic, the bank clearances for the year were $39,000,000. In 1893 they were $45,000,000. In 1894 they were $44,000,000, in 1895, $57,000,000; in 1896, $61,000,000. This shows how the city continued to expand, in spite of the bad times.

An important event in the industrial development of the region was the establishment of the present chamber of commerce of Los Angeles in 1888. This institution differs somewhat from those that bear a similar name in other cities, in the extent and variety of the work it undertakes. Its membership is not confined to men in active business, but includes all who are interested in the advancement of the city. It has 1000 members, and almost from its inception has been endowed, through the far-sighted liberality of the wealthy and progressive men of the city, with sufficient funds to carry on an active campaign of advertising and of local development. The chamber's first meetings were held in the old board of trade building on First and Broadway, which has since been torn down. In 1889 a permanent exhibit of Southern California products was opened over the Mott market on Main street, between First and Second. In 1894 the organization moved to its present quarters at Fourth and Broadway, in a building designed especially for its use. Recently it purchased a piece of property on Broadway, between First and Second streets, where its permanent home will probably be erected during the coming year.

When the chamber of commerce began work, which was just at the close of the boom, the industrial conditions of the region were in very bad shape. The city had entirely outgrown the country; the farming land had been overrun with town sites; much of it was in the hands of non-residents, who were holding it for speculation instead of for use; and so large a percentage of those actually engaged in husbandry were either ignorant of the whole art or were utterly inexperienced as to local conditions of soil and climate, that the results were far from satisfactory. A primary object of the chamber in the establishment of the display of local products was to enable the farmers to compare their work and thus gain by one another's experience in this new strange country. For this same purpose citrus fairs were held during the years from 1890 to 1895. One of these fairs, that of 1891, was sent to Chicago and exhibited to an attendance of 120,000 people in the old exposition building on the lake front. These fairs and the display made at Chicago in the Columbian exposition helped to stimulate orange culture, and to regulate and improve the industry. Other lines of horticulture and of farming were encouraged and assisted, and at the end of a few years the industrial situation had been reorganized on a substantial basis. Manufacturing had begun in various lines that were allied to the agricultural development — beet sugar, fruit canning and crystallizing, making of pipe for irrigation, etc.

A great amount of work was done by the chamber of commerce in making the possibilities of the Southern California region known in the eastern states with a view to attracting immigration; and the extraordinary increase in population during the decade from 1890 to 1900, an increase that is still actively in progress, shows how successfully the designs were carried out. This advertising was of all kinds, the distribution of printed matter, the use of space in magazines and newspapers, and. most important of all, the sending of large and striking exhibits to the great fairs of the country. At the Columbian exposition in Chicago in 1893, the Midwinter fair in San Francisco in 1894, the Cotton exposition in Atlanta in 1896, the Transmississippi exposition at Omaha in 1898 and the Pan-American at Buffalo in 1901, the chamber had independent exhibits that attracted wide attention. It also participated on a smaller scale in numerous displays in Europe and America.

No new railways were constructed into Los Angeles during this period, but an event of great commercial significance was the beginning of work on the deep-water harbor at San Pedro. As the original project for the improvement of the inner harbor for vessels of light draft drew toward its completion, agitation began for the construction of a seawall from Point

171

Fermin out into the exterior bay, to protect an area which could be used as a harbor for the largest ocean going vessels. The total sum expended on the interior improvement was about $900,000, and the depth of water attained would admit vessels drawing seventeen and eighteen feet. It was, and is, used chiefly for the lumber and coal trade of the coast, but was not practicable for the ocean commerce that was seeking outlet and inlet through this region. There being no deep-water harbor nearer than San Francisco on the north — 500 miles — and San Diego on the south — 100 miles — there was need of a harbor of refuge and a harbor of naval necessities at this point. The engineering authorities of the government conceded the justice of the claim, and in 1891 a report was submitted to congress by a board of army engineers appointed to examine the coast from Orange county to Santa Barbara, with a view to determining the best point for the construction of a harbor, and this report was unequivocally in favor of San Pedro.

In 1892 the first effort was made to secure an appropriation from congress to begin the work, but it was defeated through the declaration of the chief engineer of the Southern Pacific that no harbor could ever be constructed at San Pedro. It was decided to appoint a special commission of five eminent army engineers to review the work of the first board and report on the comparative merits of Santa Monica, Redondo and San Pedro. This body visited the locality and made a thorough investigation, and their report was in favor of San Pedro. But the Southern Pacific was still not satisfied, claiming that the war department had favored San Pedro chiefly through a desire to be consistent. All efforts to secure an appropriation for that place were resisted, and for several years the commercial men of the city were divided into two camps, for Santa Monica with the Southern Pacific, and for San Pedro against the Southern Pacific.

Finally, in 1896, a bill was introduced in the house of representatives appropriating $2,900,000 for a deep-water harbor at Santa Monica. There was a general feeling among the people of Los Angeles that the interest of the Southern Pacific in the Santa Monica project was because a harbor there would be exclusively controlled by that corporation, whereas a harbor at San Pedro would be open to competition. The Terminal road, which had extensive holdings at San Pedro, and the Santa Fe road, which was believed to be disinterested except in so far as the question of location might affect the general welfare of the region, were both determined in their opposition to the Santa Monica plan, as were also the two senators of the state and the congressman of the district. So many protests from authoritative sources against the proposed improvement were forwarded to Washington, accompanied by demands that it be changed to San Pedro, that the item was struck out of the house bill, and Los Angeles was left, as in previous years, with no appropriation for deep-water work. When the matter came up in the senate, Stephen M. White, who was a resident of Los Angeles, and a member of the senate committee on commerce, demanded that the money be appropriated for San Pedro, and when that was refused, that the whole question of location be left to a third board of engineers, one of whom should be from the navy, one from the coast survey and the other three from civil life. The commerce committee refused this compromise, and put back in the bill the appropriation for Santa Monica. The fight was then carried to the floor of the senate, and at the end of a long struggle, Mr. White's plan was adopted. The new board reported in favor of San Pedro, and the work was begun in 1899, after two years of most extraordinary and unaccountable delay.

When this work, which is the construction of a seawall 8500 feet long, is completed, Los Angeles will have at its ocean gateway a harbor that is admirably adapted for refuge and for most naval necessities, and is not without great value for commercial purposes; but to make it entirely serviceable for the latter it will be necessary to dredge out the inner harbor for several thousand feet along the docks. When that is done Los Angeles will possess one of the finest harbors in the country, and will take its share of the Oriental commerce that is destined to come to the Pacific coast.

The bank deposits of Los Angeles, which before the boom were $3,000,000 or $4,000,000, rose during the boom to $12,000,000; for a brief time they fell back to $9,000,000, but since then the rise has been almost continuous, until now they aggregate about $25,000,000. Annual clearances are now 400 per cent larger ,than they were ten years ago, which is a striking evidence of the growth of general business. The orange industry, which had its start in the orchard of William Wolfskill in Los Angeles in the 50's, has grown to mammoth proportions. To deliver the crop in the east a trainload must start every hour of the working day through more than half the year. The gross receipts in the eastern market aggregate about $15,000,000. The region covered by this industry extends from San Diego to Santa Barbara, but most of the area is commercially tributary to Los Angeles. The oil industry of Southern California also centers at Los Angeles, the product averaging three or four millions per annum, most of which is mined in the immediate vicinity of the city. In the years 1899 and 1900 Los Angeles passed through a veritable oil boom, with a vast amount of trading in securities of doubtful value. The sinking of many hundred wells stimulated manufacturing and business of all kinds, and although the first enthusiasm of the discovery has worn off, the industry is believed to be only in its beginning.

The other principal sources of income to Los Angeles, besides the two mentioned above, are: Its wholesale trade, which covers all Southern California, most of Arizona and extends well into the San Joaquin valley, the miscellaneous products of surrounding farms, such as hay, grain, vegetables, fruits, etc., the local manufactures, which since oil has been supplied as a cheap fuel, have undergone a great increase, the expenditure of travelers, who are entertained by tens of thousands every winter, and lastly, a great amount of money brought in by the never-ending stream of new-comers. These are people whose purpose it is to make their homes in Los Angeles; they buy property and build houses and put money into new enterprises for the development of the country. As long as the climate holds good, this source of supply seems likely to be limitless. It must be noted, moreover, that Los Angeles contains a large element of the retired class, whose incomes are spent in the city, but are derived from investments in the eastern states.

In the midst of the boom Los Angeles adopted a new charter (1889), but the document was faulty in providing too many elective offices and in failing to definitely locate responsibility. The city government, while far from bad, is by no means up to the standard that the city is entitled to enjoy, considering the unusual character of its population. There is no such percentage of foreign element as is to be found in most American cities, neither is there an illiterate or impoverished element. On the other hand, the exceptionally large proportion of people of comfortable means who have the time that they might devote to the duties of citizenship, gives an opportunity such as few cities enjoy for a high quality of local government. Three attempts have been made to give the city a new and adequate charter, but all have been defeated.

The mayors of the city during the latter period were: T. E. Rowan, 1892-4; Frank Rader, 1894-6; M. P. Snyder, 1896-8; Fred Eaton, 1898-1900, and M. P. Snyder at the present time. On national and state issues the city is generally Republican, although through a combination of silver Republicans and Democrats Mr. Bryan's forces carried the city in 1896, while the county went the other way by a small majority. In 1900 both city and county went heavily Republican. In local elections. Democrat and Republican alternate in the office of mayor, while the majority of the council is almost always Republican.

At the present writing, the summer of 1901, the city is growing with greater rapidity than at any time in its history, if we except the one or two years of the boom, when it added a hundred per cent every few months. That the population of 100,000 in 1900 is compounding at the rate of 10 per cent per annum the school census shows clearly enough, and the increase of business is on even a greater ratio than that of population. The southwestern region of the United States will support at least one great city, and all doubt as to where that city will be located is now at an end. The little pueblo that Governor De Neve founded 120 years ago, in order that grain for the army might be raised in California instead of imported from Mexico, has at last grown to be the active, prosperous city of his dreams. That it should some day become one of the great metropolitan centers of the nation is not a dream, but the natural outgrowth of existing conditions.

www.ingramcontent.com/pod-product-compliance
Lightning Source LLC
Chambersburg PA
CBHW060320050426
42449CB00011B/2576